LEAVING CERTIFICATE

LATER MODERN HISTORY OF EUROPE AND THE WIDER WORLD TOPIC 3

Dictatorship and Democracy
1920–1945

STEPHEN TONGE

THE EDUCATIONAL COMPANY

FOREWORD

This book covers the syllabus requirements for Topic 3 of the Later Modern European section of the new Leaving Certificate course – Dictatorship and Democracy in Europe, 1920–45. Students will examine an era of profound change in European history. Starting in the splendid Hall of Mirrors at Versailles, we finish in the ruins of Germany.

The three perspectives laid out in the syllabus are covered. The political changes that saw the rise of Fascism and Communism and the most destructive war in human history are studied. We concentrate not just on great events, but on the lives of ordinary people. The developments in society and the economy are examined in a period overshadowed by the impact of the Great Depression. We also look at the growth of anti-Semitism in Germany and the tragic suffering of the Jewish people in Europe during World War II. Developments in religion, culture and science, such as Church–state relations in the Fascist dictatorships, the control of the new mass media in Nazi Germany and the growth of cinema and radio in America and Britain, are also covered.

The three case studies (the Show Trials, the Jarrow March and the Nuremberg Rallies) are dealt with in their wider political context. A Leaving Certificate-style document question has been included with each case study. The understanding and evaluation of sources are central to the new syllabus, and throughout the book there are numerous opportunities for students to practise these skills.

Biographies of each of the key personalities are available at the end of the book, which should prove to be an invaluable aid for both Higher and Ordinary Level students.

At the start of each chapter, the syllabus elements, key personalities and key concepts that students will meet are outlined. Throughout the chapters, there are key questions designed to encourage the student to focus on and understand the main developments in the topic they are studying. They are also designed to enable students to develop a greater understanding of cause and effect. Throughout the chapter, there are short review questions that are designed to reinforce the learning outcomes. At the end of the chapter, there are a range of question types for both Higher and Ordinary Level students – source questions, paragraph answers and essays.

Throughout the book, students are encouraged to form their own opinions on events based on analysing the evidence of what they have read. The opinions of historians are included to help students to understand the topic they are studying.

In studying this topic, it is hoped that students will get a broader understanding and a greater appreciation of one of the most tragic periods in human history.

As a further aid to students, a series of podcasts on the major topics in the book can be downloaded at www.edco.ie/LCHistory

CONTENTS

WEBSITES

General Websites
www.bbc.co.uk/history/
www.channel4.com/history/
www.thehistorychannel.co.uk/site/home/
www.pbs.org/history/

Italy 1920–45
www.library.wisc.edu/libraries/dpf/Fascism/Intro.html
www.thecorner.org/hist/total/f-italy.htm
www.casahistoria.net/Fascism.html

Weimar and Nazi Germany
www.historyplace.com/worldwar2/riseofhitler/index.html
www.calvin.edu/academic/cas/gpa/
www.spiegel.de/international/germany/0,1518,531909,00.html
www.kubiss.de/kulturreferat/reichsparteitagsgelaende/englisch/stationen.htm
www.ushmm.org/museum/exhibit/online/kristallnacht/frame.htm
http://germanhistorydocs.ghi-dc.org/home.cfm

Soviet Russia, 1920–45
www.soviethistory.org/
http://lcweb.loc.gov/exhibits/archives/
www.newseum.org/berlinwall/commissar_vanishes/index.htm
www.iisg.nl/exhibitions/chairman/sovintro.php
http://gulaghistory.org/nps/onlineexhibit/

Britain, 1920–45
www.youtube.com/watch?v=L2sVareYa_c
www.bbc.co.uk/history/british/britain_wwone/jarrow_01.shtml
www.learningcurve.gov.uk/homefront/

France, 1920–45
www.spartacus.schoolnet.co.uk/France.htm
http://en.wikipedia.org/wiki/Vichy_France

World War II
www.bbc.co.uk/history/worldwars/wwtwo/
http://news.bbc.co.uk/onthisday/hi/themes/conflict_and_war/world_war_ii/default.stm
www.channel4.com/history/microsites/H/history/a-b/battle.html
www.iwmcollections.org.uk/
www.ushmm.org/
http://search.eb.com/normandy/
www.learningcurve.gov.uk/worldwar2/default.htm
www.history.com/minisite.do?content_type=mini_home&mini_id=1090

Anglo-American Culture, 1920–45
www.digitalhistory.uh.edu/historyonline/hollywood_history.cfm
www.pbs.org/jazz/time/

① Introduction: The Impact of the First World War

The First World War had a major impact on Europe. Borders changed dramatically with the creation of many new countries. Emperors and kings lost their thrones and political revolutions broke out in many countries. Let's look briefly at the war and the peace treaties that followed it.

WORLD WAR I

The war was sparked by the assassination of Archduke Franz Ferdinand, the heir to the throne of the Austrian empire, in Sarajevo, the capital of Bosnia. He was shot by a Serb who hoped to see the Austrian province become part of the Kingdom of Serbia. Austria attacked Serbia and this triggered a crisis between Europe's main powers that plunged Europe into war by the start of August 1914.

During the war, the main European powers were divided into two alliances:

- The **Central Powers** of Germany, Austria–Hungary and Turkey.
- The **Allies**, led by Britain, France and Russia. Italy joined them in 1915.

The Germans advanced into France but were stopped at the first Battle of the Marne. Trenches were then constructed by both sides. Conditions in these trenches were very poor. For the next four years, generals found it difficult to make a decisive breakthrough and battles usually resulted in heavy causalities. In 1916, two of the worst battles occurred at Verdun and the Somme. It is estimated that 1 million men lost their lives during the Battle of the Somme.

On the Eastern Front, the Germans defeated the initial Russian invasion and advanced into the Russian Empire. The Russians had more success against the Austrians, but any gains they made were usually lost when the Germans sent men to help their Austrian ally. There was fighting in the Alps between the Italians and the Austrians. In Turkey, an attempted landing by British troops was defeated at Gallipoli. The Balkans was also the scene of bloody struggles between the Allies and the Central Powers.

In 1917, two major events occurred that were to have a major impact on the course of the war:

- The United States entered the war on the side of the Allies in April. US troops only started arriving in France in 1918, but they made a decisive contribution to the Allied victory.
- Tsar Nicholas II of Russia was overthrown by a popular revolution in February. The new

Troops in trenches in World War I. Conditions were harsh for the ordinary soldier throughout the war.

government made the mistake of continuing the war. The revolutionary Lenin saw his opportunity and seized power in October. This was the world's first successful Communist revolution (see Chapter 2). His government immediately took Russia out of the war.

THE END OF THE WAR

In the spring of 1918, the Germans launched a massive offensive on the Western Front that was very successful at first. However, in August, the Germans were defeated and forced to retreat. Helped by fresh American troops, the British and the French advanced towards the German border. As their allies surrendered and the Austrian Empire collapsed, the Germans realised they were defeated. The German Emperor, Wilhelm II, was forced to abdicate (give up his throne) and the new democratic government surrendered to the Allies. At 11 a.m. on 11 November 1918, the bloodiest war in human history ended.

THE NEGOTIATIONS IN PARIS

In January 1919, the delegates from the victorious Allied powers met at Paris to negotiate a peace treaty. They faced a host of problems:

- Over 10 million people had died in the war and large parts of Europe were destroyed. There were millions of refugees and food was in short supply. It was estimated that famine threatened over 200 million people. To make matters worse, the deadly Spanish flu epidemic was raging in both the victorious and defeated countries.

- Another serious problem was the threat of the communist revolution spreading throughout Europe, helped by the chaotic conditions. The new communist government in Russia was encouraging revolution in other countries, especially Germany. The delegates were determined to stop this.

The most powerful countries at the conference were France, Britain, the US and Italy. They had different views about how to treat the defeated powers, especially Germany.

- France had suffered terribly in the war and a quarter of all Frenchmen between the ages of 18 and 30 had died. The French delegation was led by premier **Georges Clemenceau** (1841–1929), who wanted a harsh peace treaty that would protect France from a future German attack. He aimed to take as much German land as possible, weaken their army and force Germany to pay compensation for the damage caused by the war.

- The British delegation was led by Prime Minister **David Lloyd George** (1863–1945). He took a more moderate view, but was under a lot of political pressure at home to be harsh on the Germans. The main British aims were the destruction of the German navy, acquiring German colonies in Africa and getting compensation for the cost of the war.

- President **Woodrow Wilson** (1856–1924) represented the US. He wanted a just and fair peace based on his Fourteen Points. He felt that frontiers of countries should be decided on the principle of **self-determination**. This meant that transfer of territory should be on the grounds of nationality and should take account of the wishes of the people who lived there. This is why he strongly opposed the secret Treaty of London (1915), as it had promised large territorial gains for Italy in return for them entering the war on the side of the Allies. His major aim was to see an international body called the **League of Nations** set up to settle future disputes between countries. Wilson was very popular among ordinary people throughout Europe, who were inspired by his vision for post-war Europe. Unfortunately for Wilson, he faced a lot of political opposition at home from the Republican Party and from those who felt the US should stay out of European affairs.

- The Italian Prime Minister, **Vittorio Orlando** (1860–1952), hoped to gain the land promised

From left to right: David Lloyd George, Vittorio Orlando, Georges Clemenceau and Woodrow Wilson.

to Italy by the secret Treaty of London. Italy had suffered over 500,000 dead and was heavily in debt as a result of the war. Italy felt they deserved what was promised under the Treaty of London.

THE TREATY OF VERSAILLES

By June, the treaty with Germany was ready and the Germans were given no choice but to agree to what was put in front of them. On 28 June 1919, the treaty was signed by the Germans at the Hall of Mirrors in the Palace of Versailles outside Paris. The main points of the treaty were as follows.

TERRITORY

Germany lost one-eighth of its pre-war territory to Belgium, Denmark, France, Lithuania and Poland.

East Prussia was separated from the rest of Germany by Polish territory. This became known as the **Polish Corridor**. It included the German-speaking port of **Danzig**, which was controlled by the League of Nations but through which the Polish state had access to the sea.

The small **Saar** region was placed under international control for 15 years while the French exploited its coal mines.

The Germans were forbidden to station troops on the west bank of the River Rhine or within 30 miles of the east bank of the river. This was known as the **demilitarised zone**. Allied troops were to occupy this area for 15 years.

Germany and Austria were forbidden to unite as one country (this was known as the *Anschluss* in German).

New countries were formed from the old Austrian, German and Russian Empires. These included **Czechoslovakia**, **Estonia**, **Hungary**, **Latvia**, **Lithuania**, **Poland** and **Yugoslavia**.

MILITARY

The German army was reduced to 100,000 men. Conscription was forbidden. Germany's navy was limited to six battleships and they were not allowed to have an air force, tanks or submarines.

REPARATIONS

Under Article 231, or the **War Guilt Clause**, Germany and its allies were blamed for causing the war and Germany was ordered to pay reparations, or compensation, to the Allies. In 1921, the figure was fixed at £6.6 billion.

COLONIES

German colonies were taken over by the League of Nations and called **Mandates**. They were to be administered by one of the victorious countries. In reality, they passed from one colonial master to another, e.g. German East Africa became British East Africa.

THE LEAGUE OF NATIONS

The aim of this new international organisation was to preserve peace, but before it got off the ground, the League was seriously weakened when the US Senate voted against joining the organisation. It also possessed no army with which to enforce its decisions. Thus, it could do little to stop a determined aggressor such as Japan or Italy in the 1930s.

The main decisions affecting the other defeated Central Powers were also agreed during the Paris negotiations:

- The peace treaty signed with Austria was called the **Treaty of St Germain** (1919).
- The **Treaty of Trianon** (1920) dealt with Hungary and the **Treaty of Neuilly** (1919) with Bulgaria.
- The **Treaty of Sevres** (1920) was signed with Turkey, but after a war with Greece, this

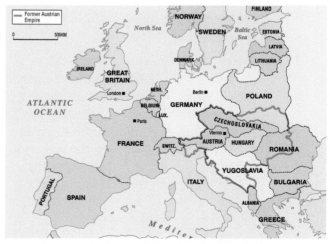

Europe in 1920. The borders of the old Austrian empire are shown in red.

agreement was replaced by the **Treaty of Lausanne** in 1923.

THE IMPACT OF THE TREATY

Popular opinion in two countries, Germany and Italy, was outraged by the agreements reached at Paris. Resentment to the treaty was very strong in Germany. Political leaders attacked the territorial losses to the new Polish state. They also pointed to how they believed Germany had been treated unfairly:

- The ban on union with Austria and the incorporation of large numbers of Germans into the new state of Czechoslovakia were seen as violations of Wilson's promise of self-determination.
- They did not believe Germany had started the war.

Many Germans hoped that one day the treaty would be torn up and Germany would become a great power again. Many extreme nationalists, such as Adolf Hitler, associated the new democratic government with the shame of the Treaty of Versailles. Reparations caused a series of economic problems that led to massive hyperinflation in 1923.

Feeling in Italy was also very hostile. The Italians were furious that the Allies had gone back on promises made to them during the war. This resentment centred on the town of Fiume. Italy was also heavily in debt, which caused economic problems after the war.

We will read more about the impact of the treaty on Italy and Germany in Chapters 4 and 5 and will see how opposition to the treaty contributed to the growth of fascism in both countries.

END OF CHAPTER QUESTIONS

1 What were the main events on the Western Front during World War I?

2 Why was 1917 an important year in World War I?

3 What were conditions like in Europe after the war?

4 What were the aims of the main Allied powers at the Paris Peace Conference?

5 What were the main points of the Treaty of Versailles?

6 Read what the historian Stéphane Audoin-Rouzeau wrote about the German reaction to the treaty and answer the question that follows:

'First, a part of the country was occupied by Allied Troops and especially by African French Troops on the left bank of the Rhine. And despite the fact that it had been impossible to enter into German territory during the war itself (that was the first humiliation), the part of the German territory occupied by Allied troops and by colonial troops coming from the French empire especially.

'The second humiliation, of course, was the restriction of the German army and the limitation of its army for the future. And, the third was the Treaty itself. The fact that German leaders were not invited to the conference, and they only had to sign the Treaty with no objection, and that they had to sign a treaty which declared clearly that Germany was responsible for the disaster in Europe and in the world. And that was, I think, going too far with Germany and that had huge consequences on German nationalism in the 20s and 30s.' (Source: www.pbs.org)

According to Audoin-Rouzeau, what humiliations did the Germans feel they had suffered? Is there any evidence that he sympathises with the German view?

7 The historian Ruth Henig wrote the following about the German reaction to the Treaty:

'It was the acknowledgement of defeat, as much as the treaty terms themselves which they found so hard to accept.'

Do you agree with Henig's verdict? Argue your case.

② Lenin's Russia, 1917–24

What do you need to know in this chapter?

Elements	Key Personalities	Key Concepts
The regimes of Lenin and Stalin	Vladimir Lenin	Communism Totalitarianism
The Soviet alternative (society and economy)		Dictatorship Propaganda

INTRODUCTION

In Chapter 1, we read that there was a communist revolution in Russia in 1917. This event saw the creation of the world's first communist society – an alternative to the dominant capitalist system. In the rest of Europe, many were inspired by this new experiment, but to others, Communism was a disease that threatened civilisation. They felt it had to be stopped by any means. This feeling contributed to the growth of Fascism.

In this chapter, we will look at how this Communist revolution occurred and the policies pursued by the leader of the revolution, **Vladimir Lenin.**

Here is an explanation of some of the terms you will meet in this chapter.

April Thesis: Lenin's revision of Marxist theory that argued that an immediate revolution was possible in Russia.

Bolsheviks: Russian Socialists who believed in using revolution to achieve political change; also called Communists.

Bourgeoisie: Marxist term for the middle class.

Cheka: The secret police.

Collectivisation: Policy of abolishing private farms and replacing them with state collective farms.

Commissar: A minister in the Communist government.

Cult of personality: Propaganda mechanism that portrayed Lenin as the father of his people and Stalin as a superman guiding the USSR to the promised land of Communism.

Industrialisation: Transforming Russia from an agricultural country to a modern industrial power.

Kremlin: Headquarters of the Soviet government in Moscow.

Kulak: Wealthy peasants, seen as enemies by both Lenin and Stalin.

New Economic Policy (NEP): Revision of Communist economic policies allowing limited capitalism.

Proletariat: Marxist term for the working class.

Provisional government: The government formed after the abdication of the Tsar in March.

Reds: What the Communists were called during the Civil War.

Soviet: Soldiers and workers' councils that ran the cities of Russia in 1917.

Treaty of Brest Litovsk: Peace treaty signed with Germany in March 1918.

USSR: Russia was renamed the Union of Soviet Socialist Republics. Sometimes it was called the Soviet Union – many contemporaries still referred to it as Russia.

War Communism: This was an economic policy that saw the rapid transformation to Communism during the Civil War.

Whites: Opponents of the Communists (Reds) during the Civil War.

KEY QUESTION

How did Lenin come to power in Russia?

RUSSIA UNDER THE TSARS

In 1914, Russia entered World War I on the side of Britain and France. Most people in Europe viewed Russia as a backward country, both politically and economically. A vast empire containing many different peoples (Russians, Ukrainians, Belarusians, Poles, Germans, etc.), it was ruled by **Tsar Nicholas II**. A kind and gentle man, he was not suited to dealing with the vast changes Russia was experiencing. Its economy was growing rapidly and the cities, especially the capital, St Petersburg, and Moscow, had seen massive growth in population. Life was tough in these cities, with most workers employed in large factories where conditions and pay were poor. Despite the growth of the major cities, the vast majority of Russians were still peasants who lived in the countryside. Most were very poor and could not read or write.

The Tsar had been reluctant to share power and would not agree to a parliament elected by the people. This led to a lot of political violence called terrorism, e.g. murders of local officials. In 1905, a popular revolution forced the Tsar to agree to the establishment of a parliament, called the **Duma**. During this revolution, soviets, or councils, were set up that controlled cities throughout Russia.

The Tsar was able to restrict the number of people who could vote to this parliament, which meant that peasants and workers were under-represented. The secret police were widely used to keep an eye on opponents of the regime, especially violent revolutionary groups like the Bolsheviks.

When World War I broke out in 1914, support for the Tsar and his government was strong. This was to change as the war continued.

WHY DID THE TSAR'S GOVERNMENT BECOME UNPOPULAR?

- In 1915, Tsar Nicholas took personal command of the army and went to the front, leaving the government in the hands of his wife, **Tsarina Alexandra**. The German-born Tsarina was

Tsar Nicolas II (1868–1918).

Key Concept Explained: Communism

Karl Marx.

Communism was based on the theories of the German economist **Karl Marx** (1818–83). He put forward his ideas in two books: *The Communist Manifesto* and *Das Kapital*. His views were based on the experiences of Europe during the Industrial Revolution in the 19th century. This had led to the creation of a large working class living in cities and working in factories owned by businessmen.

Marx argued that history was a series of class struggles between different economic groups in society. The final class struggle would happen between the workers (whom he called the **proletariat**, or the working class) and the factory owners (whom he called the **bourgeoisie**, or the middle class).

He predicted that the working class would win, which would transform society from capitalism to socialism. This would be a classless, equal society where all property was owned by the community as a whole. He believed that private property, private business, etc. should be abolished. He argued that international co-operation between workers would help to achieve these aims. He dismissed traditional religion, which he felt was an instrument for controlling the workers.

His supporters saw his ideas as a new religion, but they soon disagreed on how this change should happen. Some argued for a revolution and were called **Communists** (e.g. Lenin). They believed that all means were justified in achieving a Communist state, including terror. Those who believed this change could occur through peaceful means (i.e. through elections) were known as **Democratic Socialists**, e.g. SPD in Germany or the Labour Party in Britain.

When he came to power in Russia, Lenin and his supporters hoped that the revolution in Russia would act as a spark for further revolutions in Europe, especially in Germany.

The Communist revolution in Russia and the growth of Communist countries in many European countries, e.g. Germany and Italy, frightened many people and this contributed to the growth of fascism.

---

unpopular and was under the influence of the strange monk **Rasputin**. He dismissed ministers he did not like and brought complete discredit to the whole Tsarist system of government.

Rasputin (1869–1916) was a mysterious monk from Siberia who was able to cure the heir to the throne, Alexei, of haemophilia. This gave him great influence over his mother, the Tsarina Alexandra, affording him great political power during World War I. He was murdered by a group of nobles in December 1916, although the exact circumstances of his death are still debated by historians.

- Although Russian troops fought bravely, the army suffered heavy causalities. Many soldiers lacked proper military training and the supply of arms and artillery was inadequate. The offensive of 1916 against the Austrians had cost the Russians 1 million dead or wounded. As commander, many blamed the Tsar for these defeats.
- There was a breakdown in food supplies to the cities, with Petrograd (St. Petersburg's German name had been changed) and Moscow receiving only a third of their fuel and food requirements. Prices increased fourfold during the war.

By the start of 1917, all political parties were dissatisfied with the Tsar and his government. The main parties were as follows.

- The **Kadets** (Liberals) wanted a political system similar to Britain and were led by **Prince Lvov**.
- The **Social Revolutionaries** (SRs) wanted peasant ownership of the land. **Alexander Kerensky** was a leading figure in this party.

- The **Social Democrats** were Socialists with a large following among the workers in the cities. In 1903 they had split into the **Bolsheviks** (majority) and the **Mensheviks** (minority). The Bolsheviks were revolutionaries and were led by Lenin. The **Mensheviks** favoured peaceful change in society.

THE FEBRUARY REVOLUTION

In January 1917, in the middle of a particularly severe winter, strikes began in the capital, **Petrograd**. By February, Petrograd was paralysed by these strikes. The ordinary soldiers in the city refused to crush the strikes and instead joined the protesters. All military command within the city collapsed and the Tsar lost effective control of his capital. At the beginning of March, after taking advice from his leading generals, the Tsar decided to abdicate (resign). **A provisional government** was established under the leadership of the widely respected moderate, **Prince Lvov.** He was replaced by **Alexander Kerensky** in July. This government was to rule until a **constituent assembly** was elected that would draw up a new constitution for Russia.

The provisional government existed side by side with the **Petrograd Soviet**. The soviet had been set up during the February Revolution and quickly established itself as the real power in the city. It had full control over the railways and had the loyalty of the soldiers. It co-ordinated the activities of other soviets that sprang up across Russia at this time. At first, it was dominated by moderate Socialists and co-operated with the provisional government, but this was to change.

LENIN RETURNS TO RUSSIA

The Germans were watching events closely in Russia. German agents approached the Bolshevik leader, Lenin, who was living in exile in Switzerland. They knew if he came to power he would take Russia out of the war. In April they helped him return to Russia with financial help to stage a revolution. On his arrival, he published his '**April Theses**' in *Pravda* (the Bolshevik Party newspaper). Much to the surprise of some of his colleagues, he argued for an immediate takeover of power and advocated a policy of complete non-cooperation with the provisional government.

The provisional government made two crucial errors: it continued the war and postponed land reform. These unpopular decisions played into Lenin's hands, who called for '**Peace, Bread, Land**'.

GROWING BOLSHEVIK SUPPORT

Bolshevik support grew during the summer, as military defeats saw morale collapse and mutinies spread in the army. This was coupled with severe economic problems, such as massive inflation.

In addition, the Germans were advancing deeper into Russia and the government faced opposition from army generals who blamed it for the spreading chaos. In September 1917, the former

Alexander Kerensky (1881–1970) was born in the same town as Lenin. He was the only democratic prime minster of Russia for over 70 years.

Crowds on the streets of Petrograd in 1917. Support for the Bolsheviks grew in these chaotic conditions.

Vladimir Lenin (1870–1924) A follower of Marx he led the Bolshevik party. In 1917 he became the ruler of Russia after the October Revolution – the first successful Communist revolution. His attempt to introduce a communist economy failed and he was forced to change policy with the New Economic Policy. He died of a stroke in 1924.

commander of the Russian army, **General Kornilov**, marched on Petrograd to overthrow the government, but was defeated. The Bolshevik-controlled **Red Guards** (a military force made up of workers) helped to stop Kornilov's forces. This action gave the Bolsheviks greater support, respectability and influence. Crucially, they now were in charge of the Petrograd Soviet. The leading Bolshevik, **Leon Trotsky**, was elected chairman of the Petrograd Soviet. The Moscow Soviet also had a Bolshevik majority.

The Petrograd Soviet then set up a **Military Revolutionary Committee**, supposedly to defend the city against the Germans. In reality, it was a cover to gain control of the military in the capital in order to organise a revolution.

REVOLUTION!

On 10 October, a meeting of the Bolshevik **Central Committee** decided to stage an immediate revolution by a 10 to 2 majority. Kerensky now tried to act against the Bolsheviks, but it was too late. Trotsky issued orders for a revolution. During the night of 24–25 October, the **Red Guards**, helped by soldiers and sailors, seized most of the main buildings in Petrograd, e.g. railway stations and telephone exchanges, with little bloodshed. The members of the provisional government (except Kerensky) were arrested. By early November, Moscow and most of the larger cities had recognised the new government.

KEY QUESTION

How did Lenin establish Communist control in Russia?

THE FIRST COMMUNIST GOVERNMENT

The new government, or the **Council of People's Commissars** (Sovnarkom), was set up. Lenin was the president and there were 15 ministers. **Leon Trotsky** was Commissar for Foreign Affairs and **Joseph Stalin** was Commissar for Nationalities.

Leon Trotsky (1879–1940) planned the October Revolution and led the Communists to victory in the Civil War. A determined opponent of Stalin, he was forced into exile and later assassinated in Mexico.

Lenin speaking to a crowd in 1917.

The government acted quickly to establish its authority and popularity.

- It agreed a ceasefire with Germany (the Peace Decree).
- Private ownership of land was abolished and land was distributed among the peasants (the Land Decree).
- Banks and factories were taken over by the state. This is called **nationalisation**.
- Workers' control over factory production was introduced.
- Revolutionary tribunals were set up in place of normal courts.

However, the Bolsheviks received a setback when the elections were held for a constituent assembly, they received only a quarter of the vote. The Social Revolutionaries emerged as the largest party. It soon became clear, though, that Lenin was determined not to share power. When the assembly met in January 1918, it was closed at gunpoint.

THE RUSSIAN CIVIL WAR

In March, the **Treaty of Brest-Litovsk** was signed with the Germans. The treaty was harsh and Russia gave up the Ukraine, its Polish and Baltic territories and Finland. One-third of Russia's population, along with 80 per cent of its iron and 90 per cent of its coal, was lost. With the new border dangerously close to Petrograd, the government moved to Moscow.

Russia under Lenin.

The treaty was hugely unpopular in Russia, even among some Bolsheviks, but Lenin felt peace was necessary if the Bolsheviks were to establish control of Russia. Lenin also believed that revolution would soon spread to Germany, which would reduce the effect of the treaty.

In June 1918, discontent with the peace treaty contributed to the outbreak of civil war. The supporters of the government were called **the Reds** and their opponents **the Whites**. Lenin appointed Leon Trotsky as Commissar of War, and he proved to be an outstanding military commander.

Bolshevik forces defeated the different White generals, who rarely co-ordinated their forces and were separated from each other. By 1920, all major White forces had been defeated.

Japan, Britain, France and the US intervened on the side of the Whites, hoping to stop the spread of Communism. However, their aid was half-hearted and morale among many of the troops serving in Russia was low. This foreign intervention convinced the Bolsheviks that the capitalist powers were committed to their destruction. There was also a war with Poland that saw Russian forces defeated at Warsaw in 1920.

WHY DID THE COMMUNISTS WIN THE CIVIL WAR?

There are a number of reasons for the Reds' victory:

- The Bolsheviks were politically unified, while the Whites were divided. Supporters of the Tsar regarded SRs and Kadets as little better than the Reds.
- Most of the industry and railways remained under Bolshevik control, e.g. Petrograd and Moscow.
- The practical leadership of Lenin and Trotsky was important. For example, when it was clear that the Red Army lacked officers, 75,000 former Tsarist officers were recruited (although they were closely watched). Conscription was also introduced in the areas the Bolsheviks controlled. This meant that the Red Army outnumbered the Whites by over five to one.

- Although deeply suspicious of the Bolsheviks, many peasants saw them as a better alternative to the Whites, who would have restored their land to its original owners.
- The foreign intervention allowed the Bolsheviks to gain a lot of patriotic support for opposing the invaders.
- Terror was an important factor. Trotsky even created special cordon detachments just behind the front line to shoot deserters. Soldiers had a cruel choice: possible death if they advanced or certain death if they did not. The Cheka, or secret police, dealt mercilessly with any critics.

THE RED TERROR

During the Civil War, the Communist regime took increasingly cruel measures against its opponents. Lenin said:

We'll ask the man, where do you stand on the question of the revolution? Are you for it or against it? If he's against it, we'll stand him up against a wall.

The Cheka was set up in 1918 under the leadership of **Felix Dzerzhinsky**. In July 1918, as White armies advanced, the Tsar and his family were shot at **Yekaterinburg**. In August 1918, **Fanya Kaplan** nearly succeeded in assassinating Lenin. This gave the Cheka the excuse to start what became known as **the Red Terror**. This involved mass executions of people based not on their actions, but their class origins and beliefs (rich peasants, White officers, nobles, priests, Kadets, moderate Socialists, SRs, etc.). Guilt or innocence were completely irrelevant – what mattered was establishing complete control through fear and terror.

Execution was not the Cheka's only method; it also pioneered the development of the first modern slave labour (or concentration) camps. In total, over 100 slave labour camps were set up to deal with political opponents. Their locations were deliberately chosen to expose the prisoners to the harshest possible climate and the guards acted with unspeakable brutality. During his rule, Stalin was to expand both the number and scale of these camps.

The exact number executed during the Red Terror is difficult to estimate: it is somewhere between 100,000 and 500,000. One historian, **Orlando Figes**, has suggested that more people were murdered by the secret police between 1917 and 1924 than were killed in the battles during the Civil War.

THE COMINTERN

During its struggle for survival, the Communists believed that revolution would spread to other industrialised countries in Europe. To co-ordinate the international Socialist movement under Russian control, Lenin founded the Communist International, or **the Comintern**, in March 1919. Although no other successful socialist revolutions occurred after the Bolshevik Revolution (there were failed attempts in Germany and Hungary), the Comintern provided the Russian leadership with the means to control foreign Communist parties. From then on, Communist parties took their orders from Moscow.

KEY QUESTION

What economic changes did Lenin introduce?

WAR COMMUNISM

As we have read, when the Bolsheviks came to power, they began to introduce a wide range of new economic policies. For example, they handed factories over to the workers and gave land to peasants. This was part of a programme that intended to bring about an immediate change to Communism. It involved replacing the free market (private business) with state control over all means of **production** (farms, factories) and **distribution** (railways, shops). As many measures were introduced during the Civil War, the Bolsheviks called it **War Communism**.

In practice, War Communism meant that:
- All privately run businesses became illegal.
- Worker control of factories ended.

Relief aid being handed out to famine victims.

- All large factories passed into the hands of the government, who decided what they produced.
- Workers were now subject to strict discipline and strikers could be shot.
- Food and most other goods were rationed.
- Peasants were expected to sell their produce to the government and only keep what they needed to survive. Their food was needed to feed the workers in the cities.
- Forced labour was introduced. This was originally for class enemies (e.g. the middle class) but was later extended to workers and soldiers.

This attempt to introduce full-blown Communism proved to be a disastrous failure. Although it helped to win the war by keeping the troops supplied with food, it induced the total collapse of economic activity. For example, grain production fell from 80 million tons in 1913 to 37.6 million in 1921.

The Russian currency, the **rouble**, became worthless as the country was affected by **hyperinflation** (prices rising out of control). Workers could buy little with their wages. Peasants refused to sell their grain, as the government prices were too low. This led to food shortages in the cities. The government responded with terror – the Cheka and the Red Army were sent into the countryside to seize grain. Hundreds of thousands died as peasants resisted the government.

This government policy of seizing grain, added to bad weather and the effects of the Civil War, led to a devastating famine. About 5 million people died, with reports of cannibalism. Lenin reluctantly agreed to seek international aid, which kept the death toll from rising even further.

THE NEW ECONOMIC POLICY (NEP)

Not surprisingly, by 1921, opposition to the Communists had grown. General unrest erupted in a rebellion at the **Kronstadt** naval base (near Petrograd). Although the revolt was crushed with customary brutality, Lenin was shaken, as the sailors were traditionally loyal Bolshevik supporters. He realised that War Communism had failed and he decided to change policy. Central to the shift in policy was a realisation that if the regime was to survive, it would need to gain some support from the peasants.

He introduced the **New Economic Policy** (NEP) in order to revive the economy. Lenin had not abandoned the goal of Communism and said, 'We are taking one step backward to later take two steps forward.' The new policy signalled a return to a limited capitalist system:

- The government now took a proportion of the peasants' harvest in tax, but it was considerably lower than under War Communism.
- Peasants could now retain their excess produce and sell it for a profit.
- Small privately owned companies such as shops were allowed. Large-scale businesses such as banking and the railways remained under state control. However, these state-owned companies were now expected to make a profit.

Over the course of five years, the NEP saw industrial and agricultural output rise to pre-war levels. By 1924, privately owned business accounted for 40 per cent of Russian domestic trade. International trade also grew and inflation was brought under control. Those who took advantage of NEP in the cities were called **NEPmen**.

The NEP caused disquiet among some in the party, who saw it as a reversal of everything they believed. NEPmen were often persecuted by hostile officials who taxed them heavily. Some party members were especially unhappy that the prosperous peasants, or Kulaks, were benefiting from the policy, as they were seen as the enemies of Communism.

THE DEATH OF LENIN

In May 1922, Lenin suffered his first stroke. Over the next two years, he was to have four strokes in total. Recent evidence suggests that he may have been suffering the effects of syphilis. He was greatly weakened by his illness. He became an isolated figure and a power struggle developed between Stalin and Trotsky to succeed him.

He dictated his **political testament** in December 1922. In it, he recommended that Stalin be removed as General Secretary of the party. The party decided not to take action and Stalin was still in office when Lenin died. After a stroke in 1923, he could not speak. In January 1924, he died at the village of Gorky, near Moscow. His body was preserved in Red Square in Moscow and Petrograd was renamed Leningrad in his honour. After his death, his cult of personality grew and he became a God-like figure who could do no wrong.

An ill Lenin.

LENIN – AN EVALUATION

There is no doubt that Lenin was one of the foremost political leaders of the 20th century. His idea of a revolutionary party as a disciplined, military-style organisation served as an important model for later revolutionary leaders of the 20th century, such as Mao Zedong of China and Fidel Castro of Cuba.

Lenin's common sense (historians sometimes use the word **pragmatism**) and his ability to seize an opportunity when it arose were two of his major political skills.

- He saw that the provisional government was doomed by October 1917. Against the advice of many of his supporters, he ordered what turned out to be a successful revolution.
- He pulled Russia out of the war with Germany, which helped to strengthen his regime.
- His leadership helped to ensure victory in the Civil War, leading to the establishment of the Communist state.
- His ability to recognise when his economic policies had failed led him to abandon War Communism and replace it with the New Economic Policy.

After the collapse of Communism in 1989, a more negative opinion of Lenin grew among historians, who pointed to the fact that Lenin set up a very brutal **totalitarian** regime.

- Democracy was banned and a one-party police state was established.
- The murder of the royal family cast a shadow across the new government.
- War Communism resulted in a famine in which an estimated 5 million people died.
- The biggest criticism of Lenin was his use of terror as state policy. To Lenin and his followers, terror was necessary, as the goal of a Communist state justified any action taken. He set up the apparatus of terror (secret police, show trials, concentration camps, etc.). He devalued human life and, as we shall see in the next chapter, Stalin was to take this policy to its logical bloody climax in the 1930s.

REVIEW QUESTIONS

1 Give two reasons why the Tsar was unpopular by 1917.

2 Is it fair to say that the provisional government helped to bring about its own downfall?

3 How did the new government establish its authority and try to become popular?

4 Explain why the Treaty of Brest-Litovsk was hated in Russia.

5 Give two important reasons for the success of the Bolsheviks during the Civil War.

6 What actions did the Cheka take to ensure Communist control in Russia?

7 Why was there a famine in Russia in 1921?

8 Was the New Economic Policy successful? Explain your answer.

Lenin's Russia: Timeline

1870	Born at Simbirsk.
1903	Split in the Russian Social Democratic Party saw the formation of the Bolshevik Party, led by Lenin.
1914	Russia entered World War I on the side of the Allies.
1917	February Revolution resulted in the overthrow of the Tsar.
	April: Lenin returned to Russia.
	October: Bolsheviks seized power in a bloodless coup.
1918	January: Constituent assembly closed.
	March: Treaty of Brest-Livtosk.
	June: Outbreak of the Civil War.
	July: Murder of the Tsar and his family.
	August: Assassination attempt on Lenin. Beginning of the Red Terror.
1919	March: Comintern set up to control foreign Communist parties.
	April: Concentration camps established in Russia.
1920	Defeat of the Whites.
1921	Famine ravaged Russia, estimated 5 million died.
	March: Revolt at Kronstadt naval base.
	Introduction of the New Economic Policy.
1922	Russia officially renamed the Union of Soviet Socialist Republics (USSR).
	May: Lenin suffered his first stroke.
1924	January: Lenin died. Petrograd renamed Leningrad in his honour.

1 **Source Question**
Read the source and answer the questions that follow.

The following are excerpts from the demands of the Kronstadt sailors, dated 28 February 1921.

2. *Freedom of speech and press for workers, peasants, Anarchists and Left Socialist Parties.*

3. *Freedom of meetings, trade unions and peasant associations.*

5. *To liberate all political prisoners of Socialist Parties, and also all workers, peasants, soldiers and sailors who have been imprisoned in connection with working-class and peasant movements.*

6. *To elect a commission to review the cases of those who are imprisoned in jails and concentration camps.*

7. *To abolish all Political Departments, because no single party may enjoy privileges in the propagation of its ideas and receive funds from the state for this purpose.*

11. *To grant the peasant full right to do what he sees fit with his land and also to possess cattle, which he must maintain and manage with his own strength, but without employing hired labor.*

13. *We demand that all resolutions be widely published in the press.*

Source: www.soviethistory.org

(a) For whom do the sailors demand freedom of speech?
(b) Give two demands that are made in the case of prisoners.
(c) Why do the sailors want all political departments abolished? Which 'single party' do you think the sailors are referring to?
(d) Do you think that demand number 11 would have been popular with peasants?
(e) Would you agree that these demands are a strong criticism of Lenin and his government? Explain your answer.

2 Write a paragraph on **TWO** of following (Ordinary Level):
(a) How Lenin came to power.
(b) Why the Red Army won the Civil War.
(c) Economic policies introduced by Lenin.

3 Write an essay on **ONE** of the following:
(a) What role did Lenin play in Russian affairs? (Ordinary Level)
(b) How did Lenin establish a Communist regime in Russia? (Higher Level)

4 'Lenin's achievements are overshadowed by the brutality of his government.'
Do you agree? Argue your case.

(3) Stalin and the USSR, 1924–45

What do you need to know in this chapter?

Elements	Key Personalities	Key Concepts
The regimes of Lenin and Stalin	Joseph Stalin	Communism
		Totalitarianism
The Soviet alternative (society and economy)		Dictatorship
		Propaganda
The Stalinist state in peace and war		Cult of personality
Case Study: The Show Trials		Collectivisation

INTRODUCTION

In this chapter, we will see how Stalin transformed the USSR's society and economy. We will also read how the use of terror played a central role in Stalin's policies. We will focus on the Show Trials, which saw leading members of the Communist Party accused of fantastic crimes.

KEY QUESTION

How did Stalin become the ruler of the USSR?

RISE IN THE PARTY

After the February Revolution in 1917, Stalin returned from exile in Siberia and became editor of **Pravda**. He played little part in the **October Revolution**, although his role would be greatly exaggerated when he was in power.

After the revolution, he was appointed **Commissar for Nationalities**. During the Civil War, he served as a commander on a number of fronts, where he frequently came into conflict with Trotsky, his main rival in the party. Stalin was appointed **General Secretary of the Communist Party** in 1922. He used this position to build up his power base within the organisation, appointing his supporters to posts throughout the country.

POWER STRUGGLE

In 1924, Lenin died and a power struggle involving **Leon Trotsky**, **Lev Kamenev**, **Gregory Zinoviev** and Stalin followed. Lenin's testament, which contained damning comments about Stalin, was not made public. Both Kamenev and Zinoviev saw

Stalin with Lenin. Stalin was always careful to portray himself as a loyal supporter of Lenin and his ideas in order to become his natural heir.

Joseph Stalin (1879–1953) After Lenin's death he became leader of the USSR. He modernised the economy through a programme of rapid industrialisation. This progress came at a terrible human cost with mass executions and the use of slave labour. In World War II he led the USSR to victory over the Germans.

Here is an explanation of some of the terms you will meet in this chapter.

Gulags: The prison camp system in the USSR.

NKVD: The secret police.

Permanent Revolution: Trotsky's policy of encouraging worldwide revolution.

Purges: Removing 'enemies of the people' from the Communist Party.

Show trials: Propaganda trials held of those accused of plotting against Stalin.

Socialism in One Country: Stalin's policy of establishing socialism in the Soviet Union. It involved rapid industrialisation using Five-Year Plans.

Lenin's views as only benefiting Trotsky, who they mistakenly saw as their main rival.

The other leaders underestimated Stalin's political ability and he was never isolated during the power struggle. For example, he allied himself with Zinoviev and Kamenev against Trotsky.

A key question for party members was how the Communist regime could achieve the rapid industrialisation of Russia's backward rural economy. This would create a large working class that would be more likely to support the Communist regime. It would also make Russia militarily more powerful and better able to defend itself against its capitalist enemies. Trotsky had said the only way to do this was by encouraging revolution in other countries. He called this theory **Permanent Revolution.** Some leaders felt that rapid industrialisation was not possible and that the pace of change would have to come slowly.

Stalin disagreed with both positions and insisted rapid industrialisation was possible. Posing as the heir of Lenin, he put forward his theory of **Socialism in One Country**. He argued all that was needed was a plan and the iron will and determination that had won the Civil War. He felt that the revolution could be exported only when the country had been industrialised.

In 1925, at the **Fourteenth Party Congress**, Stalin's Socialism in One Country theory was adopted as party policy – Stalin had won. Trotsky was removed from his post as **Commissar for War**. In 1927, Trotsky was expelled from the party and two years later he was exiled from Russia. Stalin then turned on Kamenev and Zinoviev. They were expelled from the party, although they were later readmitted. By 1928, Stalin was the dominant figure in the party and was ready to implement his transformation of the USSR.

Structure of the Communist Party in Stalin's Russia

General Secretary of the Communist Party (Stalin)

↑

Politburo
Cabinet of 10 members chosen by the Central Committee for day-to-day running of the country – in reality, picked by Stalin

↑

Central Committee of the Party
Chosen at each party congress – names decided by Stalin

↑

Party Congress
At first held every year under Lenin, but more infrequently under Stalin

KEY QUESTION

How did Stalin transform the Soviet Union's society and economy?

SOCIALISM IN ONE COUNTRY

As we have seen, Stalin felt that Russia could no longer rely on world revolution. He believed that priority had to be given to the industrialisation of Russia or it could be defeated by the hostile powers that surrounded it. He said:

'We are 50 or 100 years behind the advanced countries. We must make good this lag in 10 years or be crushed.'

His strategy involved building an industrial nation with a heavy emphasis on coal, iron and vast public works such as canals. He proposed to end the **New Economic Policy** (NEP) and the destruction of all elements of private enterprise that existed in Russia. State control over agricultural production was necessary and was to be achieved through **collectivisation**.

The policy was implemented through a series of **Five-Year Plans** that began in 1928. In all, there were three plans:
- 1928–32.
- 1933–37.

- 1938–41 (cut short due to the German invasion).

As a result, the Soviet Union became a **command economy** where all decisions on what goods to produce were decided by the government. In order to achieve such rapid change in Russia in such a short period, widespread use was made of terror and propaganda.

This painting is an example of Socialist Realism – artists were expected to use their paintings to glorify the ideals of Communism using imagined scenes from everyday life. This term is misleading, as what they were painting was anything but everyday reality.

PROPAGANDA

Newspapers, radio, cinema, writers and artists were all tightly controlled by the party and all glorified Stalin and his policies. Targets set by the Five-Year Plans were declared over-fulfilled. A **cult of personality** was developed, where Stalin became a superman or God-like figure who could do no wrong.

Many towns were renamed after him, e.g. **Stalingrad**, **Stalinsk**, **Stalinogorsk**, **Stalinbad**, **Stalino**. Statues were erected throughout Russia and poems, plays and novels were written in his honour.

He was known as the *vozhd*, or leader, or was given pompous titles such as 'Father of Nations', 'Brilliant Genius of Humanity', 'Great Architect of Communism' and 'Gardener of Human Happiness' (Stalin was a keen gardener!). Soviet history was rewritten to give Stalin a more significant role in the revolution, especially at the expense of **Trotsky**.

INDUSTRIALISATION OF RUSSIA

Stalin's first Five-Year Plan emphasised heavy industry such as coal and iron. It set goals that were unrealistic, such as a 250 per cent increase in overall industrial development and a 330 per cent expansion in heavy industry. Many new industrial centres were built, particularly east of the Ural Mountains:

- Iron and steel works at Magnitogorsk.
- Tractor factories at Stalingrad and Kharkov.
- A vast plant for agricultural machinery at Sverdlovsk.
- Car factories at Moscow and Gorki.
- Oil refineries at Baku.

The model for Stalinist industrialisation was the new industrial city of **Magnitogorsk**, on the eastern slopes of the Ural Mountains. The city took its name from the high-grade magnetic iron ores in the surrounding hills. The project was to build a single steelworks capable of producing more than the pre-1917 Tsarist Empire: 5 million tons of steel and 4.5 million tons of iron.

The factory was built with the help of American engineers and was equipped with American and German machinery. By the outbreak of the war, the complex employed 45,000 people. The city, partly designed by German architects, was dominated by the steelworks and a permanent dark haze hung over it.

PUBLIC WORKS

The construction of massive public works was also a central part of the plan. Some of the schemes included:

- The White Sea-Baltic Canal.
- The Moscow-Donets railway.
- The Dnieper hydroelectric dam (prior to its construction, the Shannon Scheme had been the largest hydroelectric station in the world).
- The Moscow-Volga Canal.
- The Moscow Underground, seen by many as the greatest achievement of the period.

Propaganda hailed the projects as great successes for the new state but failed to mention that they were mainly built by slave labour.

RESULTS OF INDUSTRIALISATION

The table shows the impressive increase in output under the Five-Year Plans.

Output	1927	1933	1937
Electricity (billion kW)	5	13	36
Coal (million tons)	35	64	128
Oil (million tons)	12	21	47
Steel (million tons)	4	6	18

With the emphasis on heavy industry, there were widespread shortages of everyday consumer goods and food was rationed. Living standards for workers fell. When targets were not met, terror was used, with show trials held for managers who were accused of sabotage, e.g. deliberately destroying machinery. Workers were severely disciplined for minor offences. If absent without just cause for even a single day, they could be automatically

РЕАЛЬНОСТЬ НАШЕЙ ПРОГРАММЫ
–ЭТО ЖИВЫЕ ЛЮДИ, ЭТО МЫ С ВАМИ,
НАША ВОЛЯ К ТРУДУ, НАША ГОТОВНОСТЬ
РАБОТАТЬ ПО-НОВОМУ,
НАША РЕШИМОСТЬ ВЫПОЛНИТЬ ПЛАН.

Propaganda poster praising the achievements of Stalin and industrialisation. Note the smiling faces.

dismissed from work, have their ration cards confiscated and be evicted from their housing.

Other measures were used besides terror. Rewards such as higher wages were given to the best workers. Examples of hard work were praised, and the most famous example of this was the **Stakhanovite movement**. This was named after a miner, Aleksei Stakhanov, who mined a record 102 tons of coal during his six-hour shift.

Life was made bearable for many by the provision of work, a flat, schooling and free, albeit basic, health care. Many diseases, such as typhus, cholera and malaria, were tackled. There was far greater equality in society, which meant that careers such as doctors, teachers and engineers were opened to women. They were attracted into the workforce by new crèches and day-care centres that allowed mothers to work.

The country had been transformed from a backward, predominantly agricultural society to a major industrial power. There had been a massive population transfer from the countryside to the cities and the urban workforce had trebled in size.

Many in the West looked to the USSR as an inspiration, given the mass unemployment caused by the Great Depression. Prominent figures such as **George Bernard Shaw** and **H.G. Wells** visited Russia and praised what they saw. Shaw said, 'Were I only 18 years of age I would settle in Moscow tomorrow.'

By 1939, Russia was industrially self-sufficient and could supply its own needs. It was now one of the most powerful countries in the world and Stalin's policies helped to defeat the Nazi invasion. It is important to remember, however, that this advance came at a terrible cost. **Niall Ferguson** points out that 'for every 19 tons of steel produced in the Stalinist period, approximately one Soviet citizen was killed.'

COLLECTIVISATION

Central to Stalin's polices was the need to make agriculture more efficient. In 1928, the vast majority of the population were peasants who worked small plots of land. Production methods were backward and few farms had modern machinery such as tractors.

The First Five-Year Plan called for transforming Soviet agriculture from individual farms into a system of large state collective farms. This was called **collectivisation**. Each collective farm, called a *kolkhoz*, would have between 50 to 100 families working on it.

Stalin believed that collectivisation would make farming more efficient, thereby producing grain reserves sufficiently large to feed the growing urban labour force. It would also free many peasants for industrial work in the cities and enable the party to extend its political dominance over the remaining peasantry. Some grain could be sold abroad and the money used to buy machinery needed for the new factories.

MAN-MADE FAMINE

Peasants resisted Stalin's policies and the state responded with its usual tactic – terror. Stalin focused particular hostility on the wealthier peasants, or *kulaks*. Seen as class enemies, they were blamed for the opposition to Stalin's policies.

About 5 million people – men, women and children – were deported to the **Gulags** (see p. 23) or transported to unsettled territories in Siberia, often in the middle of winter, where most died.

Despite this policy, forced collectivisation of the remaining peasants was fiercely resisted – livestock was killed and there were revolts throughout the country. Troops were used to defeat the peasants. Determined to break peasant resistance, Stalin used famine as a state policy. His particular target was the Ukraine, the traditional bread basket of the USSR.

In 1932, Stalin raised Ukraine's grain quota by 44 per cent. This meant that there would not be enough grain to feed the peasants, since Soviet law required that no grain from a collective farm could be given to the members of the farm until the government's quota was met.

Stalin's decision and the methods used to implement it condemned millions of peasants to death by starvation. Party officials, with the aid of regular troops and secret police units, waged a merciless war against peasants who refused to give up their grain. Any man, woman or child caught taking even a handful of grain from a collective farm could be executed or deported. Peasants were prevented from leaving their villages by the secret police, the NKVD, and a system of internal passports.

The famine broke the peasants' will to resist collectivisation. The death toll from the 1932–33 famine in Ukraine has been estimated at between 6 and 7 million, although some historians think the figure is far lower, at about 2.5 million.

RESULTS OF COLLECTIVISATION

Aside from the human cost, the policy of collectivisation was a disaster, as can be seen from the decline in numbers of livestock in the USSR.

A good harvest in 1933 helped agriculture to revive. Rationing of bread and other food products was ended in 1935. By 1940, livestock levels had reached pre-1928 levels and grain, cotton and sugar production increased.

There was also increased mechanisation, as tractors and combine harvesters were supplied by many of the new factories that had been built. By 1939, well over 90 per cent of the 25 million farms that had existed in 1928 had been turned into about 400,000 collectives.

However, the human cost was truly staggering. It is difficult to calculate the numbers who perished during collectivisation, but some historians estimate the figure to be about 10 million.

REVIEW QUESTIONS

1. Explain the term 'Socialism in One Country'.
2. Give one reason why Stalin was successful in the power struggle after Lenin's death.
3. What were the Five-Year Plans?
4. How was a cult of personality of Stalin promoted in the USSR?
5. Name three public works schemes built in the 1930s.
6. At the time, why did many people in Western Europe admire Stalin's policies?
7. What was the aim of the policy of collectivisation?
8. Describe two measures taken by Stalin to deal with opposition to collectivisation.

THE PURGES

As we have read, terror had always been an essential element of policy in Communist Russia. From 1934 until 1939, Russia was to suffer another period of unprecedented cruelty that became known as the Purges, or **the Great Terror**.

Stalin became increasingly worried about opposition to his policies and his control of the party (although most of these fears were in his imagination). He wanted to remove any threat to his power. The Purges also served another useful purpose – they laid the blame for all the failures of Stalin's policies at the hands of 'traitors' and 'spies'.

The event that triggered the Purges was the murder of **Sergei Kirov** in December 1934. He was the popular Leningrad party leader and a close ally of Stalin. At the Seventeenth Party Congress in 1934, when the members of the **Central Committee** were chosen, Kirov received more votes than Stalin. On the surface, Stalin and Kirov were friends, but Stalin probably saw him as a rival. He was almost certainly assassinated on Stalin's orders. Stalin used this event as evidence of a plot against his rule and began a witch hunt against any potential enemies within or outside the party.

EVERYDAY LIFE DURING THE GREAT TERROR

The secret police, called the NKVD, arrested millions of Russians. The vast majority were innocent of any crimes. The secret police worked with great determination arresting suspects, as they knew they could be next. The arrests came in the middle of the night. This led to a climate of fear throughout the country, with everyone afraid that they would fall victim to the NKVD. Informers were everywhere. Even children were encouraged to report their parents to the authorities.

Provincial party leaders, members of the national minorities, industrial managers, former nobles, priests and other religious people were arrested. Anyone with connections or who had visited countries abroad were viewed with particular suspicion. One important target were those who were termed '**Old Bolsheviks**' – people who had been members of the party before 1917. As we shall see, many of these men were to be tried during the Show Trials. The arrest of loyal Communists made Stalin's terror different from Lenin's in that Lenin had rarely targeted Communist Party members.

The process fed upon itself as the accused confessed to often bizarre crimes under torture and named more names. Most of those arrested were shot or sent to the Gulags. In 1936, unhappy with progress, Stalin had the head of the secret police, **Genrikh Yagoda**, replaced with **Nikolai Yezhov**. Under Yezhov, the pace of terror intensified. Many Russians called the period **the Yezhovschina** – the Yezhov Era. When Stalin wanted to end the Purges, he had Yezhov removed. He was blamed for killing too many people and later shot. Yezhov was then replaced by Stalin's old friend and fellow Georgian, **Lavrentiy Beria**.

Stalin was unrepentant about the bloodletting. At the party congress in 1939, he declared that the purge 'was unavoidable and its results, on the whole, beneficial'.

Cartoon showing Yezhov crushing the enemies of the Revolution.

THE GULAGS

The majority of people arrested were not shot, but sent to **Gulags**. These were camp systems found throughout the USSR. They were designed to provide slave labour to help with the process of industrialisation. There were 476 camp complexes, each containing numerous individual camps. Conditions were extremely harsh. Prisoners, or *zeks*, received inadequate food rations and unsuitable clothing. This made it difficult to endure the severe weather in many of the camps (where the temperatures fell below 0°C six months of the year) and the long working hours (14 hours a day). The inmates were often beaten, tortured or murdered by camp guards and other inmates.

One of the best-known of the Gulag camp complexes was **Kolyma**. This was an area of Siberia about six times the size of France that contained more than 100 camps. Other than Antarctica, its climate is perhaps the most severe in the world. Over 1 million people died there from its establishment in 1931 to 1953, the year of Stalin's death. Prisoners spoke of Kolyma as a place where 12 months were winter and all the rest summer. Other large camp complexes were at **Vorkuta** and **Solovetsk**.

SLAVE LABOUR

Gulag prisoners were used as slave labour and built some of the public works schemes that we read about earlier in the chapter. They constructed the White Sea-Baltic Canal, the Moscow-Volga Canal, the Baikal-Amur main railroad line, numerous hydroelectric stations and important roads. Gulag manpower was also used for the mining of coal, copper and gold. Over 100,000 prisoners helped to build the White Sea-Baltic Canal, and tens of thousands died. When the canal was opened, it was found to be too shallow to be used by large ships.

THE DEATH TOLL

It is difficult to estimate the number of Stalin's victims. The Kremlin went to great lengths to cover up the magnitude of Soviet population losses. It concealed the results of the 1937 census when it revealed a massive drop in population – the entire census board staff were shot as spies. A 'revised' census was published in 1939, but even this revealed that roughly 10 per cent of the Soviet population was statistically missing – some 15 million victims of Stalin's reign of terror.

Other historians put the figure as high as 20 or 30 million. Left-wing historians dispute this figure and say that the number of Stalin's victims was far lower. All agree that Stalin's policies were carried out at a terrible human cost. Mass graves are discovered in Russia even to this day.

Here is what two historians have written about Stalin's crimes:

> *It is sometimes said that Stalin's crimes were necessary to modernise an antiquated [backward] country. This was precisely how he justified the costs of collectivisation to Churchill. But the human cost was out of all proportion to the gains in economic efficiency.*

Source: Niall Ferguson, *The War of the World: History's Age of Hatred*, Allen Lane, 2006.

> *Between 1929 and 1953 the state created by Lenin and set in motion by Stalin deprived 21.5 million Soviet citizens of their lives. No one in history has ever waged such war on his own people.*

Source: Dmitri Volkogonov, *The Rise and Fall of the Soviet Empire: Political Leaders from Lenin to Gorbachev*, HarperCollins, 1999.

Gulag prisoners at work.

Terror in the USSR

- Liquidation of the *Kulaks*.
- Ukrainian terror famine.
- Use of informers, secret police, the NKVD.
- Purges/show trials.
- Gulags and slave labour.
- Executions and deportations during World War II.

CASE STUDY: THE SHOW TRIALS

KEY QUESTION

What role did the Show Trials play in Stalin's Russia?

THE PURPOSE OF THE TRIALS

The Great Terror was marked by three elaborately staged show trials of former high-ranking Communists, or 'Old Bolsheviks', as they were known. Also named the **Moscow Trials**, they were propaganda trials, with the accused men portrayed as **enemies of the people**. Show trials were not new in the Soviet Union: a series of trials were staged against Russian and foreign industrial experts between 1928 and 1933, where defendants were accused of sabotage, treason and spying for foreign powers.

Stalin's aim in organising the trials was to establish complete domination over the Communist Party and to eliminate any potential threats. Many of the accused were members of the party prior to the revolution and had been opponents of Stalin in the party at some stage. Another purpose of the trials was to find scapegoats to blame for failures during the Five-Year Plans.

In all, there were three trials and like a puppet master, Stalin completely controlled what happened. The assassination of Sergei Kirov provided the excuse. The NKVD collected the 'evidence' while the arch-villain and leader of the plots, Trotsky, was conveniently in exile.

HOW THE TRIALS WORKED

The trials followed the same format.

1. The defendants were accused of incredible crimes, e.g. plotting to assassinate Stalin or working as spies for foreign countries such as Germany.
2. The defendants then confessed their guilt and were found guilty – the verdicts had been decided before the trial.
3. The proceedings were widely publicised, both at home and abroad.
4. The vast majority were then shot.

Here is an explanation of some of the language that was used during the show trials.

- **Terrorism:** Any doubt or opposition to Stalin's policies.
- **Assassins/terrorists:** Opponents of Stalin.
- **Conspiracy:** More than two terrorists.
- **Bloc/unified centre:** Co-operation between different factions opposed to Stalin.
- **Counter-revolutionary:** Working to overthrow the Communist revolution and restore capitalism.

The real star of the show was the 53-year-old prosecutor, **Andrei Vyshinsky**. He was vain, witty

Andrei Vyshinsky (1883–1954).

and intelligent and had once shared a cell with Stalin. His ex-Menshevik past made him absolutely obedient, as he himself could find himself arrested at any moment. He was notoriously unpleasant to those who worked for him.

THE FIRST SHOW TRIAL – THE TRIAL OF THE SIXTEEN

In 1936, **Lev Kamenev**, **Gregory Zinoviev** and 14 other leading Bolsheviks were put on trial. Before the trial, they had been interrogated by the NKVD to produce the required confessions. Carefully planned and stage-managed, the trial opened on 19 August in the October Hall in the House of Unions in Moscow. The 350 spectators were mainly NKVD in plain clothes, foreign journalists and diplomats. The three judges sat on a raised platform in the centre. To increase their humiliation, the 16 defendants were dressed in old and ill-fitting clothes. To reinforce the impression of their guilt and were guarded by NKVD troops with fixed bayonets. Stalin was said to be present in a gallery with darkened windows at the back of the room.

The defendants were accused of an amazing collection of often bungled crimes ordered by a shadowy conspiracy led by Trotsky, Zinoviev and Kamenev. Called the **United Trotskyite-Zinovievite Centre**, it was alleged that they had killed Kirov and had repeatedly attempted to kill Stalin and other leaders. Kamenev admitted that 'for ten years … I waged a struggle against the party … and against Stalin personally'. Some of the evidence was very weak. One defendant even confessed to being involved in the murder of Kirov when he was already in prison. The accused implicated others in their evidence and this raised the prospect of other Bolshevik leaders appearing in further trials.

In his closing speech, Vyshinsky demanded the death penalty, saying:

> These mad dogs of capitalism tried to tear limb from limb the best of our Soviet land … I demand that these mad dogs should be shot – every one of them!

Before the verdict was announced, Kamenev said, 'No matter what my sentence will be, I, in advance, consider it just.' When the judges brought in their pre-decided verdict of death, one of the defendants shouted, 'Long live the cause of Marx, Engels, Lenin and Stalin!' Appeals for mercy were rejected and all 16 were shot soon after and their property confiscated. Soviet newspapers applauded the executions and demanded more purges of counter-revolutionaries.

REACTION IN THE WEST

For six days, the defendants had willingly confessed to their crimes. This amazed Western spectators, both in Russia and abroad. This is reflected in the reaction of the British magazine *The New Statesman*:

> Very likely there was a plot. We complain because, in the absence of independent witnesses, there is no way of knowing. It is their [Zinoviev and Kamenev] confession and decision to demand the death sentence for themselves that constitutes the mystery. If they had a hope of acquittal, why confess? If they were guilty of trying to murder Stalin and knew they would be shot in any case, why cringe and crawl instead of defiantly justifying their plot on revolutionary grounds? We would be glad to hear the explanation.

Source: *The New Statesman*, 5 September 1936.

Despite the weaknesses in the evidence, the US ambassador was convinced of the defendants' guilt and wrote that most other diplomats agreed with his view. The delegation sent by the International Association of Lawyers noted in its report:

> We consider the claim that the proceedings were summary and unlawful to be totally unfounded. [...] We hereby categorically declare that the accused were sentenced quite lawfully. It was fully proven that there were links between them and the Gestapo.

Communist parties throughout Europe attacked any criticism of the trials. The leader of the British Communist Party called the trials 'a new triumph in the history of progress'.

WHY DID THE DEFENDANTS CONFESS?

Contemporary foreign observers were baffled by the sight of hardened revolutionaries willingly confessing their guilt. Why did they do it? To this day, historians are not sure.

- Torture and the fear of torture played a role. 'All means' were to be used to get confessions. The methods that were used broke the resistance of even the strongest person. When an official told Stalin that Kamenev would not confess, he became enraged and told the official not to come back until he had a confession from Kamenev.
- They may have thought that if they co-operated, their lives and those of their families would be spared. Stalin had promised Kamenev and Zinoviev that if they confessed publicly to their crimes, they and their families would not be shot. He did not honour this promise. Both men were executed and Kamenev's wife and son were killed, while Zinoviev's son, three brothers and one of his sisters were later shot.
- The accused men were loyal Communists and some may have believed that the good of the party came first, even over their own lives.

THE SECOND SHOW TRIAL: THE TRIAL OF THE SEVENTEEN

The Second Show Trial opened in January 1937 of the members of the **Parallel Anti-Soviet Trotskyist Centre.** In all, 17 men were charged. The most prominent were **Yuri Pyatakov** and **Karl Radek**. Both were former supporters of Trotsky. The rest were leading figures in the industrialisation drive.

In court, Vyshinsky called the defendants 'liars and clowns, insignificant pygmies'. The accused fell over each other to prove their own guilt. They confessed to conspiring with anti-Soviet 'Trotskyites' and having spied for Nazi Germany and Japan. This was all the more remarkable because many of the defendants were Jewish. Some of the evidence was comical – for instance, it was alleged that Trotsky's son ordered assassinations at a meeting in the Hotel Bristol in Copenhagen, even though this hotel had been demolished in 1917.

Stalin dictated the contents of Vyshinsky's summing up at the end of the trial to the prosecutor. Radek was imprisoned (where he died soon after), while most of the defendants were shot.

THE THIRD SHOW TRIAL: THE TRIAL OF THE TWENTY-ONE

The last of the show trials was staged in March 1938. This was known officially as the **Case of the Anti-Soviet Bloc of Rights and Trotskyites.** Twenty-one men stood in the dock and included prominent figures such as **Nicholas Bukharin,**

The defendants during the Second Show Trial.

Nicholas Bukharin (1888–1938) was editor of Pravda from 1918 until 1929. He was expelled from the party for opposing Stalin in 1929, but was readmitted in 1934.

Nikolai Krestinsky, **Alexei Rykov** and former chief of the secret police, **Yagoda**. In a similar vein to the earlier trials, the defendants faced a wide range of allegations, including:

- Murdering Kirov and the writer Maxim Gorky.
- Unsuccessfully trying to assassinate Lenin two decades before and plotting to assassinate Stalin as well as other Bolshevik leaders.
- Conspiring to wreck the economy and the country's military power.
- Spying for Britain, France, Japan and Germany.

An ex-Commissar for Agriculture was blamed for 'mistakes' in collectivisation and the head of the collectives was accused of selling butter containing glass. These men proved to be handy scapegoats for the failure of collectivisation.

When the trial started, Krestinsky, a former member of the Central Committee, actually pleaded not guilty.

The President: Accused Krestinsky, do you plead guilty to the charges brought against you?

Krestinsky: I plead not guilty. I am not a Trotskyite. I was never a member of the Bloc of Rights and Trotskyites, of whose existence I was not aware. Nor have I committed any of the crimes with which I personally am charged.

The next day, after a night with the NKVD, he changed his mind.

Krestinsky: In the face of world public opinion, I had not the strength to admit the truth that I had been conducting a Trotskyite struggle all along. I request the Court to register my statement that I fully and completely admit that I am guilty of all the gravest charges brought against me personally.

Source: http://art-bin.com/art/amosc_preeng.html.

After this minor setback, the trial followed the normal format, with most of the defendants admitting responsibility for fantastic crimes, and all were shot bar three minor figures. In his final speech, **Bukharin** made a strong defence of his actions. He confessed his guilt in general but denied many of the specific allegations against him, e.g. plotting to murder Lenin.

THE PURGE OF THE RED ARMY

In between the second and third trials, there was a widespread purge of the army. Historians are unsure of Stalin's motives in purging the military. He may have believed that it was necessary to remove any officers whose loyalty was in doubt to prevent a military takeover.

Civil War hero **Marshal Tukhachevsky**, the Chief of the General Staff, and other senior officers were tried for plotting with Germany and executed. Tukhachevsky's name had been mentioned in evidence during the Second Show Trial.

According to figures published in Soviet newspapers in 1987, the purge accounted for most of the leadership of the army. In all, about 50 per cent of all officers, or 35,000 men, were shot. This action seriously weakened the leadership of the Red Army and the Soviet Union was to suffer severe defeats at the hands of the Germans in 1941.

Many foreign Communists who had fled to Russia were also victims of the purges. For example, 10,000 Polish Communists were executed at the time of the Third Show Trial.

SUMMARY

In 1939, of the original 15-man Bolshevik government of 1917, only two were alive, Stalin and Trotsky. Ten had perished during the Show Trials. In 1940, Trotsky was murdered by one of Stalin's agents in Mexico. The trials made Stalin the absolute master of the Communist Party and created an atmosphere of terror throughout the USSR.

The trials served as a warning to all party members that no one was safe from arrest, while to ordinary citizens, it reinforced the message that there were traitors everywhere working against their interests, even at the top of the party. This justified the Great Terror, as these traitors allied to hostile foreign powers could end Communism.

It is difficult to disagree with the assessment of the Show Trials given by the historian Joe Lee:

Although the Show Trials of 1936–8 involved only a handful, they were the crowning glories of the entire process. They included the big three of the old guard, Kamenev, Zinoviev and Bukharin, a warning that treachery could infiltrate the highest ranks – and that any disagreement with Stalin could be seen as treachery.

Source: Joe Lee, *The Shifting Balance of Power: Exploring the 20th Century*, Sunday Tribune, 2000.

REVIEW QUESTIONS

1 Why did Stalin start the purges?

2 What groups of people were arrested during the purges?

3 What were conditions like in the Gulags?

4 Give two reasons why show trials were held between 1936 and 1938.

5 'All of the show trials basically followed the same format.' Do you agree? Explain your answer.

6 What action did Stalin take against the Red Army in 1937?

7 What impact did the purges of Soviet officers have?

THE STALINIST STATE AT WAR, 1941–45

Note: For more detail on World War II, see Chapter 10.

KEY QUESTION

How did Stalin respond to the German invasion of 1941?

NAZI-SOVIET NON-AGGRESSION PACT

Alarmed by Hitler's growing power and German expansion in the 1930s (e.g. the Munich Conference), Stalin looked for allies against a possible German attack. However, France and Britain were wary of Communism and believed that the Russian Army was weak. They dragged their feet and negotiations continued throughout the summer of 1939. The Germans took advantage and offered Stalin a deal. He agreed.

On 23 August 1939, **the Nazi-Soviet Non-Aggression Pact** was signed. The two countries promised not to attack each other. Secretly they agreed to divide Poland between them. Germany also allowed Russia to take over Latvia, Estonia, Lithuania and part of Finland. This land had been lost by Russia in 1918.

This agreement provided Russia with security in the short term and also freed Hitler from the fear of Russian intervention when he invaded Poland, and later France.

THE GERMAN INVASION OF RUSSIA

Hitler failed to defeat the Royal Air Force in the Battle of Britain in 1940 and decided to conquer the USSR instead. In June 1941, Hitler launched Operation Barbarossa, the massive invasion of Russia. Involving over 3 million men, the German attack of the Soviet Union was initially a great success – the German army inflicted defeat after defeat on the Red Army, capturing vast numbers of men. The purges had severely depleted the Red Army officer corps. Minsk and Kiev were captured and the Germans laid siege to Leningrad. In the Baltic States and in the Ukraine, German troops were welcomed as liberators from the cruelty of Stalin's rule. Despite these victories, German soldiers found the ordinary Russian soldier to be a brave and determined, if poorly led, opponent.

STALIN'S REACTION

Although he received many warnings, Stalin refused to believe that Hitler would attack. Historians have long debated why he did not act on the large number of reports reaching him of German preparations. He probably believed that Hitler would not risk a two-front war and an attack so late in the year.

His first reaction was one of deep shock. Two weeks after the invasion, he addressed the nation and took command of the army. The *Stavka*, or army supreme headquarters, was established to plan and organise Soviet forces. Stalin realised that most Russians would not fight for Communism, so he appealed to traditional Russian patriotism. Propaganda now stressed past Russian glories against Western invaders, rather than Communist successes. He also eased the persecution of the **Orthodox Church** in order to use its support in the struggle against the Germans. Stalin also started a **scorched earth policy** – retreating soldiers removed or destroyed anything that could be of value to the advancing Germans, such as crops, animals or railway cars. **Partisan units** were formed behind the German lines to wage a guerrilla campaign in the occupied territories.

THE USE OF TERROR

Stalin also relied on traditional methods, using terror to stiffen morale in the struggle against the Germans and stamp out desertion, which had become a major problem.

- The infamous **Order No. 270** prohibited any soldier from surrendering. Stalin declared, 'There are no Russian prisoners of war, only traitors.' Any soldier deserting or surrendering was to be killed on the spot. Their families would be subject to arrest and could be sent to labour camps. This order presented Stalin with a problem when his son, Yakov, was captured by the Germans. He refused a German offer of an exchange of prisoners and his son died in a German concentration camp. Nearly 150,000 soldiers were sentenced to death in 1941 and 1942. Officers whose men deserted, even through no fault of their own, were often shot.
- Over 750,000 NKVD troops operated behind the front, rooting out 'traitors' and those guilty of 'defeatism'. **Holding units** or **blocking detachments** of NKVD were set up behind troops to machine-gun anyone who retreated. **Antony Beevor** noted that the Soviets executed 13,500 of their own men during the Battle of Stalingrad.
- Widespread use was made of **penal battalions**. In total, over 400,000 men served in these during the war, where life expectancy was very short.

KEY QUESTION

How did the USSR defeat the Germans?

TOTAL WAR

All resources were directed to victory. This was made easier by the almost total control of the Soviet state over the lives of its citizens. Production of war material was moved to the east, out of the reach of the bombers of the advancing Germans. Some 16 million workers moved as well. In all, 2,500 factories were dismantled and rebuilt in the east. Soviet war production was aided by the fact that many of the new industrial cities in the 1930s had been built in the east. Factories now operated day and night. These factories made vast numbers of tanks and planes that dwarfed German production. At **Chelyabinsk**, a massive tractor factory was converted to tank production, which earned the city the nickname Tankograd, or Tank City.

Conditions for ordinary Russians were very harsh. The great majority of men between the ages of 18 and 50 were conscripted into the Red Army and over 1 million women served in the army as well. Given the shortage of men, women played an important role in both factories and on farms: over half of the workforce in factories and over three-quarters of the workers on collective farms were women.

Russian propaganda poster during the war. What message is contained in the poster?

Conditions for workers were poor. They were housed in poorly constructed and inadequately heated barracks. Accidents were common, as little emphasis was placed on safety. Food was in short supply and was strictly rationed. Workers' rations were one-fifth those of their British equivalents.

All holidays and leave were cancelled. Workdays were long, with compulsory overtime. Following Stalin's call to turn the USSR into a 'single war camp', large sections of the workforce were placed under military control. Absenteeism and lateness were treated like desertion and offenders could be sent to labour camps.

Nearly every Russian family was affected by the war, with a brother captured, a son killed in battle, cousins hanged by German forces, etc. The massive effort and sacrifice of the Russian people were motivated by patriotism and a desire for revenge. To this day, Russians call World War II the **Great Patriotic War**.

The terrible atrocities carried out by the Germans strengthened the resolve of the Russian people:

- The historian Niall Ferguson estimates that in the first few weeks of Operation Barbarossa, the Germans shot up to 600,000 prisoners of war.
- The partisan war was particularly brutal, with attacks on German troops leading to harsh German reprisals on local civilians.
- Hundreds of thousands of Jews were rounded up and shot by special SS forces called **Einsatzgruppen**.

One captured Soviet soldier told his German interrogators:

> 'We have badly mistreated our people; in fact, so bad that it was almost impossible to treat them worse. You Germans have managed to do that. In the long term the people will choose between two tyrants the one who speaks their own language. Therefore, we will win this war.'

TURNING THE TIDE

The winter of 1941 was extremely harsh, and the Germans suffered thousands of casualties from frostbite. As their advance ground to a halt outside Moscow, the Russians were able to prepare a counteroffensive, aided by supplies sent by America. Throughout the war, the Soviets relied on American aid for trucks, jeeps, aircraft fuel and radio equipment.

After making some disastrous decisions in 1941 and 1942, Stalin decided to take a less prominent role in military planning and did not interfere in the day-to-day military decision-making as much as Hitler did. Led by capable men such as **General Gregori Zhukov**, the Russians learned from their early defeats and reformed their army and improved their tactics. They copied the Germans and formed tank armies and they gained control of the air.

In 1943, the Soviets won a major victory at **Stalingrad**, where they crushed the German Sixth Army, shattering the myth of German invincibility. The following July, the German offensive at **Kursk**

Soviet troops in Berlin.

was defeated. The Russians then went on the offensive. In June 1944, a vast Russian attack drove the Germans out of the USSR and the Red Army advanced into Eastern Europe.

By 1945, Russian troops had entered Germany, where they behaved with great brutality. In April they launched their final offensive of the war and by the start of May their troops had captured Berlin and the war was over.

STALIN'S CRIMES

During the war, Stalin conducted a series of deportations of suspect nationalities. Accused of collaboration with the Germans, millions of people were uprooted and sent to Siberia and the Central Asian republics. People deported included Poles, Volga Germans, Crimean Tatars, Latvians, Lithuanians and Estonians. Wide-scale executions were carried out, the most famous of which was at Katyn Forest in 1940, when Polish officers captured during the Soviet invasion of Poland in 1939 were shot.

Perhaps one of Stalin's greatest crimes was the treatment of returning Soviet POWs at the end of the war. After suffering great cruelty at the hands of the Germans, the million or so survivors who returned to the USSR were declared traitors to the Socialist motherland. Thousands were shot outright, while many of the remainder were sent to labour camps, where a large number died.

CONTRIBUTION TO ALLIED SUCCESS

There can be little doubt that militarily, the Eastern Front was the most important theatre of the war, measured by both the scale and the numbers involved. The bulk of the German army was committed to the Eastern Front. The intensity and horror of the fighting were not matched in the west. In all, the Russians suffered 26 million dead in the war, of which 10 million were soldiers. This is much larger than the losses suffered by either the Americans or the British Empire. The Soviet victory at Stalingrad is acknowledged as the turning point of the war. Russian victories in 1944 made the successful Allied invasion of France and the conquest of Germany possible.

The historian **Richard Overy** wrote about the importance of the Eastern Front:

> It was here that the German army was defeated, and the outcome of World War II decided in favour of the Allied powers.

Source: Richard Overy, 'The Soviet-German War 1941–1945', 2003 (www.bbc.co.uk/history).

SUMMARY

For all his crimes, many Russians today see Stalin as a great war leader. His strong if harsh leadership was important in defeating the Nazis. This victory established the USSR as a major world power to rival the United States. Russia recovered most of the land lost as a result of World War I and established a network of Communist-controlled states in Eastern Europe. One result of this was the Cold War, which dominated world affairs for the next 40 years.

R E V I E W   Q U E S T I O N S

1 What was agreed in the Nazi-Soviet Non-Aggression Pact of August 1939?

2 Outline some of the successes of Operation Barbarossa.

3 Aside from terror, what steps did Stalin take to encourage resistance to the Germans?

4 What role did women play in the Russian war effort?

5 What were conditions like for ordinary Russians during the war?

6 Outline the major events in the war on the Eastern Front between 1942 and 1945.

7 Give two reasons why the performance of the Red Army improved from 1942 onwards.

8 How were returning Russian prisoners of war treated at the end of the war?

Stalin's Russia: Timeline

Year	Event	Year	Event
1879	Born in Georgia.	1936	First of the major Show Trials.
1917	Minor role in the October Revolution.	1937	Purge of the armed forces.
1922	Appointed General Secretary of the Communist Party.	1939	Nazi-Soviet Non-Aggression Pact.
1924	Death of Lenin. Power struggle between Trotsky and Stalin.	1941	German invasion of the USSR. Scorched earth policy adopted. German advance stopped at Moscow.
1928	Undisputed leader of the USSR. Introduction of the First Five-Year Plan.	1943	Defeat of the Germans at Stalingrad. Teheran Conference.
1929	Collectivisation policy introduced.	1945	Yalta Conference. Capture of Berlin and the defeat of Germany.
1932–33	Famine in the Ukraine kills millions.		
1934	Murder of Sergei Kirov led to the beginning of the Great Terror.		

DICTATORSHIP AND DEMOCRACY

DOCUMENTS A AND B:

A. This is an extract from the final speech by prosecutor Andrei Vyshinsky on 'the criminal activities of Bukharin and his fellow traitors' before the Supreme Court of the USSR, 11 March 1938.

> *Bukharin's participation in such a monstrous crime as the attempt on Lenin's life by Kaplan, the Socialist-Revolutionary terrorist, on August 13, 1918, has now been fully revealed … The court investigation established, with exhaustive thoroughness, that the Bloc of Rights and Trotskyites, as agents of the intelligence services of certain states, worked to undermine the military power of the USSR; aimed for the overthrow of Soviet power and the restoration of capitalism …*
>
> *The crimes of the accused are proved by their own testimonies, by the evidence of witnesses, by the findings of expert witnesses, and by material evidence. The entire Soviet people and all the honest men throughout the world are awaiting your sentence. Let your sentence, Comrade Judges, resound as a bell calling for new victories. The entire country demands one thing: shoot the plotters as foul dogs, crush the accursed vipers.*
>
> *The years will pass and graves of traitors will be overgrown with wild weeds and thistles, while bright rays of our sun will shine over our Fatherland as brightly as ever. Along the road cleaned of this filth, our people will march onward; headed by our great teacher and leader, Stalin, they will march towards Communism.*
>
> Source: *Soviet Russia Today*, Vol. 7, No. 2, April 1938.

B. This is an extract from Nicholas Bukharin's last plea before the Supreme Court of the USSR, Moscow on 12 March 1938.

> *I once more repeat that I admit that I am guilty of treason to the Socialist Fatherland, the most wicked of possible crimes, of the organisation of kulak uprisings, of preparations for terrorist acts and of belonging to an underground, anti-Soviet organisation.*
>
> *I categorically deny that I was connected with foreign intelligence services, that they were my masters and that I acted in accordance with their wishes.*
>
> *I categorically deny my involvement in the assassination of Kirov … According to Yagoda's testimony, Kirov was assassinated in accordance with a decision of the 'Bloc of Rights and Trotskyites'. I knew nothing about it.*
>
> *We came out against the joy of the new life with the most criminal methods of struggle. I reject the accusation of having plotted against the life of Vladimir Ilyich [Lenin], but my counter-revolutionary allies, and I at their head, endeavoured to murder Lenin's cause, which is being carried on with such tremendous success by Stalin. I await the verdict. What matters is not the personal feelings of a repentant enemy, but the flourishing progress of the USSR and its international importance.*
>
> Source: http://art-bin.com/art/obukharin.html.

1 Comprehension

(a) According to document A, what verdict does Andrei Vyshinsky demand?

(b) Give two examples from document A to show that Vyshinsky strongly disapproves of the actions of the accused men.

(c) In document B, to what crimes did Bukharin admit his guilt?

(d) According to document B, how does Bukharin try to show his support of Communism?

2 Comparison

(a) From document B, did Bukharin agree with all of the allegations made against him in document A?

(b) Which of the two sources do you think is the more reliable? Explain your answer with reference to both sources.

3 Criticism

(a) Would you agree that document A is a clear example of propaganda?

(b) What are the strengths and weaknesses of document B as a historical source?

4 Contextualisation

(a) What role did the show trials play in Stalin's Russia?
Ordinary Level (1 A4 page)

(b) How important was terror for Stalin's regime?
Higher Level (1.5 A4 pages)

END OF CHAPTER QUESTIONS

Paragraph Questions

1 Write a paragraph on **TWO** of the following (Ordinary Level):

- The policy of collectivisation.
- The Five-Year Plans.
- Stalin's leadership during World War II.

2 Write an essay on **ONE** of the following (Higher Level):

(a) To what extent did Stalin transform the society and economy of the Soviet Union? **See analysis, page 35.**

(b) How significant was the role played by the USSR in World War II?

(c) What did Lenin and Stalin contribute to Communism in Russia?

ESSAY ANALYSIS

To what extent did Stalin transform the society and economy of the Soviet Union?

SUGGESTED APPROACH

- There are no dates in the question – make sure to put them in, as they will make it easier to plan your essay and give it a better structure. The period between Stalin's introduction of the first Five-Year Plan in 1928 and the German invasion of Russia in 1941 should be examined.
- Make sure to answer the question in your introduction and then again in your conclusion.
- This is not a biography of Stalin, so don't give any detail on his rise to power.
- As it is not a political essay, don't write too much on the show trials.

SUGGESTED CONCLUSION

There is no doubt that Joseph Stalin transformed the society and economy of the USSR. He presided over a period of rapid industrial development without parallel in history. An agricultural country was rapidly changed into a modern industrial society. He brought Russia from the age of the wooden plough to the atomic age. His policy of Socialism in One Country probably saved Russia from defeat in World War II. However, these changes were accompanied with the use of terror on a truly remarkable scale unsurpassed in modern history. He created the perfect totalitarian state. An estimated 20 million people died during the years 1924 to 1939. Collectivisation was an abject failure and famine was used as a means of achieving state policy. The *Kulaks*, or wealthy farmers, were eliminated. Death camps were set up in Siberia and slave labour was widely used. Innocent people were arrested in vast numbers and tortured, executed or imprisoned. As the Russian historian **Dmitri Volkogonov** has noted, 'No one in history has ever waged such war on his own people.'

Main Points

1. Socialism in One Country	• Turning Russia into an industrial country through a series of Five-Year Plans.
2. What did industrialisation involve?	• Emphasis on coal, iron and steel. New towns built, etc.
3. Main results of industrialisation	• Massive increase in production. • Some benefits for workers
4. What was the policy of collectivisation?	• Joining smaller farms together to form collectives. • Reasons for the policy.
5. Collectivisation and the use of terror	• Destruction of the *Kulaks* and the Ukrainian terror famine. • Results.
6. Use of terror and its impact on society	• Totalitarian state/NKVD. • Vast numbers arrested and sent to Gulags. • Slave labour used to build projects.

Further essay analysis can be found on pages 103 and 120. More are available online at www.edco.ie/LCHistory.

Italy under Mussolini, 1922–45

4

What do you need to know in this chapter?

Elements	Key Personalities	Key Concepts
The origins and growth of the Fascist regimes in Europe	Benito Mussolini	Fascism Dictatorship Propaganda Personality cult
Wartime alliances		
Church–state relations under Mussolini and Hitler		Totalitarianism Anti-Semitism

INTRODUCTION

One of the direct consequences of World War I was the growth of a new political movement called **Fascism**. In this chapter, we will look at the country where Fascism was born, Italy, and the career of the man who invented it, Benito Mussolini.

Italy had been unified as one country in 1870. It was ruled by a king and major decisions were made by an elected parliament, but until 1913, only wealthier Italians could vote. The country was poor, with a large division between the richer north, where most of the industry was located, and the poor agricultural south. At the turn of the century, over 50 per cent of the population could not read or write and over 500,000 Italians were emigrating every year, mainly to the United States.

In 1915, Italy joined World War I on the side of the Allies. Italy was promised large amounts of land by the secret Treaty of London at the expense of the

Austrian Empire and therefore hoped to gain great power status. However, the war did not go well for the Italians. They suffered a heavy defeat at Caporetto in 1917 and in total Italy lost over 500,000 men. Despite this, Italy emerged on the victorious side at the end of the war.

KEY QUESTION

How did Mussolini come to power in Italy?

CONDITIONS IN ITALY AFTER WORLD WAR I

There were widespread political and economic problems in Italy after World War I.

- There was a lot of dissatisfaction with the **Treaty of Versailles**. The country had gained the regions of Trentino, South Tyrol and Istria,

Here is an explanation of some of the terms you will meet in this chapter.

Corporate State: policy that called for co-operation between the different classes – in reality a cover for fascist control.

Il Duce: the leader – the title given to Mussolini when he ruled Italy.

Lateran Treaties: agreement between Mussolini and the Pope that recognised the Vatican State.

March on Rome: the event that saw Mussolini seize power.

Rome-Berlin Axis: alliance with Hitler signed in 1936.

Salo Republic: the German-backed government that Mussolini controlled between 1943 and 1945.

Squadristi/Blackshirts: Mussolini's uniformed followers.

but Italians felt that this was not enough. Many believed that Italy should receive all the land promised to them under the **Treaty of London** of 1915, e.g. Dalmatia had been awarded to Yugoslavia. Italian nationalists who hoped that Italy would now become a great power felt betrayed. They called it the 'mutilated victory'.

- This resentment was symbolised by the town of **Fiume**. Italians were outraged that the town, with a significant Italian population, had been made a Free City under the control of the League of Nations. In 1919, the war hero, writer and poet **Gabriele D'Annunzio** seized Fiume. He set up a Fascist-style regime with the Roman salute, speeches and marches. His occupation of Fiume lasted until he was removed by Italian troops in January 1921.

- The economy had failed to recover after the war. Unemployment rose to 2 million and ex-soldiers who had left the army found it difficult to get jobs. Prices were rising quickly (this is called inflation) – between 1919 and 1921 there was a 50 per cent increase in prices.

- As a result of the economic problems and inspired by the Bolshevik takeover in Russia, there was also widespread industrial unrest in Italy. This culminated in a general strike in September 1920 where 500,000 workers occupied factories throughout Italy. In some factories, workers' councils were formed that were similar to the soviets set up in Communist Russia. This period of industrial

unrest became known as the **Two Red Years**. Conditions were just as bad in the countryside, where farmers formed **Peasant Leagues** to defend their interests against landlords. These leagues frequently resorted to violence.

- There was also a lot of political instability. Between 1919 and 1922, there were a number of weak coalition governments, with five different prime ministers. These governments did not seem able to tackle Italy's political and economic problems. Many Italians lost faith in democracy and looked to a strong leader that would solve Italy's ills.

THE START OF THE FASCIST PARTY

Against this background, in March 1919, **Benito Mussolini** formed his political party, known as the **Fascio di Combattimento**, or **combat groups**, in Milan. Mussolini was a well-known journalist and political writer and had been a strong supporter of Italy's involvement in World War I. The following are some of his views.

- Although he was a former Socialist, his movement was opposed to Socialism and Communism.

- He promised to bring order and to end strikes.

- He wanted to make Italy a great power. He strongly attacked the Treaty of Versailles. Mussolini was a supporter of D'Annunzio's occupation of Fiume.

- He criticised the weak democratic governments that governed Italy and argued that only a strong ruler – **a dictator** – could solve Italy's problems.

Mussolini used symbols borrowed from the Roman Empire, including the fasces, where it was a symbol of authority and which the party

Fasces – the symbol of the Fascist movement and a symbol of authority in ancient Rome. It was chosen because it reflected the Fascists' belief in law and order and their hope of recreating the glories of ancient Rome. Much of the ritual of Italian Fascism was borrowed from the Roman Empire.

was named after. His uniformed followers wore black shirts and were called the *squadristi*, or **Blackshirts**. Their motto was 'I don't give a damn'. Their role was to create an impression of order, loyalty and discipline and to fight opponents of the party. Many of Mussolini's early followers were university students and ex-army officers who were attracted to the movement by a sense of adventure and a dislike of traditional politics. Fighting between the Fascists and their left-wing enemies became common in towns and villages throughout Italy.

The party grew slowly at first, winning only 2 per cent of the vote in the 1919 election. In order to win over more supporters, Mussolini moderated his polices to appeal to the middle classes. He stopped his attacks on the Catholic Church and the monarchy. One of Mussolini's main political gifts was his ability as a public speaker. His speeches won many followers to the party.

In 1921, Mussolini turned his movement into a proper political party called the **National Fascist Party**. He was helped when the powerful Socialist Party split into two when more extreme members left to form the Communist Party in January 1921.

INCREASING POPULARITY

In the 1921 elections, the Fascists won 35 seats and Mussolini was elected to parliament. Although overall the result was disappointing, in some provinces Fascist candidates topped the polls.

Focus on Fascism

Fascism was the political philosophy that was most associated with Mussolini's Italy. It spread to other countries such as Germany, Spain and France. It developed for a number of reasons.

- The political and social changes brought about by World War I, e.g. change in governments, defeat in war.
- Dissatisfaction with the Treaty of Versailles. In Germany, the treaty was seen as too harsh, while many Italians felt they did not get the reward their sacrifices deserved.
- The spread of Socialism and Communism after the revolution in Russia.
- The economic problems after World War I, e.g. unemployment.
- A loss of faith in the democratic system, as it failed to tackle these political and economic problems.

There were differences between Mussolini and Hitler, but Fascism in both countries had the following characteristics.

- **Authoritarian:** Believed in strong government, order and a powerful leader – a dictator.
- **Anti-democratic:** Opposed democracy, which was seen as weak, indecisive and unable to protect the interests of the people.
- **Totalitarian:** The state was all-powerful. Loyalty to the state was the responsibility of the citizen. Secret police and terror were used to keep control of the population. Propaganda was widely used to encourage loyalty.

- **One-party state:** There was no place for any party other than the Fascist Party. All other political parties and trade unions were banned.
- **Cult of personality:** The leader could not be criticised. He had an almost God-like status: Il Duce in Italy, Der Führer in Germany. Image created by propaganda.
- **Anti-Communist/Socialist:** Extremely hostile to these political groups, which they saw as disloyal to their countries and disruptive to society. In both Germany and Italy, this was an important reason for the growth of support for Fascist parties.
- **Economic self-sufficiency:** Countries should develop their own industry and agriculture and not rely on imported goods. This was seen as important in developing the greatness of the state.
- **Extreme nationalism:** Great emphasis was placed on building up the strength and prestige of their country. This led to aggressive foreign policies in both Italy and Germany.
- **Racism:** As a result of nationalism, there was an intolerance of any racial group that was seen as different or not loyal. In Italy, it led to discrimination against Germans and Slavs and later Jews. In Germany, Jews were the target – this is called anti-Semitism.

Fascism is sometimes referred to as the 'anti' philosophy, as it can be best understood by what it opposed rather than what it advocated (anti-democratic, anti-Communist, anti-Semitic, etc.).

Many wealthy industrialists and landowners started to give significant financial support to the Fascists because of their anti-Socialist policies. Membership also began to increase dramatically (see table).

The Fascists held massive rallies to intimidate their opponents and to remove local officials they disliked. Throughout Italy, left-wing party and newspaper offices were attacked and burned. It is estimated that about 2,000 people were victims of political violence in the years between 1919 and 1922 – most at the hands of Blackshirt mobs. There was a lot of sympathy for Mussolini among the police and the army. As a result, they often turned a blind eye to Fascist violence while coming down hard on political violence from the left. In August 1922, the Blackshirts helped to break a **general strike** called by the Socialist Party. For more and more Italians, Mussolini seemed like the man who would save Italy from the Communist menace and return it to greatness.

THE MARCH ON ROME

In October 1922, convinced by other leading Fascists that it was now time to act, Mussolini demanded that he be appointed prime minister. He announced his intention to march on the capital, Rome. His followers began to occupy towns throughout north and central Italy in preparation for a seizure of power. On 28 October, Prime Minister **Luigi Facta** asked **King Victor Emmanuel III** to declare a state of emergency and

King Victor Emmanuel III (1869–1947), Hitler and Mussolini. His motives in appointing Mussolini are unclear. Many historians argue that he feared that if he did not, there would be a military takeover and that he would lose his throne to his cousin.

Growth in Fascist Party Membership	
1919	17,000
1920	30,000
1921	100,000
1922	300,000

use the army. The troops in Rome were loyal to the king and could have crushed the Fascists. However, fearing civil war, the king refused and Facta resigned. Mussolini refused to serve under another prime minister. The king gave in and appointed him prime minster at the age of 39. His Fascist supporters then staged a victory march through Rome – the myth of the Fascist revolution had been born.

Mussolini marches through Rome. This picture was a propaganda stunt, as he was already in power.

KEY QUESTION

How did Mussolini establish a dictatorship?

THE 1924 ELECTION

When appointed prime minister, Mussolini led a coalition government in which Fascist MPs were a small minority. His government contained all of the major parties except the Socialists and Communists. He also served as Minister for Foreign Affairs and the Interior (justice). The latter ministry gave him control of the police. Over the

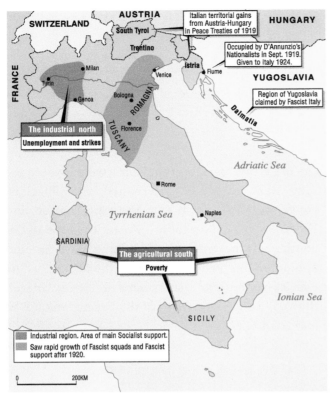

Map of Italy showing land gained at the end of World War I.

Cartoon criticising Mussolini after the murder of Matteotti. What is the central message of the cartoon?

next four years, Mussolini gradually set up a one-party state.

The Blackshirts were formed into the **Volunteer Militia for National Security** and paid by the government. They now had a free hand to attack Mussolini's political enemies. He set up a **Fascist Grand Council** which introduced laws for Italy without consulting the non-Fascists in the government.

In November 1923, the **Acerbo Law** was passed that said that the party with the greatest number of votes in a general election (as long as it was over 25 per cent) would receive two-thirds of the seats in parliament. This law was broadly welcomed by most Italians, as it would end weak and indecisive coalition governments. In January 1924, Mussolini's popularity increased when he negotiated the return of **Fiume** to Italy. The April election was a great victory for the Fascists, who received 65 per cent of the votes cast. There is little doubt that the result reflected the fact that Mussolini was popular among many Italians, but he was not taking any chances. The election was marred by the violence of Mussolini's followers

and the rigging of votes (cheating) in the countryside, particularly in the south. Many known political opponents were prevented from voting by Blackshirts. Political violence during elections was nothing new in Italy, but Mussolini had taken it to a new level. As a result of the election, he now had control of the parliament.

THE MURDER OF MATTEOTTI

Soon after the election, Mussolini suffered a major political setback. In June, the moderate Socialist leader **Giacomo Matteotti** was abducted in broad daylight by Blackshirts and later murdered. After the election, he had made a very critical speech in parliament attacking the Fascists' tactics. Historians are unsure whether Mussolini ordered the kidnapping and murder, but at the time it was widely believed that he was responsible.

The murder placed Mussolini in a very weak political position. There was an outcry in the press and non-Fascist MPs resigned from the parliament in protest. Known as the **Aventine Secession**, this boycott was a mistake, as it weakened their ability to remove Mussolini. The king, who still had the power to sack Mussolini, refused to act, as it could mean the Socialists coming to power. Mussolini recovered and survived the crisis.

THE ESTABLISHMENT OF ONE-PARTY RULE

In January 1925, Mussolini announced his intention to set up a dictatorship. Press freedom was ended and the police and Fascist militia increased their violence against opponents of the regime. The wooden club and castor oil came to symbolise Fascist violence. A law was introduced on Christmas Eve, 1925 which stated that only the king could dismiss Mussolini as prime minister. Mussolini now had the sole responsibility to introduce laws.

In November 1926, after a failed attempt on Mussolini's life, all political parties except the Fascist Party were banned. The Fascist Grand Council, which Mussolini controlled, replaced the parliament. This spelled the end of parliamentary democracy in Italy. At local level, elected mayors were replaced by Fascist officials. Mussolini was now the dictator of Italy, or **Il Duce** – the Leader.

K E Y   Q U E S T I O N

What was life like in Mussolini's Italy?

TOTALITARIANISM

Mussolini talked of the state having total power over the lives of its citizens – this became known as **totalitarianism**. Propaganda and terror played important roles in creating the totalitarian state.

- **Propaganda** was used to develop a **cult of personality** around Mussolini. In 1925, all independent newspapers were closed. The remaining newspapers were told to print his name in capital letters as DUCE. Newspaper editors were expected to praise his successes and play down his failures. The image portrayed of Mussolini was tightly controlled. Backed by the slogan 'Mussolini is always right', he was presented as a man of destiny working tirelessly for the Italian people – a superman. His picture was to be seen on posters on buildings throughout the country. All cinemas had to show official newsreels supporting the regime before every film.
- Once he became dictator of Italy, Mussolini took action to deal with political criticism. The death penalty was brought in for political crimes. A secret police, the **OVRA**, was

established. It held suspects without trial, tapped phones and read mail. A special court was set up to try those who were judged to be a danger to public safety. Ten people were executed for political crimes between 1927 and 1940 and over 5,000 people were sent to prison camps. Some of the camps were located on remote Mediterranean islands where conditions were tough but not severe.

One by-product of the strict nature of Mussolini's regime was the destruction of the Sicilian Mafia. Over 10,000 suspected members were arrested and many more emigrated to the US. However, Italy never became a truly totalitarian state and the government was more content with appearance rather than reality. In Mussolini's Italy, life was far more tolerable, even for enemies of the regime, than in Stalin's Russia and Hitler's Germany.

THE CORPORATE STATE

Mussolini wanted to show that Fascism would bring a new society to Italy that could provide an example to the rest of the world. He introduced what became known as the **corporate state**. His aim was to promote co-operation between employers and workers and to end class warfare. This would provide an alternative to socialism and capitalism – 'a third way'.

In the different areas of the economy, workers and employers were organised into **corporations, e.g. textiles**. They were expected to work together to settle disputes over pay and working conditions. Strikes and lockouts were not allowed. Catholic and Socialist trade unions were banned and Fascist-controlled unions negotiated for the workers.

By 1934, there were 22 corporations for each of the major industries. This system had admirers in many countries, e.g. Britain and Ireland. In reality, the Fascist Party was in full control. It also ensured the control of employers over their employees. While the employers were free to choose their own representatives, the Fascist Party chose the leaders of the Fascist trade unions.

To compensate them for their loss of freedom, workers had access to such benefits as free

Mussolini with one of his pet lions. Why do you think Mussolini would want this picture to be taken?

Benito Mussolini (1883–1945) Mussolini set up the Fascist party in 1919. He seized power after the March on Rome in 1922. He joined the war on the side of Germany in 1940 but the war went badly and in 1943 he was removed from power. In 1945 he was captured while trying to flee Italy and executed.

Sundays, annual holidays with pay, social security, sports and theatre facilities and cheap tours and holidays.

CONTROL OF THE YOUNG

Like Hitler, Mussolini made sure that the Fascists exercised a lot of control over the young. This is called **indoctrination**. He saw children as the Fascists of the future.

- He wanted boys to grow into brave soldiers who would fight for the glory of Italy.
- Girls were expected to be good mothers who would provide Italy with a population that a great power was expected to have.

A portrait of Mussolini hung in every classroom. Children chanted Fascist slogans such as 'Believe, Obey, Fight'. They were taught that Mussolini was the only man who could lead Italy back to greatness. History textbooks were rewritten to focus more exclusively on Italian history. In 1931, all teachers had to swear an oath of loyalty to the party. Despite tight political control, Mussolini did

spend more money on education and this helped to rapidly reduce the illiteracy rate.

After school, boys were encouraged to attend Fascist youth movements such as the **Balilla**. Set up in 1926 for boys between the ages of eight and 15, it placed great emphasis on loyalty to the Duce and physical training involving gymnastics and sport. From the age of 11, members were shown how to use rifles. Girls attended similar organisations, such as the **Piccole Italiane** for girls aged eight to 14 years old. These organisations were important in developing loyalty to Mussolini's totalitarian state.

MUSSOLINI AND THE ECONOMY

Propaganda played a major role in Mussolini's economic policy, with all of his decisions hailed as successes. The truth was more mixed.

- Mussolini wanted Italy to become **self-sufficient** in agriculture, thereby reducing Italy's need for wheat exports. In 1925, he called for a victory in the **'battle for grain'**. Rich farmers did well out of this policy, as they were guaranteed a good price for the wheat they produced. Grain imports did fall, but wheat became expensive, causing the price of bread to rise, which affected the poor.
- Mussolini insisted on keeping the value of the lira strong against other countries. This policy was a failure, as it made Italian exports sold to other countries more expensive. This caused unemployment and in 1936 Mussolini was forced to reduce the value of the lira.
- Public work schemes were important for the government. As well as their prestige value for the regime, they had the added benefit of employing a lot of people.
  * The **Pontine Marshes** – an area of mosquito-infested marsh outside Rome – were drained. Towns, villages and roads were built on the reclaimed land.
  * Other major projects included the development of hydroelectric plants and the building of new motorways, or *autostrada*.
  * The railways were electrified and the regime prided itself on technological achievements such as building the world's fastest sea plane.

1 Why were Italians unhappy with the Treaty of Versailles?

2 Explain why Socialism was an important political movement after the war.

3 What were Mussolini's main political aims?

4 Give two reasons why Mussolini's party grew in popularity after 1921.

5 Give two reasons why the Fascists were successful in the 1924 election.

6 Why was the murder of Matteotti very serious for Mussolini?

7 How was propaganda used to promote a cult of personality?

8 What was the corporate state?

9 What actions were taken by the Fascists to ensure that young people were loyal to Mussolini?

10 Outline some of the major economic policies pursued by Mussolini.

THE ROMAN QUESTION

Possibly Mussolini's greatest achievement was the agreement he reached with the Pope in 1929. In a country where nearly everyone was born a Catholic, relations between Church and state were important. The position of the Catholic Church had long been a source of controversy in Italy. The Church had lost a lot of territory during the process of Italian unification. After the capture of Rome that completed this process in 1870, the Pope had called himself 'the prisoner of the Vatican' and called on Catholics not to vote in Italian elections. This dispute became known as the **Roman Question.** After 1870, many governments pursued **anti-clerical** policies, reducing the power of the Church in Italian life, especially in education.

The **Roman Question** bitterly divided Italians. After the war, there had been an attempt to end the quarrel. In 1919, the Pope had ended the ban on Catholics voting in elections, but a final settlement on the Vatican failed because of the king.

KEY QUESTION

How did Mussolini handle Church–state relations in Italy?

MUSSOLINI AND THE CATHOLIC CHURCH

Mussolini was not religious and did not believe in God. At first he had been strongly opposed to the Catholic Church. However, as we have seen, Mussolini moderated his attitude. He knew that the Church retained the affection of many Italians and realised the benefits of reaching an understanding with the Church. He wanted to create a strong and united Italy and wanted to end a quarrel that divided the country.

The Church shared his anti-Communism. Although deeply concerned by the actions of Mussolini's government, especially against Catholic organisations, the Church regarded Fascism as the lesser of two evils facing Italy.

Mussolini made a number of gestures designed to win the approval of the Church. He had his children baptised and went through a religious marriage ceremony with his wife of 10 years. His social policy, especially his opposition to divorce and abortion, won approval from the Church.

THE LATERAN PACTS, 1929

Pope Pius XI wanted to reach an agreement with the government that would end the 60-year-old dispute. In 1926, negotiations began that resulted in the 1929 **Lateran Pacts**, which were named after the Lateran Palace in the Vatican. The future **Pope Pius XII** played an important role in reaching an agreement with Mussolini.

The pacts involved a settlement of the **Roman Question** and a **concordat** that regulated relations between Church and state in Italy.

- The **Vatican** (a tiny state of 109 acres) was created as an independent sovereign country.
- The Church was compensated for the land that it lost during the process of Italian unification.
- Catholicism became the state religion of Italy and religious instruction was made compulsory in all schools. Divorce was banned.
- The Church guaranteed that Church-run bodies would not get involved in politics. Priests were not allowed to join any political party.
- All bishops had to be Italian and take an oath of loyalty to the state.
- The Pope was forbidden to interfere in international disputes involving Italy.

This agreement became known as **the Conciliation** in Italy. The pacts ended a 60-year-old feud between Church and state and brought Mussolini's regime great prestige, both nationally and internationally. The historian Adrian Lyttelton wrote about the significance of the pacts:

> *Mussolini's solution of the Roman Question was a personal triumph which enormously increased his prestige and popularity, both at home and abroad … The conquest of Catholic opinion gave the regime a much wider social base than it had previously possessed.*

Source: Adrian Lyttelton, *The Seizure of Power – Fascism in Italy 1919–1929*, Weidenfeld & Nicolson, 1987, p. 419.

TENSION BETWEEN CHURCH AND STATE

As a result of the agreement, Mussolini had largely succeeded in silencing any independent Church criticism of his actions and the Church gave a lot of support to his regime. However, this did not mean that there were no tensions. In 1931, Mussolini became involved in a dispute with **Pope Pius XI** over the Church organisation **Catholic Action**. He accused it of interfering in politics and sought to destroy it, but his actions were strongly criticised by the Pope. In the end, a compromise was reached that ended the dispute.

Pope Pius XI condemned the **totalitarian** doctrine. The writings of many leading Fascists, including Mussolini, were put on the **index** of books that Catholics were forbidden to read. The Church opposed the introduction of the Racial Laws against **Italian Jews** in 1938. Under these laws, marriage between Jews and Italians was forbidden. They were not allowed to own important industry and were banned from certain occupations, such as the army. However, these anti-Jewish laws were not enforced strictly until the Germans occupied Italy in 1943. The Church, especially **Pope Pius XII**, played an important role in saving many Italian Jews from the Holocaust. However, many historians have criticised the Church's role in Fascist Italy and have argued it could have done more to oppose Mussolini.

KEY QUESTION

How did Mussolini conduct his foreign policy?

FOREIGN POLICY SUCCESSES

Mussolini wanted to recreate the glories of ancient Rome and make Italy a major player in European and world politics. He said, 'My objective is simple. I want to make Italy great, respected and feared.' He hoped to make Italy the dominant power in the Mediterranean, which he referred to as 'our sea'.

In 1923, Mussolini occupied the Greek island of **Corfu** after Italian members of a commission deciding on the Greek-Albanian border were shot. This decisive action proved popular with Italians. The League of Nations condemned the occupation, but Mussolini stood firm and Italy received compensation for the murder.

In 1924, he negotiated the return of **Fiume** to Italy, which was a major foreign policy success. In 1926, Italy established a protectorate (political control through a puppet government) over **Albania**. In doing this, Mussolini hoped to dominate the Adriatic Sea. For the rest of the 1920s, Italy played a prominent but cautious role in international diplomacy.

At first, Mussolini viewed the rise of Hitler with disquiet. In 1934, the first meeting between Hitler and Mussolini in Venice was a failure. The same year, after an attempted revolt by Austrian Nazis, Italian troops were rushed to the **Brenner Pass** to prevent any German intervention in Austria. In 1935, the **Stresa Front** was formed between Italy, Britain and France to oppose German rearmament carried out in defiance of the Treaty of Versailles.

THE INVASION OF ABYSSINIA

In October 1935, soon after the formation of the Stresa Front, Mussolini ordered the invasion of **Abyssinia**. This aggressive act was to have important consequences. Mussolini invaded Abyssinia for a number of reasons.

- He wanted Italy to gain glory and prestige by building up an overseas empire.
- He hoped to gain revenge for the defeat Italian forces had suffered at the hands of the Abyssinians in 1896.

Abyssinia was one of the few independent African countries and a member of the League of Nations. The invasion brought international condemnation, though France and Britain were reluctant to take action against Mussolini, as they did not want him

Hitler and Mussolini at the Munich Conference in 1938.

to become an ally of Hitler. The French and British foreign ministers proposed a secret agreement that would see Mussolini keep part of the country. When this was made public, the foreign ministers were forced to resign. Economic sanctions imposed by the League of Nations were agreed, but were only half-heartedly applied.

ALLIANCE WITH HITLER

Mussolini was enraged by the response of the League of Nations, especially the British and the French. The very thing the British and French had feared happened – Hitler and Mussolini, the two dictators, became allies. In 1936, both countries intervened on the side of **General Franco** in the Spanish Civil War. Over 70,000 Italian troops were sent to Spain. Later the same year, Mussolini formed an alliance with Hitler that became known as the **Rome-Berlin Axis**.

He abandoned his protection of Austria and supported Hitler's takeover of the country in 1938. The same year, fearful of war, he helped to negotiate the **Munich Agreement** that awarded the **Sudetenland** to **Germany**. In 1939, Mussolini occupied **Albania** and the **Pact of Steel** was signed, which drew Italy and Germany closer together. This pact committed both countries to support the other if one of them became involved in a war. However, when World War II broke out, Mussolini declared Italy's neutrality. Despite all the propaganda about Italy's greatness, the country was completely unprepared for war.

ITALY AND WORLD WAR II

In 1940, believing that German victory was inevitable, Mussolini joined the war and invaded France. This invasion descended into farce, as the Italian troops only advanced a few hundred yards. Italian involvement in World War II was to prove disastrous and contributed directly to Mussolini's removal from power.

The Italians suffered a number of embarrassing defeats.

- In North Africa, an Italian invasion of Egypt was crushed by British forces and Italy lost Abyssinia in 1941.

- In October 1940, jealous of Hitler's success, Mussolini invaded Greece. This attack was defeated and Italian troops were forced back into Albania.

These defeats forced the Germans to send troops to both North Africa and the Balkans to help the Italians. Italian troops were poorly led and equipped. Italian war production was very small in comparison to Germany or the Allies.

FALL FROM POWER

Mussolini's popularity among ordinary Italians declined and it became clear that the war was deeply disliked in Italy. There were frequent strikes in the industrial north of the country. Mussolini made fewer and fewer public appearances. In May 1943, Italian and German forces surrendered in North Africa. Allied troops then invaded Sicily, where they were greeted as liberators. Rome was bombed for the first time in the war. Many leading Fascists now turned against Mussolini. On 24 July 1943, there was a revolt in the Fascist Grand Council and the next day Mussolini was removed from power by the king and arrested. Italy changed sides, and in response the Germans occupied most of the country.

Mussolini was imprisoned in a mountaintop hotel but was rescued in a daring raid by German paratroopers. Mussolini was installed by the Germans as the ruler of northern Italy. Called the Italian Social Republic, it was more commonly known as the **Salo Republic**, as his headquarters was at the town of Salo. Mussolini was no longer a powerful dictator and relied on the Germans to remain in power.

In April 1945, as the Allies advanced through northern Italy, Mussolini tried to flee to Switzerland with a convoy of Germans, disguised as a German soldier. The convoy was stopped near the border and he was recognised and captured by anti-Fascist Italian partisans. On 28 April 1945, he was executed along with his mistress, Clara Petacci. Their bodies were then displayed upside down in a square in Milan. The arrogant dictator had met a humiliating and brutal end. His death marked the end of Fascism in Italy.

SUMMARY

Mussolini took advantage of post-war economic and political problems to come to power in Italy. He promised to make Italy great, defeat Communism and restore order among the political chaos that was post-war Italy.

Once in power, he proceeded cautiously to establish a dictatorship. It was only in 1926 that he could be called a full-blown dictator. He used terror to maintain control and propaganda to promote a cult of personality.

Throughout the 1920s and 1930s, he became a respected international statesman, enjoying a lot of popularity at home. His corporate state was admired throughout Europe. His regime was popular and brought some benefits to Italy.

However, his aggressive foreign policy and his alliance with Hitler were his undoing. The war saw him become an increasingly unpopular figure. After the Allies invaded Italy, he was removed from power. Installed as a German puppet ruler, he was later executed by his own countrymen.

Here are two historians' assessments of Mussolini:

Though his Fascist regime may be credited with some positive achievements especially in its early years, its crude belief in political violence … and its praise of war as something inherently beautiful and beneficial did untold harm and ultimately turned any positive achievements to dust and ashes.

Source: Denis Mack Smith, *Mussolini*, Weidenfeld & Nicholson, 1977.

'In the final analysis, the problem with Benito Mussolini was that he turned out to be no more than an ambitious intellectual from the provinces who believed that his will mattered and who thought that he was a Duce. His supporters thought that he was always right. However in the most profound matters … he was, with little exception, wrong.'

Source: Richard Bosworth, *Mussolini*, Hodder, 2002.

REVIEW QUESTIONS

1 Before Mussolini came to power, why had there been a lot of tension between the Church and state in Italy?

2 What was agreed between the Pope and Mussolini in the Lateran Pacts? Why was this treaty a significant agreement?

3 What issues caused disagreement between the Church and state after 1929?

4 Why did the Italians invade Abyssinia in 1935? What impact did the invasion have on Mussolini's foreign policy?

5 How did the Italian army perform during World War II?

6 Account for Mussolini's fall from power in 1943.

7 Read the views of the two historians on page 46. Would you agree that they are both very critical of Mussolini? Explain your answer.

Mussolini's Italy: Timeline

1883	Birth of Mussolini.
1914	Supported Italy's entry into the war.
1919	Formation of the Fascio di Combattimento.
1921	35 Fascist MPs elected.
1922	March on Rome – Mussolini appointed prime minister.
1923	Acerbo Law passed.
1924	Fascists won general election. Murder of Matteotti.
1926	All political parties except the Fascist Party banned.
1929	Lateran Pacts signed with the Pope.
1935	Italians invaded Abyssinia.
1936	Rome-Berlin Axis signed.
1940	Italy entered World War II.
1941	Italians defeated in Greece and North Africa.
1943	King Victor Emmanuel III removed Mussolini from power.
1945	Captured by partisans and shot.

Source Question

1 Read the following account of the March on Rome from the British *Manchester Guardian* newspaper from Monday, 30 October 1922.

On Saturday, while Mussolini ordered a general mobilisation of his more or less armed force of nearly half a million, the Cabinet decided upon measures of resistance.

Orders to the military are not to forbid Fascist forces from leaving the provinces, only to forbid their entrance to Rome. The entrances to the capital are occupied by troops who have put up barriers of barbed wire as a measure of caution.

Bloodshed has occurred in Cremona, where some Fascists have been killed, but generally the situation is regarded without great anxiety, some confidence being placed in the political sense and patriotism of the Fascists.

The Cabinet had asked for more drastic military measures but the King today refused to approve martial law in order to avoid conflict. Theatres are shut, and newspapers suspended, but the Rome population is quiet.

The King has begun consultations with the Speaker of the Lower House, Signor Denicola, and with the President of the Senate, as well as with Mussolini and the Right wing leader, Signor Salandra.

Source: *The Guardian* (www.guardian.co.uk).

(a) Mention two orders that were given to the military.
(b) Why was the situation 'regarded without anxiety'?
(c) What did the cabinet ask the king to do and why did the king refuse?
(d) Other than Mussolini, name two people the king had begun consultations with.
(e) What was the main result of the March on Rome?
(f) Do you think this is an objective source? Explain your answer.

2 Write a paragraph on **TWO** of the following:
 ● Why Mussolini came to power in Italy in 1922.
 ● How Mussolini established a dictatorship in Italy.
 ● The Lateran Pacts, 1929.
 ● Italy and World War II.

3 Write an essay on **ONE** of the following:
 ● Why was Mussolini an important figure in Italian history? (Ordinary Level)
 ● What factors led to the origins and growth of Fascism in Italy between 1919 and 1929? (Higher Level)

4 'Mussolini showed great skill in handling relations with the Catholic Church.' Do you agree? Argue your case.

(5) Weimar Germany, 1919–33

What do you need to know in this chapter?

Elements	Key Personalities	Key Concepts
Economic and social problems of the inter-war years; Germany and Britain	Adolf Hitler	Inflation
	Joseph Goebbels	The depression
Origins and growth of the Fascist regimes in Europe		Democracy
		Communism
		Fascism
		Dictatorship

INTRODUCTION

In this chapter, we will look at the economic and social problems faced by the new German democracy created after World War I that was called Weimar Germany. We will see how these problems led to the growth of the Nazi Party, led by Adolf Hitler, and the destruction of democracy in Germany.

KEY QUESTION

What effect did defeat in World War I have on Germany?

THE NEW REPUBLIC

As World War I drew to a close, morale in the army and at home collapsed. A series of defeats led to strikes throughout Germany. Soldiers, sailors and workers formed councils, or soviets, copying what had happened in Communist Russia.

As part of the Allied conditions for a German surrender, the Kaiser (emperor), William II, abdicated in November 1918 and went into exile in Holland. A republic was proclaimed, with the

Here is an explanation of some of the terms you will meet in this chapter.

Article 48: Allowed the president to pass laws without the consent of parliament.

Chancellor: Prime minister.

Hyperinflation: Prices rising out of control.

KPD: Communist Party.

Putsch: Rebellion.

Reichstag: Parliament.

Reparations: Payments demanded by the Allies after World War I.

Spartacus Revolt: Communist revolt in Berlin in 1919.

Wall Street Crash: Fall in value of shares in New York that had worldwide economic implications, especially for Germany.

War Guilt Clause: Blamed Germany for causing World War I.

moderate Socialist leader **Frederich Ebert** as chancellor (prime minster). The first act of the new government was to sign the armistice, or ceasefire, with the Allies and acknowledge defeat in the war.

The new republic faced a host of problems.

- Over 2.5 million Germans had died in the war and 4 million were wounded.
- Economic problems were numerous, including rising prices, unemployment and a shortage of food caused by an Allied naval blockade of German ports.
- Both the left and right wing of German politics were unhappy. On the left, there were many who hoped to see a Communist revolution similar to Russia. On the right, many powerful groups in society, such as army officers and the civil service, were unhappy that Germany had surrendered and had a shaky loyalty to the new republic. Some were completely hostile and viewed the government with contempt. They saw the surrender as an act of treason and the men who agreed to it became known as the **November Criminals**.
- To make matters worse, Germany faced the prospect of a harsh treaty that was being negotiated in Paris at the time.

THE SPARTACUS REVOLT

In January 1919, the Communist **Spartacus League**, led by **Karl Liebknecht** and **Rosa Luxemburg**, began a revolt in Berlin. It seemed as if the worldwide revolution that Lenin had predicted had begun. The new Weimar

Fighting on the streets of Berlin in 1919. The early years of the Weimar Republic saw great political chaos.

government crushed the revolt ruthlessly, using the army and the **Freikorps** to defeat the revolutionaries. The Freikorps was a volunteer militia (army) set up to defend Germany's eastern borders. It was made up of ex-army men and was strongly anti-Communist. Liebknecht and Luxemburg were shot. In Bavaria, another Communist revolt was defeated with Freikorps help in May.

THE NEW CONSTITUTION

Despite the Spartacus Revolt, in the election of January 1919, the majority of Germans voted for parties that favoured the new democratic republic. In February 1919, the German parliament met at Weimar to draw up a new constitution. The town was chosen because it was peaceful compared to revolution-torn Berlin, had plenty of food and was a signal to the Allied peacemakers in Paris. The Germans hoped that the Allies would treat a new, peaceful German republic more leniently than the Kaiser's government that had led Germany into World War I. The new republic became known as Weimar Germany because the new constitution was drawn up at the town.

Under the constitution:

- Germany was to be a federal country similar to the US, with states such as **Prussia** retaining considerable control over their own affairs, e.g. the police.
- The parliament, or **Reichstag**, was to be elected by both men and women over the age of 20. It had control of matters such as income tax, defence and foreign affairs.
- The head of the government was the chancellor, who was appointed by the president.
- The president was the head of state, who was elected every seven years. Ebert was the first president. He was succeeded by **General Paul von Hindenburg** in 1925. It was a largely ceremonial position with few powers. However, under Article 48, the president could declare a state of emergency and allow the chancellor to rule by decree. This meant that he could pass laws without getting the approval of parliament. This article became very important in the 1930s.

President Hindenburg (1847–1934) was a WWI general who was elected president in 1925. He disliked Hitler, but was persuaded to appoint him as chancellor in 1933.

- The conservative **German People's Party (DVP)** was backed by businessmen.
- The **Centre Party** represented the interests of Catholics in Germany.

The parties that were opposed to the new republic were as follows.

- The **Communist Party** (KPD) was formed from the Spartacus League and wanted to see the establishment of a Soviet republic along the lines of the USSR.
- The **German National People's Party** (DNVP) campaigned for a return of the monarchy.
- The **National Socialist German Workers' Party** (NSDAP) was an extreme nationalist and racist party, better known as the Nazis.

The electoral system was fair but meant that it was impossible for one single party to gain an overall majority. This led to many coalition governments.

Broadly speaking, there were two main groups of parties, one in favour of the new republic, one against. The parties that supported the new republic were:

- The **Social Democrats** (SPD) were moderate Socialists and were the most popular party in Germany until 1932.
- The liberal **German Democratic Party** (DDP) had strong support among the middle classes.

THE IMPACT OF THE TREATY OF VERSAILLES

The terms of the Treaty of Versailles came as a complete shock to the German people and virtually all sections of political opinion denounced the treaty. It was called the **Diktat** (the dictated peace), as Germany had been given no choice but to sign.

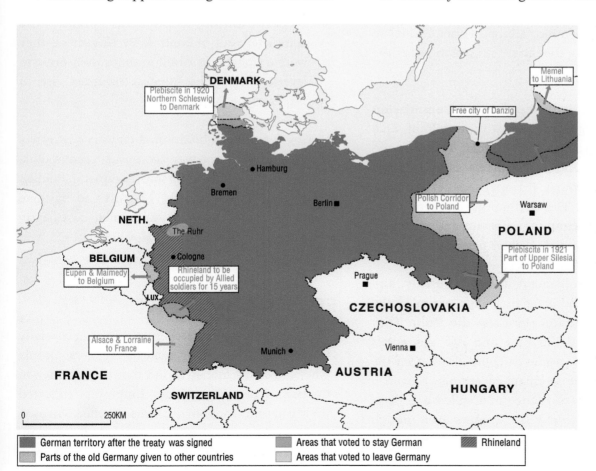

Territory lost by Germany at the Treaty of Versailles.

Political violence continued. In 1920, a right-wing politician, **Wolfgang Kapp**, led a revolt in Berlin backed by the Freikorps. The army refused to crush the revolt and the government fled to Stuttgart. The revolt, or **putsch**, collapsed when the trade unions in the city called a general strike. At the same time, a failed Communist revolt in the Ruhr left over 1,000 dead. Right-wing assassinations claimed the lives of over 200 people, including two leading politicians associated with the Treaty of Versailles, **Matthias Erzberger** and **Walther Rathenau**.

A 100 billion mark note. Money became worthless during the hyperinflation.

KEY QUESTION

What was the impact of the hyperinflation of 1923?

THE FRENCH OCCUPATION OF THE RUHR

Even the strongest opponent of the republic might have grown to accept it if it had provided a decent income for its citizens. However, the republic suffered two economic failures without equal in German history, the first of which was the hyperinflation of 1923.

In 1921, the **Allied Reparations Commission** presented the government with a bill of £6.6 billion, to be paid mainly in gold. This demand added to the economic problems caused by the defeat in World War I. Prices rose quickly (this is called **inflation**). The German government could not afford the reparations payments and at the end of 1922 they defaulted on their payments.

The French government reacted quickly and 70,000 French and Belgian troops occupied the industrial heartland of Germany, **the Ruhr**. They intended to seize the coal and use the goods produced by the factories as compensation for the money owed. The German government began a policy of passive resistance and called a general strike. It agreed to pay the workers even though they were on strike, and in order to do this it printed money.

THE IMPACT OF THE OCCUPATION

The economic effects of the occupation were catastrophic.

- The loss of production in the Ruhr caused factories to close elsewhere in Germany and unemployment rose from 2 per cent to 23 per cent.
- The amount of money collected in tax collapsed and the government financed its activities by printing money – this is the major cause of inflation. Paying the workers in the Ruhr further fuelled this inflation.
- **Hyperinflation** followed as prices rose completely out of control. By November, they were a staggering 1 billion times their pre-war levels! This is the greatest recorded rise in prices in the 20th century.

During a period of inflation, a country's currency loses value. After the war, there was a remarkable decline in the value of the mark against the dollar. In April 1919, you needed 12 marks to buy one dollar. In September 1923, one dollar cost nearly 99 million marks and by November 1923 you needed over 4 trillion marks!

EFFECTS ON EVERYDAY LIFE

The rise in prices hit everyone hard, especially those on fixed incomes such as teachers. People who had saved money found that their money in the bank was now worthless. Employees collected their wages in shopping baskets or wheelbarrows, as so many banknotes were needed to make up their wages. The number of zeros on banknotes grew and grew. The highest-value note printed during the inflation was a 500 trillion mark note – it was worth less than a pre-war 1,000 mark note.

The British *Daily Mail* newspaper reported on 29 July 1923:

> *In the shops the prices are typewritten and posted hourly. For instance, a record player at 10 a.m. was 5,000,000 marks but at 3 p.m. it was 12,000,000 marks. A copy of the* Daily Mail *purchased on the street yesterday cost 35,000 marks but today it cost 60,000 marks.*
>
> Source: Richard Evans, *The Coming of the Third Reich*, Penguin Press, 2004.

Germany literally came to a halt as businesses and local governments could not afford to pay their workers. For example, by September 1923, 60 out of the 90 tram routes in Berlin had stopped working. The impact on ordinary people can be seen by the rise in the price of rye bread, a staple food:

Month	Price (in marks) for 1 kilo
January	163
July	2,000
1 October	9,000,000
5 November	78,000,000,000
19 November	253,000,000,000

At the height of the hyperinflation, over 90 per cent of the expenditure of an average family went on food. Families started selling their possessions to make sure they had something to eat. In some cities, crowds rioted and looted food shops.

A NEW CHANCELLOR

During the dark days of 1923, **Gustav Stresemann** was appointed chancellor and his policies helped to transform the fortunes of Weimar. Although his government lasted only 100 days, he remained as foreign minister in successive coalitions until his death in October 1929. He took the crucial step of ceasing financial support to the general strike in the Ruhr and introduced a new and stable currency, the **Rentenmark** (soon renamed the Reichsmark), which restored confidence. One Rentenmark was equal to 1 trillion of the now-worthless marks. This ended the hyperinflation and a stable exchange rate was established with the dollar.

Despite strong criticism from German nationalists, Stresemann agreed to meet Germany's reparations obligations, come what may. In return, the Allies agreed to look at the reparations and set up a committee under the American banker **Charles Dawes**. His proposals, called the **Dawes Plan**, set a moderate scale of payments, rising from £50 million to £125 million after five years. The French also agreed to end the occupation of the Ruhr. In America, a loan of $800 million was raised, mainly to help German economic recovery.

THE 'GOLDEN ERA' OF THE WEIMAR REPUBLIC

For the next five years, American loans poured into Germany, the economy boomed and Weimar Germany prospered. In the late 1920s, Germany was seen by many as the US of Europe – industrial and modern. It was home to some of the biggest corporations in Europe, such as the huge electrical company **Siemens**, the financial giant **Deutsche Bank** and the car manufacturer **Mercedes-Benz**. Culturally, it was famous for its writers, architects and composers and it had the largest film industry in Europe. It also had some of the best universities in the world.

Marlene Dietrich (1901–92) was one of the most famous film stars of her day and in 1930 left Germany and went to Hollywood. She was strongly opposed to the Nazis and supported the US during World War II.

In 1929, the **Young Plan** (named after an American businessman) greatly reduced the amount of reparations to £2 billion and extended payments over a period of 59 years.

R E V I E W Q U E S T I O N S

1 Outline some of the problems facing the new German republic at the end of World War I.

2 What was the Spartacus Revolt in Berlin?

3 How did Weimar Germany get its name?

4 Why did the French occupy the Ruhr in 1923? What impact did the occupation have on Germany?

5 Outline two major decisions taken by Gustav Stresemann to end hyperinflation.

6 What were the Dawes and Young Plans?

K E Y Q U E S T I O N

What was the economic and political impact of the Great Depression on Germany?

THE WALL STREET CRASH

Gustav Stresemann's death in 1929 could not have come at a worse time for the young republic. For all its outward signs of prosperity, the German economic recovery was based on shaky foundations, as it had largely been financed by loans from the US.

- State governments paid the wages of their staff and their activities with the help of these loans.
- Large firms depended heavily on American loans.
- German banks took out American loans to invest in German businesses.

If something happened to the US economy, Germany would suffer. In 1929, this is exactly what occurred. In late October, there was panic selling on the **New York Stock Exchange** on Wall Street in reaction to a business crisis in America. Over the course of one week, $30 billion was wiped off the value of shares. This event became known as the **Wall Street Crash** and had severe economic effects for both the US and Europe.

EFFECTS ON GERMANY

In the US, businesses collapsed, unemployment rose quickly and American demand for imports fell. American banks saw their losses mount. Loans to Germany ended and they started calling in their short-term loans, which much of the German economy had been financing itself with for the past five years.

In response, German firms began to cut back drastically. Industrial production fell quickly and by 1932 it was worth 40 per cent less than its 1929 level. To make matters worse, in 1931, a number of banks went out of business. As the table shows, unemployment rose dramatically.

By the start of 1933, over 6 million people, or roughly one in three workers, was unemployed. Rates were even higher in the industrial areas of Germany such as the Ruhr. Matters were made worse by the fact that the drastic fall in people's income caused a collapse in tax revenues. Soon many of the unemployed were not even in receipt of benefits, as state governments did not have the money to pay them. Crime and suicide rates rose sharply. Throughout Germany, men could be seen on street corners with placards around their necks reading 'looking for work of any kind'. People deserted the democratic parties in droves and turned to either the Communists or the Nazis.

Year	Number unemployed (average)	Per cent of workforce unemployed
1929	1,899,000	8.5
1930	3,076,000	14.0
1931	4,520,000	21.9
1932	5,603,000	29.9

THE RISE OF THE NAZIS

The Nazi Party was led by **Adolf Hitler**, who had served in the German army in World War I. After the war he remained in the army in Bavaria and was ordered to spy on the small **German Workers' Party**. He soon joined the party. In 1920, the party was renamed the **National Socialist German Workers' Party (NSDAP)** with Hitler as leader. Hostile commentators soon christened it the Nazi Party. It became clear that Hitler had a gift for public speaking, or oratory. His speeches attacked Versailles, the November Criminals, Jews and Socialists.

The party acquired a newspaper, the *Volkischer Beobachter* (The People's Observer), to spread its message. In 1921, the **Sturmabteilung**, or SA, was set up under the command of **Ernst Röhm**. Known as the Brownshirts because of their uniform, their job was to protect party meetings and attack political opponents. Four years later, the **Schutzstaffel** (SS) was founded to act as Hitler's personal bodyguard.

Hitler was strongly influenced by Fascism in Italy. Like Mussolini, or Il Duce, he took the title of **Der Führer** – The Leader. His party promised to:

- Tear up the Treaty of Versailles and make Germany great again.
- Unite all German speakers together in one country.
- Destroy Communism and Socialism.
- Set up a dictatorship and replace democracy, which they saw as weak.

They were also racists and saw the Germans as the master race. Jews and Slavs were racial enemies. Hitler believed that only Germans should be allowed to be citizens of Germany and he promised to smash the 'power' of Jews in Germany.

THE BEER HALL PUTSCH

Inspired by Mussolini's March on Rome, Hitler attempted to seize power by marching on **Berlin** in November. As Germany descended into economic chaos with the hyperinflation of 1923, the time seemed right. On 8 November 1923, his

Hitler during his trial after the Beer Hall Putsch. The judge was sympathetic to Hitler and gave him a light sentence.

Adolf Hitler (1889–1945) A gifted public speaker he led the National Socialist party. The Great Depression made his party popular and in 1933 he was appointed chancellor. In 1939 he started World War II when he attacked Poland. During the war he ordered the mass murder of the Jewish people. In 1945 he committed suicide as Germany neared total defeat.

attempted takeover was halted when the police in Munich opened fire, killing 16 Nazis. This event became known as the **Beer Hall Putsch**. Hitler was arrested and sentenced to five years in jail but only served nine months. While in prison he wrote *Mein Kampf*, his autobiography.

One major result of the failed revolution was a change of tactics. Hitler realised that violent revolution would not succeed and decided to achieve power by legal means. He had not abandoned his aim of establishing a dictatorship, but he understood it was essential to win mass public support through the use of propaganda and public speeches.

He reorganised the party and established his authority. The greeting **'Heil Hitler'** was made compulsory for party members. However, the economy was prospering and support for the Nazis was very low. In the 1928 election, the Nazis only gained 2.5 per cent of the vote and 12 seats in the Reichstag. The Nazis would have remained a small extreme group but for the Great Depression.

As a result of the economic downturn, the 1930 election saw the Nazis make their electoral breakthrough, increasing their seats in the Reichstag to 107 deputies, while the Communists won 77. Both parties were opposed to the democratic system.

THE HUNGER CHANCELLOR

The government was widely viewed as completely failing to tackle the economic situation. The chancellor was the Centre politician **Heinrich Brüning**. He cut government spending in order to reduce inflation and keep German exports competitive (cheap). He increased taxes, lowered government salaries and reduced unemployment assistance. While these policies reflected sound economic thinking at the time, it only worsened the situation and unemployment continued to increase. A banking collapse in 1931 made matters even worse. Brüning was so unpopular that he was nicknamed the 'hunger chancellor'.

Nazi election poster. The text reads 'Smash the world enemy', the enemy being international high finance.

THE END OF PARLIAMENTARY DEMOCRACY

Given the lack of popular support for his policies, Brüning found it difficult to get a majority in the Reichstag. He relied on Article 48, which gave the president emergency powers to get laws passed. By 1932, parliament was being largely ignored.

The Nazis continued to grow and the Brownshirts now numbered 400,000 men. Political violence intensified and 155 people were killed during 1932 in clashes in the largest state, Prussia.

In May 1932, **Franz von Papen** replaced Brüning as chancellor and called an election for July. The Nazi election campaign organised by **Dr Joseph Goebbels** used propaganda, mass meetings, posters and marches. Hitler flew throughout Germany speaking to as many as seven audiences a day. In order to attract more support, some of the party's more extreme views, e.g. anti-Semitism, were toned down.

The election was a resounding victory for the Nazis, who became the largest party in the Reichstag, winning 37.6 per cent of the vote and 230 seats. Their Communist enemies got 89 seats. A majority of Germans had voted for non-democratic parties. Moderate parties such as the DDP and DVP were annihilated. Political violence intensified, with 12 people killed on the day of the polls.

WHO VOTED FOR THE NAZIS?

Why did millions of Germans turn to the Nazi Party as an answer to Germany's problems?

- Protestant middle-class voters who had traditionally voted for the DVP or the DDP had lost confidence in the Weimar Republic with the onset of the Great Depression. They were also fearful of spreading Communist influence.
- Conservative older voters believed Hitler would restore the traditional values of the German past, e.g. order, morality and discipline.
- Hitler's strongly nationalist views appealed to many voters who saw the hated Treaty of Versailles as the source of all Germany's difficulties.

- Although the party did not do as well among the working class, it still managed to capture a significant vote among workers. About 40 per cent of Nazi voters were workers.
- The Nazi message had a strong appeal to the young and women. Between 1928 and 1930, there was a 4 million increase in the electorate. Roughly a quarter of those who had voted Nazi in 1930 had not voted before.

Nazi support was strongest in the Protestant and rural areas of northern and eastern Germany, e.g. East Prussia. Although Catholics also voted for the Nazis, a Protestant voter was twice as likely to support the Nazis as his Catholic counterpart.

THE CRISIS DEEPENS

Some of the advisors to the president, including **General Kurt von Schleicher**, wanted to include the Nazis in government. They hoped to bypass the Reichstag completely and bring in a right-wing authoritarian (strict) government. The loss of confidence in democracy was spreading throughout Germany.

Negotiations began between President Hindenburg and Hitler about possible Nazi participation in government. Hitler refused any offer of coalition unless he was appointed chancellor. Hindenburg disliked Hitler, whom he called '**the Bohemian corporal**', and the talks broke down.

Another election was called for in November 1932 and the result saw the Nazi vote fall by 2 million and their number of seats to 196. The party was also in serious financial difficulties and it seemed that its inevitable march towards power had been halted. However, it was soon to be rescued by external events.

HITLER APPOINTED CHANCELLOR

It was clear that von Papen had little popular support and he had lost the support of the army. In December 1932, General Kurt von Schleicher replaced von Papen as chancellor.

Von Papen wanted to return to power and began to plot against von Schleicher. In January 1933, it was decided to get rid of von Schleicher and to try and get the Nazis into government. Hitler agreed the terms of a coalition government in which he would hold the post of chancellor. Von Papen had great influence over a reluctant Hindenburg and was able to persuade him to agree. On 30 January 1933, Hitler was appointed chancellor by the president, with von

Herman Göring (1893–1946) was a World War I fighter ace. He was seen as a moderate by many – the acceptable face of Nazism. But as Richard Evans wrote, 'The appearance was deceptive; he was as ruthless, as violent and as extreme as any of the leading Nazis.'

Brownshirts march in Berlin on the night Hitler was appointed chancellor.

Papen as his vice-chancellor. Nazi propaganda called this event the **Seizure of Power** and it marked the beginning of their rule of Germany. We will read more about this in Chapter 6.

The Collapse of Weimar

Wall Street Crash 1929

▼

Created economic chaos in Germany – massive unemployment

▼

Weak coalitions failed to tackle the solution

▼

Loss of faith in **democracy**

▼

Increased support for **Communists** and **Nazis**

▼

President Hindenburg was a more powerful figure than the parliament and he appointed the chancellor

▼

Hitler appointed **chancellor**

SUMMARY: WHY DID THE WEIMAR REPUBLIC FAIL?

There were a number of reasons for the collapse of the Weimar Republic.

 It was a republic born out of defeat. Many within influential groups in society, such as the army, big business, the civil service and the judiciary, disliked the new democratic republic and blamed it for accepting the hated Treaty of Versailles. They would have preferred if Germany was still ruled by the Kaiser and they felt little loyalty to the new state.

 During the 14 years of the Weimar Republic, there were 20 separate coalitions. The longest government lasted two years. This political chaos caused many to lose faith in the new democratic system.

 The crucial factor that accounts for the failure of the republic was the economic problems that Weimar Germany faced. The hyperinflation of 1923 caused many Germans to lose faith in democracy. This faith was partly restored by the economic stability of the 1920s, but destroyed by the onset of the Great Depression. Rising unemployment and a sense of hopelessness saw many turn to the Nazis, who became the largest party in 1932. Many Germans now accepted that a dictatorship was required to deal with Germany's economic problems and to combat the growing threat of the Communists.

Historian Richard Evans believes that:

the political effects of the depression hugely magnified those of the previous catastrophe of the hyperinflation and made the Republic seem as if it could deliver nothing but economic disaster.

REVIEW QUESTIONS

1 Explain what happened during the Wall Street Crash.

2 What was the Beer Hall Putsch of 1923?

3 How did the Nazi Party copy Mussolini's Fascists?

4 'The polices of Chancellor Brüning were a disaster.' Do you agree? Explain your answer.

5 What role did Joseph Goebbels play in the election campaigns of the Nazi Party?

6 Give two reasons why the results of the 1932 election were significant.

7 Why was President Hindenburg such an important figure after 1930?

8 Explain why so many Germans voted for the Nazis.

Weimar Germany: Timeline

1918	Kaiser Wilhelm II abdicated – Germany becomes a republic. Germany defeated in World War I.
1919	Communist Spartacus Revolt crushed in Berlin. New Constitution drawn up at the town of Weimar. Treaty of Versailles signed – great German resentment at the terms. Hitler joined the German Workers' Party.
1920	Failed Kapp Putsch.
1923	French occupied the Ruhr. Hyperinflation made money worthless. Stresemann appointed chancellor. Hitler attempted to seize power – the Beer Hall Putsch.

1924	Dawes Plan agreed – economic stability returned to Germany.
1929	Wall Street Crash – beginning of the Great Depression.
1930	Heinrich Brüning appointed chancellor. Nazis made breakthrough in 1930 election, with 107 seats.
1932	Von Papen appointed chancellor. July election results a great success for the Nazis – 230 seats. November election saw fall in Nazi vote to 196 seats. Unemployment topped 6 million.
1933	Hitler appointed chancellor by President Hindenburg.

END OF CHAPTER QUESTIONS

1 Study the diagram of election results in Weimar Germany and answer the questions below.

Note: Weimar Parties were committed to democracy.

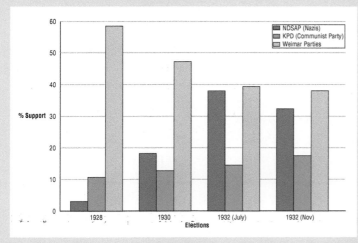

% Support

Legend: NDSAP (Nazis), KPD (Communist Party), Weimar Parties

Elections: 1928, 1930, 1932 (July), 1932 (Nov)

(a) Can you explain why the election results after 1928 show a major decline for the Weimar parties?

(b) Comment on the performance of the NDSAP (the Nazi Party).

(c) How did many Germans react to the growth of the KPD (the Communist Party)?

2 Write a paragraph on **TWO** of the following topics. (Ordinary Level)
- The hyperinflation of 1923.
- The 'Golden Era' of the Weimar Republic.
- The economic and social effects of the Great Depression on Germany.

3 Write an essay on the following.
(a) Why did Adolf Hitler become a popular figure in Germany? (Ordinary Level)
(b) To what extent did Germany's social and economic problems lead to the rise of Hitler and the Nazis? (Higher Level)

8–10 Bullet Points.

Monday 10th Feb

⑥ The Nazi State

What do you need to know in this chapter?

Elements	Key Personalities	Key Concepts
The Nazi state in peace and war	Adolf Hitler	Fascism, anti-Semitism
Church–state relations	Joseph Goebbels	The *Herrenvolk*, dictatorship
Anti-Semitism and the Holocaust		Propaganda, the cult of personality
		Totalitarianism, the Reichskirche

Here is an explanation of some of the terms you will meet in this chapter.

Anti-Semitism: Hatred of the Jewish people.
Der Führer: Hitler's title; means 'the leader'.
Enabling Act: This law gave Hitler the power to rule by decree.
Gestapo: Secret police.
Gleichschaltung: Policy of bringing all areas of German society under the control of the party.
Herrenvolk: The master race.
Holocaust: Systematic destruction of the Jewish race.
Kristallnacht: Attacks on German Jews in November 1938.
Lebensraum: Living space in Eastern Europe for German settlers.

Night of the Long Knives: Purge against the SA and other enemies of the regime.
Nuremberg Laws: Anti-Jewish laws passed in 1935.
Protective custody: Imprisonment in a concentration camp.
Reichskirche: Unified Protestant Church set up in 1933.
SA/Brownshirts: Hitler's uniformed followers, led by Ernst Röhm.
SS: Hitler's elite bodyguard, led by Heinrich Himmler. Grew to control the police and the concentration camps.
Third Reich: Name the Nazis gave to their state.
Volk: The German people.
Volkgemeinschaft: The people's community – a new Germany where class barriers would be removed. Very important aspect of Nazi policy.

INTRODUCTION

In the next two chapters, we will examine a number of different aspects of the Nazi regime. In this chapter, we will read how the Nazis established a dictatorship in Germany and the control they exercised over the life of Germans. The chapter will finish with an examination of Nazi anti-Semitism that led to one of the most tragic and evil actions in history – **the Holocaust**.

How did the Nazis establish a totalitarian state in Germany?

Most of Hitler's first cabinet consisted of non-Nazis. Von Papen and his allies in the DNVP thought that they could control Hitler. They believed that the responsibility that power brought would moderate the Nazi movement. Von Papen said, 'We've engaged him for ourselves.' Events were to prove how wrong they were.

At first, there were only two Nazi ministers in the cabinet, **William Frick** and **Herman Göring**. However, through their posts they controlled the police throughout Germany. Göring brought the Prussian police under his control and in February enrolled the SA as part-time policemen. The SA were now free to attack their political enemies, especially the Communists and Social Democrats. Their newspapers were closed down, their offices raided, their meetings attacked and their members beaten up. To win over the army, Hitler promised that he would tear up the military clauses of the Treaty of Versailles.

THE REICHSTAG FIRE

On 27 February 1933, a young Dutch Communist, **Marinus van der Lubbe**, set fire to the **Reichstag** building. Hitler saw the fire as an opportunity to strike at his enemies and claimed that the fire was the signal for a Communist revolt. This has led many historians to suspect that the Nazis may have started the fire themselves, but recent research points to van der Lubbe acting on his own.

An emergency law, **The Decree of the President for the Protection of People and State**, was passed. Usually known as the **Reichstag Fire Decree**, it suspended basic human rights and gave the police increased powers to arrest suspects. This law formed the basis of police power in Germany and helped to create a totalitarian state. Waves of arrests followed and over 10,000 Communists were detained. Beatings and torture were commonplace. As the prisons were filled to bursting point, cellars and disused warehouses were used to hold suspects. In March 1933, the first concentration camp was set up at **Dachau** near Munich.

The Reichstag on fire. The Nazis falsely claimed that this was the signal for a Communist revolt.

THE ENABLING ACT

Elections were held in March in 1933, which saw the Nazis receive 44 per cent of the vote. Hitler then announced that he would seek a further emergency law called the **Enabling Act** that would allow the government to pass laws without seeking the approval of parliament or the president. The Act would mean a change to the constitution, which required the support of two-thirds of the Reichstag. Therefore, the Nazis needed the support of other parties. To intimidate MPs, SA mobs surrounded the **Kroll Opera House** where the vote was held and Communist MPs were prevented from entering the building. Given the background of political and economic chaos, most parties, including the Centre Party, supported the bill and it was passed by 444 votes to 94. Only SPD deputies voted against the law. The Act formed the legal basis of the Nazi dictatorship. It was renewed in 1937 and made permanent in 1943.

THE END OF OPPOSITION

The Nazis were now free to carry out their policy of bringing all aspects of German political and social life under the control of the party. The Nazis used the term *Gleichschaltung* to describe this process.

- Nazi terror increased, with all political parties targeted, even those that had voted for the Enabling Act.
- One by one, political parties were banned or dissolved themselves.
- The Communists were banned on 7 March 1933 and the Social Democrats on 21 June 1933. The Conservative (DVNP), Catholic (Centre) and the Liberal parties dissolved themselves.
- In May, all trade unions were disbanded, their leaders arrested and their members forced to join the Nazi-controlled **German Labour Front**.
- On 14 July 1933, the NSDAP became the sole legal party in Germany. Goebbels noted in his diary, 'We are the masters of Germany.'

THE POLICE STATE

A secret police, the **Gestapo**, was established and quickly acquired a feared reputation. Its task was to watch enemies of the regime, such as

Concentration camp inmates in 1933.

Communists, Socialists and Jews. Criticism of the regime could result in arrest or **protective custody**, followed by torture and detention in a concentration camp.

These camps were first set up in 1933 and run by the SS to house political prisoners and what were termed 'anti-social elements', such as criminals. As well as **Dachau**, other camps included **Buchenwald (near Weimar)**, **Flossenburg (in northern Bavaria)** and **Sachenhausen (near Berlin)**.

The camp population varied greatly. In the summer of 1933, it reached 100,000 but quickly fell to a few hundred that winter. It topped 60,000 in 1938, mainly swelled by Jewish prisoners after *Kristallnacht* (see p. 71) and then fell again to 20,000 by August 1939. Conditions were harsh, with arbitrary and unpredictable violence a feature of everyday life. Prisoners had to rise before dawn and random roll calls were used to harass them further. They were at the mercy of the whims of their SS guards. When World War II broke out, the camp population exploded and a new type of camp, an extermination camp, was set up to eliminate the Jews and other racial enemies of the Nazis (see p. 136).

THE NIGHT OF THE LONG KNIVES

The brutality of the regime was reflected in the action Hitler took against his own supporters – the Brownshirts. By the summer of 1934, the SA's

Ernst Röhm (1887–1934), leader of the SA, was murdered during the Night of the Long Knives. Also seen in the photograph to the left of Hitler is Heinrich Himmler, who was leader of the SS. Originally set up as Hitler's bodyguard, the SS soon came to dominate many aspects of German life, acquiring an infamous reputation in the process.

numbers had swollen to 3 million men. Containing many violent thugs, they were disliked by most Germans and seen as the unacceptable face of the regime.

They were led by **Ernst Röhm**, who had been a loyal follower of Hitler since the early days of the party. Röhm had many enemies within the Nazi Party. Himmler, Göring and Goebbels were jealous of the power he had and his close relationship with Hitler. They plotted against Röhm, working to convince Hitler that Röhm was planning a revolt against him.

The army were also worried about Röhm. The SA greatly outnumbered the army and Röhm had openly spoken about making the SA the new army of Germany. Such talk alarmed army generals.

Hitler was persuaded to take action against the Brownshirt threat. On the night of 29–30 June 1934, units of the SS arrested the leaders of the SA, who were quickly executed. The Nazis also took the opportunity to settle scores with other political opponents, such as **General Kurt von Schleicher**. Both he and his wife were gunned down in their home.

Hitler's action was popular with Germans. As Ian Kershaw wrote, 'He took what many thought was ruthless but necessary action to crush the leadership of the SA, an increasingly unpopular sector of his own movement.'

The organisation was fatally weakened and the SS, led by **Heinrich Himmler**, became a far more important organisation. In August 1934, Hindenburg died and Hitler combined the offices of president and chancellor. Hitler was now **Der Führer** (The Leader), with absolute control of Germany.

KEY QUESTION

What was life like in Nazi Germany?

ECONOMIC SUCCESS

One major factor that contributed to Hitler's popularity among Germans was the economic prosperity Germany enjoyed in the 1930s. Hitler was aided by the policies of his economics minister, **Hjalmar Schacht**, who was a financial genius. Unemployment, which had topped 6 million in 1932, had fallen to under 1 million by 1937. A number of measures contributed to the reduction in unemployment, including:

- Massive public work schemes that saw the construction of dams, *autobahns* (motorways) and railroads.
- The Nazis also embarked on a programme of rearmament, leading to a large increase in the production of steel, tanks and planes.
- After 1935, the army was greatly expanded, further reducing the numbers of those who were unemployed.

The German economy greatly expanded its economic and industrial output. An improving world economy also helped, but no other country in the world could boast such an impressive economic performance in the 1930s.

The confidence of this new Germany was reflected in the **Berlin Olympics** of 1936, which were billed as a showpiece of German excellence. While there was little unemployment by 1938, average wages did not reach 1929 levels until 1941. Nevertheless, most workers were grateful to Hitler and the Nazis for ending the economic hardship of the Weimar years.

LIFE FOR THE WORKERS

As we have seen, all trade unions in Germany were banned and replaced by the Nazi-controlled **German Labour Front**. Working hours were increased and factory workers lost the right to strike. However, the Nazis were well aware that the working class had traditionally supported the Social Democrats or the Communists and they knew they had to gain their support. They put great stress on reaching out to workers by involving them in the people's community, or *volkgemeinschaft*, that they claimed they were creating.

Poster advertising the Volkswagen. The caption reads, 'Save 5 marks a week if you want to drive your own car.'

May 1 became a paid national holiday. A leisure arm of the German Labour Front was created, called **Strength through Joy**. It was designed to control how workers spent their spare time and their holidays.

- It organised activities such as sports and provided cheap tickets so that workers could go to plays in theatres or attend concerts.
- It organised affordable holidays for workers in Germany and abroad. This was very popular among workers. Many of them had never taken a holiday outside of their local area. They could now go skiing in the Bavarian Alps or go on cruises to the Azores, Canaries or the Norwegian fjords.
- The organisation was also involved in introducing a car that workers could afford. The **Volkswagen** (People's Car) was designed by Ferdinand Porsche and cost 990 marks – about 35 weeks' wages for the average worker. Workers paid 5 marks a week into an account, but the outbreak of the war meant that no one actually got a car.

THE YOUNG IN NAZI GERMANY

Hitler was aware of the importance of indoctrinating the young people of Germany with the Nazi message. As in Mussolini's Italy, emphasis was placed on the role of boys as the future soldiers of the Reich, while girls were taught the virtues of motherhood.

Schools were required to educate their pupils 'in the spirit of National Socialism'. Teachers were expected to be members of the **National Socialist Teachers' League** and by 1936 over 97 per cent were members. They had to be careful what they said in class – if they criticised the regime, they could lose their job and end up in prison.

From an early age, children were taught to be loyal to Hitler. A letter from a headmaster of a school in the town of Wismar gives us a good idea of what school life was life at the time:

A picture of Adolf Hitler is hanging on the wall in almost every classroom. Teachers and pupils greet each other at the beginning and end of every

Group of Hitler Youth with Hitler.

Nazi poster showing a contented and happy Nazi family. The slogan reads, 'A nation helps itself!'

lesson with the German greeting (Heil Hitler). The pupils listen to major political speeches on the radio in the school hall.

After-school activities were also tightly controlled. Boys joined the **German Young People** at age 10 and progressed on to the **Hitler Youth** at 14. Girls joined the **League of Young Girls** at age 10 and the **League of German Maidens** at 14. The Hitler Youth quickly became the largest youth organisation in the world. It was like a militarised version of the Boy Scouts. Members were taught to be loyal to Hitler and there was an emphasis on clean living, competition, teamwork, hiking, sport and so on. There was also training in the use of weapons.

THE ROLE OF WOMEN

In Germany, life for women was traditionally seen to revolve around motherhood and the home. This was summed up in the phrase '***Kinder, Kirche, Kuche***' (children, church, cooking). After World War I, this changed as women enjoyed much greater freedoms and many pursued professional careers. The Nazis sought to reverse this new trend.

Propaganda stressed that it was a woman's duty to support her husband and raise children. Large families were encouraged, with medals awarded to women with four children or more. The

propaganda poster above shows this idealised Nazi version of the role of women.

Women were encouraged to leave the workforce and stay at home. Many were offered financial incentives to quit their jobs. University entrance was restricted and promotion became difficult. By 1939, few women were to be found in professional jobs such as medicine. Despite these restrictions, Hitler was a popular figure among women in Germany.

During the war, the Nazis needed women to work in the factories, as most of the men were in the army. They had to reverse their policies and by 1944 over half of the industrial workers in Germany were women.

1. How did the Nazis exploit the Reichstag fire?
2. Why was the Enabling Act so important in establishing a dictatorship in Germany?
3. Describe what conditions were like in concentration camps.
4. What was the significance of the Night of the Long Knives?
5. What measures did the Nazis take to tackle unemployment?

6. Explain why the Strength through Joy organisation increased support for the Nazi regime.
7. 'The Nazis placed great stress on controlling the young.' Do you agree? Support your answer with evidence.
8. In Germany, what measures were taken to introduce the Nazis' views on the role of women?

KEY QUESTION

How did Hitler handle relations with the Churches?

HITLER AND THE CHURCHES

About two-thirds of Germans were Protestant, while the rest were Catholic, with a small Jewish minority. The north and the east were mainly Protestant, while the south and west tended to be Catholic. Church attendance was in decline, especially in the big cities. Overall, it tended to be higher among Catholics than Protestants. Despite this fall in observance, most Germans still felt a deep loyalty to their Church.

The Churches had been highly suspicious of the Weimar Republic, which had placed great stress on individual freedom. The Churches believed this undermined traditional morality and religious values. They were prepared to work with the new regime and shared the anti-Communist views of the Nazis. Most failed to realise the vast gulf that existed between Nazi policies and Christianity until it was too late.

Hitler had been brought up as a Catholic but had rejected its teachings. For the Nazi Party to fully control German life, he knew he needed to remove the hold the Churches had on their flocks. Their role in education and their influence over the young were particular targets. He was determined to make sure that they did not interfere in politics. Some of his followers called for extreme measures that would have seen a return to pagan German beliefs. Hitler was sensible enough to realise the strength of loyalty that many Germans felt to their Church and avoided an all-out conflict. His long-term aims are debated, but it is probable that he aimed to destroy the Churches.

CONTROLLING THE PROTESTANT CHURCHES

The vast majority of Protestants were Lutherans, although some were Calvinists. At the time the Nazis came to power, each region of Germany had its own independent self-governing Protestant church. There were 28 in total. The Nazis wanted to create one unified Protestant church that would be easier to control. It was not difficult for the Nazis to establish authority over Protestants, as they had a long tradition of state control going back to the Reformation. In July 1933, the 28 regional Protestant churches were replaced by a single church, or **Reichskirche**, known officially as the **German Evangelical Church**.

The **German Christian Movement** became influential within the Church. Hitler supported this movement, as he saw it as a means for the Nazis to gain control of the Reichskirche. The group combined Christianity with racism and anti-

Bishop Ludwig Müller gives the Nazi salute.

Semitism and called for the removal of the 'Jewish' Old Testament from the Bible. Their leader, **Bishop Ludwig Müller**, became head of the Reichskirche. Pastors of Jewish origin were removed from the Church. Bishop Müller allowed the Gestapo to monitor the contents of the sermons given by pastors (priests) and ordered all Protestant youth groups to join the Hitler Youth.

Many pastors within the Church were worried about the German Christian Movement and the spread of Nazi influence. A number had protested at the measure that excluded pastors of Jewish origin from the Church. The **Confessing Church**, under the leadership of **Martin Niemöller** and **Dietrich Bonhoeffer**, was set up to oppose Nazi policies. This group was banned in 1937. Over 700 pastors were arrested, including Niemöller, who was sent to a concentration camp. Hitler himself lost interest in the German Christian Movement when it became clear that it had failed to replace traditional Christianity.

THE CATHOLIC CHURCH

For Hitler and his supporters, the international nature of the Catholic Church was viewed with deep suspicion. Were Catholics loyal to Germany or to the Pope in Rome? Unlike Protestants, Catholics had traditionally had their own political party, the Centre Party. Given the greater loyalty of Catholics to their Church, the Nazis decided to proceed slowly. In 1933, the Catholic Church was willing to work with the new regime and a concordat, or agreement, was signed in July.

Freedom of worship and Catholic education in schools were guaranteed and Catholic organisations were to be protected. In exchange, the Church promised to withdraw from politics and the Centre Party was disbanded. As in Mussolini's Italy, this agreement brought the new regime important international recognition.

ANTI-RELIGIOUS POLICIES

However, the Nazis soon broke the concordat.

- The Gestapo kept a close eye on former Catholic politicians and monitored the content of sermons. They persecuted the Jesuits, Catholic Action (a religious and social movement) and various other Catholic organisations. Some Church property, such as land owned by monasteries, was seized.
- Particular pressure was put on Catholic youth groups, which were viewed as rivals to the Hitler Youth. By 1938, the majority had been banned.
- A number of different methods, including intimidation, were used to get parents to stop sending their children to schools run by the Church. By 1939, over 10,000 Catholic schools had been closed. Priests as well as Protestant pastors were forbidden to teach.
- A propaganda campaign was waged to discredit the Church. Hundreds of priests and monks were arrested, often on trumped-up allegations of homosexuality or financial corruption. Their trials were given front-page coverage, with headlines such as 'Houses of God degraded into brothels and dens of vice'.
- Violent attacks on religious targets were also common. Anti-religious posters were placed on churches and statues were destroyed. A few bishops were shot at or had their houses ransacked by SA mobs.

WITH BURNING ANXIETY

Pope Pius XI was deeply worried by the Nazi violations of the concordat. In 1937, he condemned the Nazi regime in a papal encyclical (letter) called *'Mit Brennender Sorge'* (With Burning Anxiety). The encyclical was smuggled into Germany under the noses of Gestapo agents.

Copies were secretly printed and hundreds of helpers in cars, on motorbikes or bicycles distributed copies to priests. Pope Pius XI credited its authorship to his Secretary of State, Cardinal Pacelli, who later became **Pope Pius XII**.

Despite the Nazis' policies, Hitler's popularity among Catholics was largely unaffected. He was not personally blamed for many of the measures, which were largely seen to be the work of local Nazi officials.

A cartoon from a French magazine criticising the concordat.

ACCEPTANCE AND RESISTANCE

The vast majority of the Protestant and Catholic Church leadership reached a compromise with the state rather than risk more violent measures. They did not challenge the state's anti-Jewish legislation and its actions, such as *Kristallnacht*. Many historians have been highly critical of this lack of action by the Churches.

However, there was resistance from Christians to some Nazi policies. Attempts to remove crucifixes from schools in Oldenburg and Bavaria were defeated by considerable local opposition.

Protests were also made by some senior bishops. These included **Cardinal Faulhaber** of Munich and, most famously, **Bishop von Galen** of Munster, who led a vigorous campaign against the Nazi euthanasia programme. An organisation called T4 had been set up to kill mentally and physically disabled people – 'useless eaters', as Hitler called them. In 1941, von Galen publically attacked this Nazi euthanasia programme. It was officially abandoned, although it secretly continued.

Committed Christians played a prominent role in the opposition to Hitler. During the war, many clerics were arrested and a large number were executed. These included **Dietrich Bonhoeffer** and the Jesuit **Alfred Delp**, who were both executed in 1945. In Poland, the Nazis waged a brutal campaign against the Catholic Church, executing about 3,000 members of the clergy.

The Lutheran pastor Dietrich Bonhoeffer (1906–45) paid with his life for his opposition to the Nazis. He was executed at the Flossenburg concentration camp in April 1945.

NAZI POLICY – SUCCESS OR FAILURE?

Despite the persecution, the clergy still managed to maintain a strong influence over their flocks. During the 1930s there was no significant decline in Church membership, while an increase occurred during World War II. The majority of Germans remained Catholic or Protestant. The historian Ian Kershaw concludes that Nazi policy categorically failed to reduce religious allegiances. One positive result of the treatment of the Churches by the Nazis was a breakdown of hostility between Catholics and Protestants, which led to much closer co-operation between the two groups after World War II.

REVIEW QUESTIONS

1 Why did the Nazis want to reduce the power of the Churches? Why did Hitler proceed cautiously when taking action against them?

2 What was the purpose of setting up the Reichskirche?

3 Explain why the Nazis supported the German Christian Movement.

4 How did some Protestants resist the spreading Nazi influence in the Reichskirche?

5 What was agreed in the concordat of 1933?

6 Explain some of the measures taken against the Catholic Church.

7 What evidence was there to suggest that many German Catholics were loyal to the Pope?

8 Why did the majority of Church leaders not attack the Nazi state?

9 Give two examples of successful religious opposition to Nazi policies.

10 How successful were the Nazis in reducing Church membership?

KEY QUESTION

What were conditions like for Jews in Germany in the 1930s?

Nazi anti-Semitism – three phases

Gradual exclusion from German life – to encourage emigration

▼

Persecution more violent as Jews lose the protection of the law, e.g. *Kristallnacht*

▼

The destruction of the Jews of Europe – the Holocaust

NAZI ANTI-SEMITISM

While most Germans felt they were better off under the Nazis, there was one group that definitely was not – the Jewish community. The Jewish population of Germany numbered over 500,000 in 1933. They were successful in business and the professions, especially medicine and law. Many of the best professors in German universities were Jewish. They tended to live in the larger towns, with the majority of Jews found in Berlin, Frankfurt, Hamburg or Breslau. On the other hand, 95 per cent of towns and villages had no Jewish population at all.

In Germany, anti-Semitism was traditionally based on three factors:

○ Jealousy at the economic success of the Jewish community.

- The fact that they were not Christian – some held the Jews responsible for the death of Christ.
- They were not seen as being true Germans and their loyalty was questioned. Some blamed Jews for Germany's defeat in World War I, while others saw Communism as being controlled by Jews.

The Nazis added a new factor – racial theory. Central to Nazi ideology was the belief in the superiority of the **Aryan race**, or master race. In German, the term is the *Herrenvolk*. The Nazi ideal was the tall, blond-haired, blue-eyed Nordic race. The Nazis wanted to purify the German race to achieve this ideal appearance. The main obstacle to this aim was the subhuman, or *Untermenschen*, who threatened to pollute the Aryan race. The main category of subhuman was the Jews. To the Nazis, the Jews were the enemies of the Aryan race. The Nazi policy against the Jews gradually became more brutal as time wore on and as the aims of Nazi policy changed from encouraging Jewish emigration to mass murder.

EXCLUDING JEWS FROM GERMAN LIFE

When the Nazis came to power, they passed a series of measures that targeted the Jewish community in Germany.
- In April 1933, a boycott of Jewish-owned shops was organised. Although the boycott was called off due to international pressure, this marked the beginning of an official policy of state persecution in Germany that was to get steadily worse.
- The same month, the **Law for the Restoration of the Professional Civil Service** was passed. This law was aimed at all political opponents and Jews who worked for the government. Anyone with one or more Jewish grandparent was retired from the civil service. This law also affected teachers, judges and professors.
- Jews were barred from the legal and medical professions. Jewish doctors were gradually prevented from working in public hospitals and from treating Aryan patients.

Albert Einstein (1879–1955) did not return to Germany when Hitler came to power. His house was attacked and his theories were banned from German universities.

- The German Evangelical Church removed pastors who were not of Aryan descent.
- In 1935, Jews were banned from the armed forces.

In 1933 alone, this persecution led to an exodus of over 40,000 Jews from Germany. Many Jewish academics were among this number, including 20 Nobel Prize winners. The famous physicist **Albert Einstein** refused to return to Germany.

THE NUREMBERG LAWS

The persecution continued across the country. Offensive slogans were painted on walls and shop windows. Signs reading 'Jews not wanted here' were strung across streets or displayed in the windows of bars, cafés and shops. Jews were banned from swimming pools and public baths. Public places bearing Jewish names were changed and statues of famous German Jews were removed. The names of dead Jewish soldiers were removed from war memorials.

At the party rally of 1935, a new set of laws were introduced that further worsened matters for

Jews. Called the **Nuremberg Laws**, they made Jews second-class citizens in Germany.

- **The Law for the Protection of German Blood and German Honour** prohibited marriages and extramarital sexual intercourse between Jews and Germans.
- **The Reich Citizenship Law** stripped Jews of their German citizenship. They now became 'state subjects'.

Under the laws, a Jew was defined as having three or four Jewish grandparents. This definition was racial and did not take into account whether the person was religious or not. To the Nazis, Jews who had become Protestant or Catholics were still defined as Jews.

A brief break from persecution came during the 1936 Olympics, when all anti-Jewish notices were removed from Berlin in order to create a good impression for foreign visitors.

KRISTALLNACHT

On the night of 9–10 November 1938, a violent outburst of anti-Semitism was organised by Goebbels. This was in response to the murder of a German diplomat, **Ernst vom Rath**, in Paris. He had been shot by a Jewish student, Herschel Grynszpan, who was outraged at the treatment of

Kristallnacht – the interior of a destroyed synagogue.

his family, who had just been deported from Germany to Poland. While the police stood by, the SA, SS and Hitler Youth burned down synagogues and Jewish-owned shops. Nearly every synagogue in Germany was attacked and over 7,500 Jewish businesses were damaged. They broke into Jewish homes throughout the Reich, terrorising and beating men, women and children. Ninety-one Jews were murdered and many committed suicide. Over 30,000 were arrested and taken to concentration camps, although they were soon released.

Because of the amount of shattered glass, this event became known as ***Kristallnacht***, or 'the Night of Broken Glass'.

Although the Nazis liked to portray the event as a popular uprising, there was little enthusiasm among the German population at large for what had occurred. To add insult to injury, the Nazis decided to collectively fine the Jewish community 1 billion marks for the murder of vom Rath. Göring commented, 'I must confess I would not like to be a Jew in Germany.' As the graph on p. 72 shows, the rate of Jewish emigration accelerated after *Kristallnacht*. Several schemes were examined for removing the remaining Jewish population from Germany, including a scheme for resettlement on the island of Madagascar off the coast of Africa.

TAKING OVER JEWISH BUSINESSES

In 1933, there were about 100,000 Jewish businesses in Germany, the majority being small or medium enterprises, with another 50,000 one-man businesses. By April 1938, some 60 per cent had passed into the hands of Germans, usually at a fraction of their value. A wide variety of methods was used to close a business or to bring about a change in ownership. These included SA or Gestapo intimidation, the withdrawal of loans, demands from the tax or foreign currency offices or frequent health inspections. Pressure could also be put on customers or suppliers.

After *Kristallnacht*, a number of laws were passed that made it practically impossible for Jews to operate in business. They were banned from owning shops and the transfer of ownership of Jewish businesses to Aryans (Germans) increased. As we will read in Chapter 7, the persecution was to get far worse during World War II.

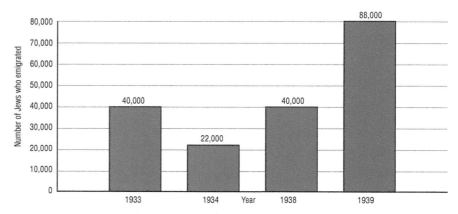

Emigration of Jews from Germany, 1933–39 (selected years).

R E V I E W   Q U E S T I O N S

1 Describe the Jewish community in Germany in 1933.

2 Explain Nazi racial theories and how they affected the Jews.

3 Explain why so many Jews left Germany in 1933.

4 How was everyday life for Jews affected by anti-Semitic measures?

5 Why were the Nuremberg Laws important?

6 'Kristallnacht showed the brutality of the Nazi regime.' Do you agree? Support your answer with evidence.

7 Outline some of the measures taken to drive Jews out of business in Germany.

HITLER'S FOREIGN POLICY

KEY QUESTION

How did Hitler's foreign policy lead to World War II?

Despite the brutality of his regime, there is little doubt that Hitler was a popular figure among Germans. The economic success and the sense of pride the Nazis created among the Germans, backed by some effective propaganda, help to partly explain this.

Historians are agreed that his foreign policy successes in the 1930s were also crucial. As we read earlier, Germans felt they had been harshly treated by the Treaty of Versailles (see page 3).

When Hitler came to power, he promised to tear up the treaty and make Germany a great power again. He also promised to unite all German speakers together in a Greater Germany – long a dream of many German nationalists. He also wanted to create a German empire in Eastern Europe and thereby acquire land for German settlers in Poland and Russia. This was called **Lebensraum**, or living space. In the words of Niall Ferguson:

> *Hitler wanted not merely a Greater Germany: he wanted the greatest possible Germany.*

He was an **opportunist** who took advantage of events for his own benefit. One of his main tactics was to use the threat of war to achieve his aims. He knew that his potential foes, France and Britain, were reluctant to go to war. The memory of the slaughter in World War I was strong in both countries and they were prepared to compromise to avoid another war.

EARLY YEARS IN POWER

Hitler had to proceed cautiously at first – his regime was viewed with great suspicion and Germany was isolated internationally. In 1933, Hitler protested at the fact that the Allies had not disarmed after World War I and Germany left the disarmament conference and the League of Nations. At the same time, he intensified the programme of secret rearmament that had begun under the Weimar government.

In July 1934, an attempt by Austrian Nazis to overthrow the government of their country was crushed. Hitler at first supported the attempted takeover but disowned the action when it was clear it would fail. Italy reacted with great hostility to the prospect of Austria falling into Nazi hands and Mussolini rushed troops to the border with Austria.

HITLER BEGINS TO DISMANTLE THE TREATY OF VERSAILLES (1935)

After World War I, **the Saarland** had been placed under the control of the League of Nations to allow the French to exploit its coal fields for 15 years. In January 1935, over 90 per cent of the population voted to return to German control. This was a major propaganda boost for Hitler, who could claim that his policies had the backing of the German people. In March 1935, Hitler announced that Germany was going to reintroduce conscription and create an army of over half a million men, using the excuse that the other powers had not disarmed. He also said that Germany was going to build up an air force (**the Luftwaffe**) and expand its navy. These actions were against the terms of the Treaty of Versailles but were popular in Germany.

Britain, Italy and France formed the **Stresa Front** to protest at this action, but took no concrete action. This united front against Germany was weakened by the actions of Britain, who felt that Germany had been harshly treated at Versailles, and there was a lot of sympathy for the German actions. They were also anti-Communist and were more worried about Stalin. Fearing an expensive naval arms race with Germany, the British concluded a naval agreement with Hitler that limited the German navy to 35 per cent of the size of the Royal Navy, though no limit was placed on the number of submarines that Germany could develop.

THE RHINELAND (1936)

Under the Treaty of Versailles, Germans were forbidden to station troops in the Rhineland. Most people now expected the Germans to break this rule and send troops into the Rhineland: the question was when? Most thought it would happen after the Olympics that were due to be held in Berlin that summer. They were wrong. On 7 March 1936, in one of his many Saturday surprises, Hitler announced that his troops had entered the Rhineland.

The British were not prepared to take any action, and the French would not act without British support. The force that Hitler had sent into the

---

The Path to World War II, 1933–39

1933: Germany left the League of Nations

▼

1935: Reintroduction of conscription

▼

1936: Troops sent into the Rhineland

▼

1938: *Anschluss* with Austria

▼

1938: Munich Conference and the occupation of the Sudetenland

▼

1939: Takeover of the Czech lands

▼

1939: Crisis with Poland over Danzig

▼

1939: Nazi-Soviet Non-Aggression Pact

▼

1939: Germany invaded Poland – World War II begins

German troops in the Rhineland.

Rhineland was small, but he had gambled and won. Hitler concluded that Britain and France were weak and that he could get away with more aggressive actions.

ALLIANCE WITH MUSSOLINI (1936)

In 1935, Mussolini attacked **Ethiopia**, destroying what remained of the Stresa Front. Hitler ignored international protests and supported the Italians. This new co-operation was strengthened with the outbreak of the Spanish Civil War in June. Both Hitler and Mussolini sent aid to **General Franco**, who was fighting against the democratically elected government of Spain. This closer co-operation between the two Fascist dictators led to an alliance known as the **Rome-Berlin Axis**. It was an agreement to pursue a joint foreign policy. Both pledged to stop the spread of Communism in Europe. This relationship became closer in 1939 with the signing of the **Pact of Steel**.

THE *ANSCHLUSS*

The Allies had prevented a union between Austria and Germany after World War I. Hitler had long wished to bring the land of his birth under German control and there was a strong Nazi Party in Austria. One result of the new alliance between Mussolini and Hitler was the dropping of Italian opposition to expanding German influence over Austria. In February 1938, the Austrian prime minister, **Kurt von Schuschnigg**, met Hitler at **Berchtesgaden** in the Alps. At the meeting, the Austrian chancellor was threatened and bullied and forced to place leading Austrian Nazis in his government. On his return to Austria, Schuschnigg tried to stop the spreading German influence by calling a referendum. This enraged Hitler and von Schuschnigg was forced to resign. German troops 'were invited in' by the new prime minister, the Austrian Nazi leader **Arthur Seyss-Inquart**.

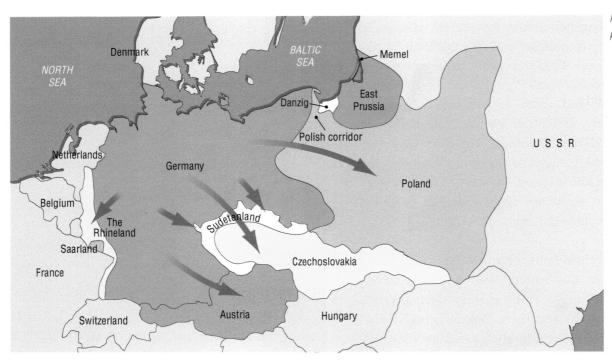

Hitler's foreign policy successes.

Hitler in Vienna in March 1938. He was greeted by large crowds when he travelled to the land of his birth.

When Hitler returned in triumph to Vienna, he was greeted by enthusiastic crowds. He announced that Austria and Germany were one, 'once and forever indivisible'. This event became known as the **Anschluss (union)**.

Again, the British and French did not act. The new prime minister in Britain was **Neville Chamberlain**. He decided to follow a policy that was called **appeasement**: giving in to Hitler's reasonable demands in order to prevent another European war from breaking out. It was a popular policy in Britain at the time.

THE SUDETENLAND, CZECHOSLOVAKIA (1938)

The next target for Hitler was the country of **Czechoslovakia**. It was the only democracy in Eastern Europe. It contained a lot of industry and had a good army. Its population was made up of a number of different national groups, including a large German minority numbering over 3 million people. They lived mainly in an area known as the **Sudetenland** and resented Czech control.

Hitler decided to use the grievances of the Sudeten Germans to bring the area under German control. He encouraged the Sudeten Germans to demonstrate against Czech rule and demand more control of their own affairs. He secretly set the date of 1 October 1938 for war with Czechoslovakia if the issue was not resolved. Throughout the summer of 1938, the crisis grew worse. If Germany attacked Czechoslovakia, it would mean a general European war, as the Czechs were allied with France. Chamberlain hoped to avoid this and felt that there was some justification in the German demand for the region. He flew to Germany and met Hitler twice, at **Berchtesgaden** and **Bad Godesberg**. Just when it seemed an agreement had been reached, Hitler made new demands and it looked as if war was inevitable.

THE MUNICH CONFERENCE

Mussolini knew Italy was not ready for war and he proposed a conference with Britain, France, Germany and Italy to settle the dispute. This met at **Munich** on 28 September 1938. The Czechs were not invited, even though the talks were about their country. Hitler also presented the demands of his allies, Hungary and Poland, for Czech land. The British and French agreed to Hitler's demands and it seemed as if peace had been preserved. The Czechs were now virtually powerless to resist the Germans.

THE END OF APPEASEMENT

In March 1939, Hitler took over the rest of the Czech lands after encouraging the **Slovaks** to declare independence under German protection.

Significantly, this was the first non-Germanic land that Hitler had seized. This occupation outraged public opinion in Britain and marked the end of appeasement. Britain guaranteed that if Poland and other Eastern European countries were attacked, they would come to their aid.

In the same month, the German-speaking town of **Memel**, lost after World War I, was taken back from **Lithuania**.

THE POLISH CORRIDOR (1939)

Under the Treaty of Versailles, the newly created state of Poland was given economic control of the German-speaking port of **Danzig** and the **Polish Corridor** had been created in order to give it access to the sea. This had separated **East Prussia** from the rest of Germany.

Hitler now demanded the German-speaking town of **Danzig** from Poland. Backed by the British guarantee, the Poles refused to compromise. Hitler accused the Poles of mistreating the German minority who lived in their country. Nazi propaganda made up or greatly exaggerated stories of attacks on Germans living in Poland.

Danzig was not the real issue for Hitler: he wanted to destroy Poland in order to gain what he called living space (*Lebensraum*) for the German people and create an empire in the east.

THE NAZI-SOVIET NON-AGGRESSION PACT

Tension grew as the summer wore on. Britain, France and Germany were trying to gain the support of the USSR in the event of war. Stalin did not trust Britain and France and felt they were encouraging Hitler to attack Russia. He had been greatly angered by the Munich Conference and was therefore prepared to listen to German offers of an alliance in August 1939.

Up to that point, Nazi Germany and the Soviet Union had been bitter enemies. The world was stunned to learn that they had reached an agreement on 23 August 1939. Called the **Nazi-Soviet Non-Aggression Pact**, both countries promised not to attack each other. Secretly, they divided Poland and Eastern Europe between them.

WONDER HOW LONG THE HONEYMOON WILL LAST?

British cartoon attacking the Nazi-Soviet Non-Aggression Pact. This pact was also known as the Molotov-Ribbentrop Pact after the foreign ministers of Germany and the USSR. What do you think the message of the cartoon is?

For the Soviet Union, it also allowed them more time to prepare for war and they gained a lot of territory in Eastern Europe. Germany was assured that if they attacked Poland, they would not have to face a two-front war.

WAR

Hitler hoped that the news of the pact with Russia would stop France and Britain from going to war if Germany attacked Poland. He was therefore surprised when Britain and Poland concluded a mutual defence treaty. Then Mussolini informed him that Italy was unprepared for war and he briefly postponed the invasion of Poland. A flurry of diplomatic activity achieved nothing and on 1 September 1939, Germany invaded Poland. On 3 September, Britain and France declared war on Germany. World War II had begun.

SUMMARY: NAZI GERMANY

The Nazis established a brutal dictatorship in Germany centred around Adolf Hitler. The police state he created saw the Gestapo monitor the population and concentration camps were used to imprison opponents. The racial policies of the Nazis ultimately led first to the exclusion of German Jews from the life of their own country and then to the Holocaust.

Despite this, there is little doubt that right up to the defeat of the Third Reich, Hitler remained a popular figure with most Germans. Some of the following factors help to explain this.

- The economic success of the 1930s caused many to support the government.
- Many genuinely believed that Hitler was creating a new Germany – a people's community – breaking down barriers between the classes in Germany. They took pride in the idea that Germans were a superior race to others.
- His foreign policy created a strong Germany, and the victories of the Wehrmacht up until the battle of Stalingrad in 1943 had inspired great confidence among the German people.
- The propaganda machine created by Dr Josef Goebbels, which we will read about in the next chapter, succeeded in creating a favourable impression of the Führer.

As a politician, Hitler took advantage of situations for his own benefit. He could be cautious and patient when the issue demanded such, as with the Churches. However, his extreme racist and nationalist ideology was morally bankrupt. It plunged Europe into the worst war in history and resulted in untold misery for millions of people.

END OF CHAPTER QUESTIONS

Source Question

1 Read the following source and answer the questions below.

This is an extract from an account by the French ambassador of the treatment received by the Czech president, **Emil Hacha**, in Berlin in March 1939. Study it and answer the questions that follow.

Immediately on arrival, Hacha was taken to the Chancellery where Herr Hitler, Field-Marshal Goering, Herr von Ribbentrop were waiting for him.

Note: Ribbentrop was the German foreign minister.

The Führer stated very briefly that the time was not one for negotiation … that Prague would be occupied on the following day at 9 o'clock. With that, the Führer wrote his signature and went out. It was about 12:30 a.m.

For hours on end Dr Hacha declared that he could not sign the document.

The German ministers were merciless. They literally hunted Dr Hacha round the table on which the documents were lying, pushing pens into his hand, continually repeating that if he continued in their refusal, half Prague would lie in ruins from aerial bombardment within two hours …

President Hacha was in such a state of exhaustion that he more than once needed medical attention from the doctors, who, by the way, had been there ready for service since the beginning of the interview. At 4:30 in the morning,

Dr Hacha, in a state of total collapse, and kept going only by means of injections, resigned himself with death in his soul to give his signature.

Source: The Avalon Project.

(a) What did Hitler state to President Hacha?
(b) What pressure did the German ministers use to force Hacha to sign?
(c) Why did Hacha need medical attention?
(d) What do you think of the Germans' actions? Support your answer with evidence from the account.

2 Write a paragraph on **TWO** of the following topics. (Ordinary Level)
   (b) How the Nazis established their control of Germany.
   • The Night of the Long Knives.
   (c) Anti-Semitism in Nazi Germany.
   • Hitler's foreign policy.

3 Write an essay on the following.
   (a) What was life like in Nazi Germany? (Ordinary Level)
   (b) What actions did Hitler take to reduce the power of the Churches in Germany? (Ordinary Level)
   (c) What were the main characteristics of the Nazi state in Germany between 1933 and 1939? (Higher Level; Leaving Certificate question)
   (d) To what extent did the Nazis establish control over the Churches in Germany? (Higher Level)

4 'Hitler was to blame for World War II.' Do you agree? Argue your case.

1-2 Pages   due 6th of March

(7) Propaganda in Nazi Germany

What do you need to know in this chapter?

Elements	Key Personalities	Key Concepts
Nazi propaganda – state control and use of the mass media Case study: The Nuremberg Rallies	Joseph Goebbels Leni Riefenstahl	Cult of personality Totalitarianism

KEY QUESTION

What steps did the Nazis take to establish state control over the mass media?

INTRODUCTION

In March 1933, **Dr Josef Goebbels** was appointed Reich Minister for Popular Enlightenment and Propaganda. During the Third Reich, he played a crucial role in influencing and controlling the opinions of the German people. He sold the Nazi message, and in the words of **Niall Ferguson** he was 'the evil genius of twentieth-century marketing'.

Goebbels's main themes were to:

- Promote the German nation and the sense of community among the German people (the *Volk*).
- Develop the **Führer principle** – the cult of personality around Hitler as the leader who could do no wrong.

Poster of Hitler with the caption 'Ein Volk, Ein Reich, Ein Führer' (One People, One Country, One Leader). The cult of personality around Hitler was carefully developed during the Third Reich.

- Encourage pride in the **Aryan race** and promote Nazi racial teaching.
- Develop hatred of the Jews and rid the nation of all Jewish influences in areas such as literature.
- Maintain public morale and incite hatred of the enemy during World War II.

Goebbels knew that for propaganda to be effective, he had to gain control of the media. Unlike today, there was no TV, so newspapers, cinema and the radio were the main targets. What mattered was getting across a positive message about Hitler and the Nazis to the German people and creating acceptance of the new state. Control of the media would allow the Nazis to present events as it suited them. Criticism of the Nazis would not be tolerated and inconvenient facts would not be published.

Dr Josef Goebbels (1897–1945) was an excellent public speaker and proved to be a talented propaganda minister. Strongly anti-Semitic, he played a large role in creating the climate of hatred towards the Jews of Germany.

RADIO

Radio had become very popular during the 1920s and Goebbels realised the importance of what he called this 'most modern instrument for influencing the masses'. He noted, **'We must not allow**

technology to run ahead of the Reich, but rather the Reich must keep pace with technology.' The **Reich Radio Chamber** was set up to give the propaganda ministry complete control of content and the hiring and firing of staff. Everyone working in radio had to be a member of the new organisation. All stations were controlled by the **Reich Radio Company**, with the propaganda ministry providing the news bulletins directly to stations.

Goebbels knew the importance of mass radio ownership so that people could hear the Nazi message and he encouraged radio ownership. Cheap sets called Volksempfänger (the People's Radio) were built. This policy meant that by 1939, over 70 per cent of households owned a radio – the highest percentage in the world. The sets were purposely designed to only receive local German stations, although in practice they could receive foreign stations such as the BBC with some difficulty. During the war, listening to foreign stations such as the BBC was a criminal offence, although it was difficult to stop it.

Poster advertising the Volksempfänger. The slogan reads, 'All of Germany hears the Führer' with the people's radio.

Collective listening was encouraged. **Radio wardens** would arrange for a speech by Hitler to be broadcast over loudspeakers in schools, factories or offices and they monitored reaction. However, it would be a mistake to think that all radio programmes were made up of Nazi propaganda. Goebbels knew that the German people would not tolerate this and he told radio managers 'don't become boring'. For example, popular music rather than classical music dominated most radio programmes.

LITERATURE

Controlling what people read was also important. The Nazis were determined to monitor the content of books and to make sure that it agreed with Nazi ideology. They were suspicious of modern literature, most of which they saw as undermining traditional values and German society. They labelled it Jewish even if the authors were not. In May and June 1933, university students throughout Germany, together with members of the SA, organised various countrywide actions to 'cleanse' libraries of what was termed 'un-German' literature. These were mainly books by authors who were Jewish or held left-wing views. This campaign led to a wave of public book burnings, the most notable of which took place in Berlin in May 1933. Works by world-famous authors such as **Heinrich** and **Thomas Mann**, **Ernest Hemingway** and **Sigmund Freud** were among those destroyed.

Beginning in September 1933, the control of literature was centrally organised by Goebbels's **Reich Chamber of Culture**. It censored texts and barred certain individuals from writing. In total, about 2,500 writers left Germany during the Nazi period.

The infamous burning of suspect books by Nazi mobs in 1933.

NEWSPAPERS

As a former journalist, Goebbels took a keen interest in newspapers. He believed that the objective of the press was to get people to 'think uniformly, react uniformly, and place themselves body and soul at the disposal of the government'. In 1933, 200 SPD and 35 Communist newspapers were closed. Instructions were given to newspapers on the size of headlines and photographs that should or should not appear, etc. Journalists the Nazis did not like could not work in newspapers. By 1935, 1,300 Jewish or left-wing journalists had been sacked or had fled the country. Publishing houses owned by Jews were taken over. For example, the Jewish **Ullstein** publishing family was forced to sell its newspapers at a fraction of their value to the Nazi publishing company, **Eher Verlag**. The same company took control of much of the Catholic press in the mid-1930s and ended up owning over 80 per cent of the newspapers in Germany. Goebbels received massive payments from this company, including a summer house in an exclusive district of Berlin.

Controlling what the Germans heard and read			
Radio	Newspapers	Film	Literature
• All stations controlled by the Nazis. • Cheap radios to spread the message.	• Opposition journalists fired and criticism not permitted. • Nazi Party newspapers such as the *Volkischer Beobachter*.	• Tight control over actors and directors. • Censorship introduced.	• 'Un-German' books burned and removed from libraries. • Books censored. • Authors forced to leave Germany.

Front page of the Volkischer Beobachter, *the official Nazi Party newspaper.*

The main Nazi party newspaper was the **Volkischer Beobachter** (The People's Observer). It was printed in four regional editions and was distributed to all civil servants. It was one of the first newspapers in the world to use colour.

FILMS

Germany had the largest film industry in Europe that technically was the equal of Hollywood. After the Nazis came to power, many leading actors and directors left Germany. Some were attracted by the money Hollywood had to offer, while others were escaping persecution because they were Jews. However, the majority stayed and cinema remained a popular leisure activity in Germany. As with other areas of the media, control of the industry was established by the creation of a new body, the **Reich Film Chamber**. Anyone who worked in the industry had to be a member of this organisation, while the **Reich Cinema Law** of 1934 introduced strict censorship of films. Goebbels was interested in films and believed that they provided the German people with an important form of entertainment and escapism from everyday life. He did not want to turn them off by too much propaganda content. As the table

shows, on the surface, the vast majority of films made were non-political.

Type of films in Germany			
Year	Comedies	Dramas	Political
1934	55%	21%	24%
1938	49%	41%	10%

However, all films were expected to follow general Nazi principles set down by the Reich Film Chamber, such as praising leadership, glorifying war, depicting Jews as villains, etc. Films such as **The Eternal Jew** and **The Jew Suss** played an important role in spreading anti-Semitism. From 1938, all cinemas had to show newsreels before a film – not surprisingly, most of the content was propaganda.

During the war, films were used (as in all countries) to boost morale and German cinemas continued to operate until the very end of the war. One of the last films released was a colour historical drama called **Kolberg**. It was produced by Goebbels and was designed to increase Germans' determination to fight.

THE 1936 OLYMPICS

Possibly the Nazis' greatest propaganda success was the staging of the 1936 Olympics in Berlin. Nazi and Olympic flags hung everywhere throughout the city. The athletics were held in a 110,000-seat stadium, which was the biggest ever built for an Olympics. Hitler attended almost every day, underlining the significance of the games. When he arrived in the stadium, the crowd rose in salute to greet him and he watched events with great enthusiasm.

Coverage of the games was transmitted on radio in around 50 languages throughout the world, with over 100 US stations alone covering the games. It was even televised on an experimental basis in the Berlin area.

After the success of her film *The Triumph of the Will* (see page 85), **Leni Reifenstahl** was commissioned by the International Olympics Committee

Here is an explanation of some of the terms you will meet in this chapter.

Documentary: a factual film made about an event or a person.

Fuhrer Principle: cult of personality that promoted Hitler as the leader guiding Germany to greatness.

Propaganda: controlling all media to present a view favourable to the government.

Reichsparteitag: Reich National Party Convention – the official name for the annual Nuremberg Rally.

The Triumph of the Will: Film record of the 1934 Nuremberg Rally.

Volksempfanger: cheap radio sets designed to encourage mass radio ownership.

Volksicher Beobachter: the People's Observer – the main Nazi party newspaper.

Themes of Nazi propaganda
- Anti-Communism.
- Cult of personality – Der Führer.
- The people's community.
- Economic success.
- The Aryan master race.
- Anti-Semitism.
- Nationalism and hatred of Versailles.

While Owens's success may have been disappointing to some Nazi racists, overall the games were a tremendous success both on and off the track. Germany won the most medals and foreign visitors left with a positive impression of the country and the Nazi regime. This favourable impression had been helped by the suspension of the anti-Jewish campaign in the press and on the radio and the removal of anti-Jewish signs and slogans from the streets.

to produce a documentary about the Olympics. The result, called *Olympia*, is considered by many to be the greatest sports documentary ever made. As with her earlier work, *The Triumph of the Will*, there is still controversy about the film today as to whether it is a documentary or Nazi propaganda.

The games were famous for the success of the African-American athlete **Jesse Owens**. He won four gold medals and broke three Olympic records. To many, his success shattered the myth of German racial superiority that was so important to the Nazis. It has been said that Hitler was so annoyed at Owens's success that he left the stadium and would not shake his hand. This is a legend made up by US newspapers, as Owens himself said:

> *Hitler didn't snub me – it was Roosevelt who snubbed me. The president didn't even send me a telegram.*

REVIEW QUESTIONS

1 What were Goebbels's main aims?

2 What was the Volksempfänger?

3 Why was there a series of book-burnings throughout Germany in 1933?

4 What was the role of the Reich Chamber of Culture?

5 Outline some of the major developments in cinema in Nazi Germany.

6 Were the Berlin Olympics a propaganda success for the Nazis?

7 Give evidence to support the view that Goebbels was very good at his job as propaganda minister.

THE PURPOSE OF THE NUREMBERG RALLIES

Rallies were common and played an important role in Nazi Germany. They combined popular festival, military parade, political meeting and sacred occasion. They were designed to emphasise the importance of the people's community and the contribution of each individual to the national will. They also gave a sense of order and discipline and made for an excellent propaganda spectacle. The rallies in Nuremberg were the most important of all. Held in early September, they involved hundreds of thousands of participants, with representatives of all party organisations, including the SS, the SA, Hitler Youth and the army.

The Nuremberg Rallies served a number of propaganda purposes.

- Their primary purpose was to strengthen the personality cult of Adolf Hitler. The rally was designed to portray Hitler as Germany's saviour.
- They demonstrated the dynamism and energy of National Socialism.
- They created the impression that the regime was popular, commanding the unlimited enthusiasm and loyalty of the general population.

WHY WAS NUREMBERG CHOSEN?

The national party rally of the Nazi Party, or to give it its title, the **Reichsparteitag** (National Party Convention), was first held in Munich in 1923. Weimar was the venue in 1926. In 1927, Nuremberg was selected, as it was situated in the centre of Germany, with the local stadium serving as an ideal venue. The Nazis could also count on a well-organised local party and the co-operation of the sympathetic local police. The Nazis later claimed that Nuremberg had been chosen because of the city's historical association with the medieval **Holy Roman Empire**.

Once in power, the scale of the rallies held in the first half of September increased dramatically. Nuremberg became known as the 'City of the Party Rallies'. The number of participants grew to over 1 million people. The 1934 rally lasted a week, with over 500 trains bringing participants from all over Germany. The rallies were now known officially as the **Reichsparteitage des deutschen Volkes**, or the National Congress of the Party of the German People. This name was chosen to represent the unity between the German people and the Nazi Party.

Each year, the rally had a different title, which usually related to a recent foreign policy success.

- The 1933 **Rally of Victory** was a celebration of the Nazis coming to power.
- The 1935 **Rally of Freedom** marked the reintroduction of conscription and breaking free from the Treaty of Versailles.
- The 1936 **Rally of Honour** was named after the German invasion of the demilitiarised Rhineland, which the Nazis saw as restoring German honour.
- In 1937, the **Rally of Labour** referred to the reduction of unemployment in Germany since the Nazis came to power.
- The *Anschluss* with Austria saw the 1938 rally named as the **Rally of Greater Germany**.
- The 1939 **Rally of Peace** was supposed to show Germany's commitment to peace, but it had to be cancelled when Germany invaded Poland.

EVENTS DURING THE RALLIES

As we have read, the most important reason for the Nuremberg Rallies was the almost religious focus on Adolf Hitler. Throughout the week of the party congress, there were numerous parades that usually followed the following format.

- Members of a party organisation such as the SA marched in front of Hitler at the rally grounds just outside the city or through the centre of the old town.
- Once a parade was over, the participants then listened to a speech from Hitler.

Here is a selection of some of the events from the 1938 party congress.

- **September 6: Day of the Opening of the Party Congress**
  Official opening of the party congress and reading of Hitler's proclamation.
- **September 7: Day of the Reich Labour Service**
  Review of the Labour Service on the Zeppelin Field. Parade of the Reich Labour Service through Nuremberg city.
- **September 8: Day of Fellowship**
  Torchlight parade of political leaders.
- **September 9: Day of the Political Leaders**
  Meeting of the National Socialist Women's Association.
- **September 10: Day of the Hitler Youth**
  Review of the Hitler Youth on the Zeppelin Field.
- **September 11: Day of the SA and SS**
  Mass meeting on the Zeppelin Field. Parade through Nuremberg.
- **September 12: Day of the Armed Forces**
  Review and mass meeting of the army. Closing ceremony of the party congress.

Sometimes important policy was announced at the rallies. The 1935 rally is remembered for the **Nuremberg Laws** that made Jews second-class citizens (see p. 70). At the 1937 rally, Hitler met the brother of the Japanese emperor, symbolising closer relations between both countries. Hitler used speeches during the 1938 rally to put pressure on the Czechs over the Sudetenland.

THE NAZI PARTY RALLY GROUNDS

Central to events was the rally grounds. Originally, one stadium had been used for the rallies, but once in power, the rally grounds were greatly extended to incorporate a number of venues. In 1934, architect **Albert Speer** was given the task of creating an overall plan for an area of 11 square kilometres. Hitler intended for the buildings at the party rally grounds to stand for thousands of years. When World War II began, the construction work was abandoned and some of the projects remained unfinished.

The most important parts of the rally grounds were as follows.

1. **The Zeppelin Field**: The Zeppelin Field was named after the site of the landing of one of Count Zeppelin's airships in 1909. It was the central venue for staging the party parades. Speer redeveloped the site, building a large grandstand 360 metres wide. The field provided space for up to 200,000 people. At night, the 'Cathedral of Light' was created when over 150 particularly strong floodlights beamed up into the sky, providing spectacular effects.

The Zeppelin Field during the 1935 rally.

2. **The Luitpold Hall**: Built originally in 1906, the Nazis rebuilt it to be used exclusively for their party congress. Albert Speer had the front of the building remodelled and the interior modernised. The hall provided space for 16,000 people.

The front of the Luitpold Hall.

3. **The Luitpold Arena**: Originally designed as a park, it was enlarged to hold over 150,000 people. At one end was the Ehrenhalle, a war

The Cathedral of Light at the 1937 party rally.

The Municipal Stadium.

memorial built in 1929. Thousands of SS and SA men gathered at the Luitpold Arena to participate in a ceremony honouring the Nazi dead at the Ehrenhalle. The other end of the Luitpold Arena was a grandstand with a speaker's platform and three tall swastika banners.

4. **Municipal Stadium**: This had been built in the 1920s as part of a sport and leisure complex and held 50,000 spectators. It was the scene of march-pasts by the Hitler Youth. The stadium is still in use and was one of the venues for the 2006 World Cup.

A new railway station was built and there was also a camp zone to house participants during the rally. During the war, it was used as a prisoner of war camp. Because of the outbreak of the war, a number of buildings planned by Speer were not completed, including a 50,000-seat **Congress Hall** modelled on the Colosseum in ancient Rome. The most ambitious project was to build the 400,000-seat **German Stadium**, but work had only started on the foundations when the war started.

The centre of the historic city was also used for parades, which were reviewed by Hitler in the central marketplace that was renamed **Adolf-Hitler Platz** in 1933.

THE TRIUMPH OF THE WILL

Hitler commissioned the young actress and director **Leni Riefenstahl** to make a record of the 1934 rally. She had made a film of the 1933 rally called *Triumph of Faith*, but it had not been successful.

Hitler at the 1934 Rally.

Hitler salutes marchers in the centre of Nuremberg.

Hitler issued orders that she be provided with all the resources that she required. A crew of 120 worked on the film with 30 cameras. The most modern techniques, such as telephoto lenses and wide-angled photography, were used. The resulting film, **The Triumph of the Will**, was, in the words of the historian Richard Evans, 'a documentary like none before'. Without any commentary, it portrayed the power, strength and determination of the German people under Hitler's leadership. The film was noted for its presentation of vast disciplined masses moving in perfect co-ordination. It was released in 1935 to widespread praise not only in Germany, but also abroad. Goebbels described it as 'a magnificent cinematic version of the Führer'. It was awarded the Gold Medal at the Venice Film Festival in 1935 and the Grand Prize at the World Exhibition in Paris in 1937.

Controversy rages to this day as to whether it is a piece of propaganda or a brilliant example of cinema. In an interview in 1964, Riefenstahl defended the film:

> *Everything in it is true. And it contains no commentary at all. It is history. A pure historical film. It reflects the truth that was then in 1934, history. It is therefore a documentary. Not a propaganda film.*

Source: www.kamera.co.uk.

Many commentators disagree and accuse the film of using spectacular filmmaking to promote a system that became a by-word for evil. Today in Germany, the movie is classified as Nazis propaganda and banned except for educational purposes.

Leni Riefenstahl shooting The Triumph of the Will.

Leni Riefenstahl (1902–2003) Making her name as an actress and film director, her work impressed Hitler. In 1934 she made a documentary of the Nuremberg party Rally called *The Triumph of the Will*. After the war she was unable to work as a director because of her association with Nazis.

REVIEW QUESTIONS

1 Why was Nuremberg chosen as the site for Nazi Party ralllies?

2 Why were the rallies useful propaganda spectacles for the Nazis?

3 Explain why the rally had a different title each year.

4 What basic format did events follow during the rally?

5 Describe some of the important venues at the rally grounds outside Nuremberg.

6 'The Triumph of the Will is a work of Nazi propaganda.' Do you agree? Outline two reasons to support your answer.

DOCUMENTS A AND B:

A. This is an extract from the diary of William Shirer describing the 1934 Nuremberg rally.

I am beginning to comprehend some of the reasons for Hitler's astounding success. Borrowing a chapter from the Roman [Catholic] church, he is restoring spectacle and colour and mysticism to the dull lives of 20th Century Germans. This morning's opening meeting ... was more than a gorgeous show, it also had something of the mysticism and religious fervour of an Easter or Christmas Mass in a great Gothic cathedral. The hall was a sea of brightly coloured flags. Even Hitler's arrival was made dramatic. The band stopped playing. There was a hush over the thirty thousand people packed in the hall. Then the band struck up the 'Badenweiler March' ... Hitler appeared in the back of the auditorium and followed by his aides, Göring, Goebbels, Hess, Himmler and the others, he slowly strode down the long centre aisle while thirty thousand hands were raised in salute.

Source: www.historyplace.com.

B: This is a picture from the 1934 rally

QUESTIONS ON THE DOCUMENTS

Comprehension

(a) According to document A, what does the author say Hitler brought into the lives of Germans?

(b) According to document A, in what ways was Hitler's arrival made more dramatic?

(c) In your opinion, what impression of Nazi Germany does document B attempt to create? Support your answer with evidence from the picture.

Comparison

(a) Documents A and B both support the view that Hitler was a popular figure in Germany.' Do you agree? Use evidence to support your answer.

(b) Which document do you think is the more effective source on the Nuremberg Rallies? Explain your answer.

Criticism

(a) What are the strengths and weaknesses of diaries as sources of information for historians?

(b) In your opinion, how reliable are pictures as evidence about events from the past?

Contextualisation   *To be done when Word Arrives...*

How did the Nuremberg Rallies help bring support to the Nazi regime in Germany? (Leaving Certificate question)

Higher Level: 1.5 A4 pages
Ordinary Level: 1 A4 page

END OF CHAPTER QUESTIONS

1   What important role did Joseph Goebbels play in Nazi Germany? (Ordinary Level)

2   What contribution did Joseph Goebbels and/or Leni Riefenstahl make to Nazi propaganda? (Higher Level; Leaving Certificate question)

3   To what extent did the Nazis establish state control over the mass media in Germany? (Higher Level)

8 Britain, 1920–45

What do you need to know in this chapter?

Elements	Key Personalities	Key Concepts
Economic and social problems of the inter-war years	Winston Churchill	Protectionism
	John Maynard Keynes	The Depression
Society during World War II: the Home Front		
Case Study: The Jarrow March, October 1936		

INTRODUCTION

In the 19th century, Britain was the world's leading economic and political power, with a vast empire spanning the globe. By the turn of the 20th century, it had been overtaken economically by both the US and Germany. Nonetheless, Britain was still a major force in the world economy, with London a key financial centre. Many in Britain believed that the reasons for their economic success were sound financial management of the nation's finances, a strong currency backed by gold (called the **Gold Standard**) and free trade. The economic problems Britain faced in the 1920s and 1930s were to challenge these traditional views.

Within the country, there was a wide gap in wealth between the prosperous south and poorer north of the country. There were also serious class divisions between the upper, middle and working classes. Politics had traditionally been dominated by the Liberals and the Conservatives. However, after World War I, the Labour Party grew in popularity

and replaced the Liberals as the main rivals of the Conservatives.

KEY QUESTION

What were economic conditions like in Britain after Word War I?

BRITAIN AFTER WORLD WAR I

World War I, or **the Great War**, as it was known, had left over 750,000 men dead and millions injured. The war had cost a lot of money that the British government had borrowed, mainly in America. Repaying the loans reduced the amount of money the government had to spend on improving services or helping the poor.

When the war ended in 1918, the coalition government, led by **David Lloyd George**, called a a general election, promising 'a land fit for heroes to live in'. His government, made up of the Conservatives and his Liberal Party, won a massive majority, though most of the MPs were Conservatives.

The government immediately began the process of returning soldiers to civilian life. This was called **demobilisation**. By the summer of 1919, over 4 million men had left the army and most found jobs in the post-war industrial boom. During the war, women had replaced men in factories and played a vital role in the war effort. They were now let go and by 1921 there were fewer women employed in industry than there had been in 1913.

ECONOMIC DIFFICULTIES

Soon a number of serious economic problems developed. Controls that limited prices, wages and profits during the war were removed. This led to inflation, which reduced what workers could buy for their wages. Soon there was industrial unrest, with a large number of strikes as workers looked for higher wages. Unions were determined to protect the position of workers and they formed a powerful alliance of miners, railwaymen and transport workers. During 1919 and 1920 there were over 2,000 strikes, including a national strike of railway workers.

In the coal mines, there were particularly poor relations between the miners and the mine owners. This was made worse with the end of the post-war boom in 1921, with unemployment rising to 2 million. The mine owners looked to cut wages, leading to a bitter industrial dispute. The owners won when the other unions would not back the miners.

Lloyd George's government did try to improve conditions for workers. It increased the amount of money paid in sickness and unemployment benefits and increased the number of those who were eligible for these payments from 3 million to 12 million workers. However, the payments were still small and workers who lost their jobs still faced real hardship.

THE FIRST LABOUR GOVERNMENT, 1924

In 1922, Lloyd George was replaced by the Conservative **Andrew Bonar Law**. The following year, Law had to resign due to ill health and was

Here is an explanation of some of the terms you will meet in this chapter.

Appeasement: British policy of giving into Hitler's demands in order to prevent war.

Beveridge Report: influential government report that led to the foundation of the Welfare State.

Chancellor of the Exchequer: name given to the Minister of Finance in Britain.

Free Trade: no taxes placed on imported goods – traditional British trade policy.

General Strike: when trade unions join together to stage a nationwide strike.

Gold Standard: a policy where a country's currency was backed by gold.

Protectionism: the introduction of taxes (tariffs) on imports to make them more expensive thereby helping domestic industry by reducing competition from imported goods.

The Abdication Crisis: in 1936 King Edward VIII gave up his throne to marry a twice-divorced American.

Trades Union Congress (TUC): organisation representing the different British trade unions.

Ramsay MacDonald (1866–1937) was the first Labour prime minster of Britain.

Stanley Baldwin (1867–1947) was one of the most important political figures of the inter-war period.

succeeded by his fellow Conservative, **Stanley Baldwin**.

The Conservatives did badly in the election of December 1923, partly because of economic problems and industrial unrest in the country. The Labour Party were the winners and led by **Ramsay MacDonald** formed its first-ever government with the support of the Liberals. The new government introduced a number of moderate reforms but could not nationalise (bring under government control) the mines or the railways as it had promised before the election. Its main reform was the **Housing Act**, which by 1932 helped to overcome a severe post-war housing shortage.

The moderation of the government did little to lessen the fear of Socialism, especially in the Conservative Party. Many people looked to the USSR and equated Socialism with revolution, bloodshed and chaos. These suspicions seemed to be confirmed when the government decided to establish diplomatic relations with the USSR. In 1924, a proposed trade agreement between both countries was bitterly attacked by the Conservatives.

By the autumn of 1924, it was clear the government was doomed. Matters came to a head when it was accused of interfering in the course of justice when a charge against a left-wing editor

was dropped. The Liberals withdrew support from the government and a new election was called. The election was famous for the publication of the **Zinoviev Letter**. Almost certainly a forgery, the letter claimed to be from the leading Russian Communist Gregory Zinoviev and set out plans for a Communist revolution in Britain. It created a 'red scare' and helped to ensure victory for the Conservatives.

KEY QUESTION

Why was there a General Strike in Britain in 1926?

THE CAUSES OF THE GENERAL STRIKE OF 1926

The pattern of poor relations between employers and workers continued, especially in the mines. The new Chancellor of the Exchequer (Minister of Finance), **Winston Churchill**, announced a return

Strikers during the General Strike.

to the **Gold Standard**, which had been dropped during World War I. It was hoped that this would increase confidence in sterling (the British currency) and restore London as the financial capital of the world. This was to prove to be a disastrous decision.

Winston Churchill (1874–1965) From a very wealthy background he had served in government during World War I. In 1926 he was finance minister during the General Strike. In 1940 he was appointed Prime Minister and provided very good leadership during the war. He lost the post-war election but served another term as prime minister in the 1950s.

While it made the British currency stronger, it made the price of exports more expensive in other countries. Demand for British exports fell and industry suffered, especially coalmining. In response, mine owners wanted to reduce wages and increase working hours. The unions refused to agree and the miners' leader, **A.J. Cook**, coined the phrase 'not a penny off the pay, not a minute on the day'. With no sign of compromise on either side, the miners went on strike.

The **Trades Union Congress**, which represented unions from different sectors of the British economy, threatened to call a nationwide strike of workers, or **general strike**, in support of the miners. The government demanded that the TUC call off the general strike. The TUC refused and the strike began on 4 May 1926. For the only time in British history, most of the workforce (over 1.5 million people) went on strike in support of one particular group of workers. Throughout the country, many feared that the strike was the start of a Communist takeover.

THE DEFEAT OF THE STRIKE

The government was determined not to back down. It had been planning for the possibility of the strike for nine months. Using emergency powers and with the help of volunteers, food supplies and a reduced train service were maintained throughout the country. It also waged an effective propaganda campaign against the strike. The government was able to portray itself as a force for moderation, while the strikers were portrayed as extremists. Baldwin said, 'The general strike is a challenge to Parliament, and is the road to anarchy and ruin.'

It soon became clear that the strike lacked public support and the leadership of the TUC was divided. Contrary to government claims, most were moderate Socialists who had hoped that the government would compromise before the strike began. They now found themselves in a very difficult position.

- Not intending to take on the government politically, they had completely underestimated the determination of the government to defeat the strike.
- Running short of funds, there was also a strong possibility that the strike was illegal and the unions could be sued for damages by the employers.

The strike collapsed after nine days, and on 12 May the TUC accepted defeat. Baldwin called on employers to take back their employees without any reprisals, although this did not always happen. The miners were left to fight on without support and held out until December, when they were forced to accept reduced wages and increased hours.

THE RESULTS OF THE STRIKE

In 1927, the government passed the **Trades Disputes Act**, which made this type of strike illegal. Unions suffered a loss of membership, but the moderates now dominated the leadership of the TUC. Industrial relations improved as both employees and employers increasingly looked for compromise in disputes.

It would be unfair to see the Conservatives as totally opposed to social reform. The government improved pensions and in 1928 finally gave the vote to women on equal terms to men. Nonetheless, the Conservatives lost the 1929 election, with the Labour Party under MacDonald returning to power. One of the reasons the Labour government had been elected was its promise to tackle unemployment, which had stood at 1 million, or 10 per cent of the workforce. The new government was soon to face a far greater economic crisis – **the Great Depression**.

A coalmining town in the 1920s. Traditional industries such as coalmining were to be hit very hard by the Great Depression.

R E V I E W   Q U E S T I O N S

1 What impact did World War I have on Britain's society and economy?

2 Why were there so many strikes in the years immediately after World War I?

3 Why did the Labour government of 1924 only last a year?

4 Explain why there was a general strike in 1926.

5 How would you describe the government's reaction to the strike?

6 Give two effects of the general strike.

K E Y   Q U E S T I O N

How did the British government deal with the economic problems caused by the Great Depression?

DEPRESSION

The **Wall Street Crash** occurred in 1929 (see p. 54). The government's economic situation deteriorated rapidly as world trade shrunk. Unemployment spread to all of the major industries, rising sharply to 2.6 million by 1931.

This presented the government with a severe problem. Rising unemployment meant increased public expenditure to pay unemployment benefit. This threatened the stability of the nation's finances and placed the Labour government in a dilemma. On the one hand, it was the party of the working man; on the other hand, it wanted to demonstrate that the party could manage the country responsibly, and the test of this was maintaining the nation's finances.

Unemployment in Britain, 1929–33					
Year	1929	1930	1931	1932	1933
Number unemployed	1.2 million	1.9 million	2.6 million	2.7 million	2.5 million

Source: Stephen Lee, *Aspects of British Political History 1914–1995*, Routledge, 1994, p. 112.

The government lacked any real economic knowledge, with MacDonald unsure how to tackle the economic difficulties. In 1931, a financial crash throughout Europe made matters worse and saw the value of the pound fall considerably. In July 1931, **the May Report** commissioned by the government predicted economic disaster unless there were severe tax rises, cuts in public sector pay and a 10 per cent reduction in unemployment benefit.

THE FORMATION OF THE NATIONAL GOVERNMENT

When MacDonald made it clear that he intended to implement the recommendations of the report, he found that he was opposed by most of his cabinet colleagues. For the Labour Party, the report was not an acceptable solution. On the advice of **King George V**, MacDonald then transformed his government into a national government made up of his few supporters in the Labour Party, the Conservatives and the Liberals. The rest of the Labour Party saw MacDonald's move as a betrayal and he was expelled from his own party.

The cutbacks were implemented a month later. The election of the same year resulted in massive backing for the national government, with over 500 pro-government MPs elected, the vast majority of whom were Conservatives.

DIFFERENT TO WEIMAR GERMANY

At the height of the crisis, nearly 25 per cent of the working population was unemployed. In contrast to Weimar Germany, where the Great Depression led to the collapse of democracy, this did not happen in Britain.

The ease with which a national government had been formed to deal with Britain's economic crisis pointed to the deep political stability of the British political system. There was very little support for the political extremes of Fascism or Communism.

- The **British Union of Fascists** was founded by the former Labour Party minister **Sir Oswald Mosley** in 1932. Although modelled on the Italian and German parties, it failed to make any significant impact. Its violent tactics and anti-Semitism were deeply unpopular with the British public and its membership fell from 35,000 in 1935 to under 5,000 in 1937.
- The **Communist Party** also failed to attract much support, even in an era of high unemployment. It followed instructions from Moscow and annoyed many of its supporters when it cut connections with the British Labour Party and the TUC. Though influential in a few areas, it remained outside the mainstream of British politics, with its peaceful and non-revolutionary traditions.

A further factor was the success of the government's policies in dealing with the crisis.

- The government left the **Gold Standard,** causing the value of the pound to fall. This made it easier for exporters to sell their goods in other countries.
- It abandoned the traditional British policy of free trade for protection. It placed tariffs (taxes) on imports to encourage industry at home.
- Interest rates were cut, which made it cheaper for businesses and individuals to borrow money.

THE DEPRESSION EASES

These measures helped to deal with the worst of the Depression and Britain recovered quite quickly

March of Fascists in London. Unlike in Germany or Italy, Fascism never became a significant movement in Britain.

and giving in to 'reasonable' German demands. By 1939, it was clear that this policy, called **appeasement**, had failed and Britain guaranteed Poland its support in the event of a German attack. On 1 September 1939, Hitler attacked Poland and two days later, Britain declared war on Germany.

REVIEW QUESTIONS

1   What effect did the Great Depression have on Britain?

2   Explain how a national government was formed in 1931.

3   Give two reasons why Britain did not suffer the same political difficulties as Germany in the 1930s.

4   What measures did the government introduce to tackle the economic crisis?

5   What was the abdication crisis?

6   What was appeasement?

from its economic problems. It was also helped by the fact that its economy had not performed as well as Germany or the US in the late 1920s, so it was not as severely affected as those countries were by the economic downturn.

In 1933, unemployment fell by 1 million and by 1934 the worst of the economic crisis had passed. The tough measures taken in 1931 were reversed. Income tax was reduced, unemployment benefit was increased and the salaries of public servants returned to their pre-1931 levels. In 1935, the crisis was over by the time Ramsay MacDonald resigned as prime minister, to be replaced by Baldwin.

THE ROAD TO WAR

In 1936, Baldwin showed great skill in handling the **abdication crisis**. This occurred when the new king, **Edward VIII**, wanted to marry a divorced American, **Wallis Simpson**. The marriage of the king to an American commoner was not acceptable to the British establishment. Baldwin opposed it because he felt it would damage the monarchy. Edward refused to abandon the woman he loved and abdicated (gave up his throne) in favour of his brother, **George VI**.

The following year, Baldwin resigned and was replaced by **Neville Chamberlain**. By now, domestic issues were being overshadowed by events in Europe. Chamberlain felt he could prevent war in Europe by negotiating with Hitler

CASE STUDY: THE JARROW CRUSADE

KEY QUESTION

What was the background to the Jarrow March?

SPECIAL AREAS

The improving economic picture was darkened by the problem of mass unemployment that affected traditional industrial areas such as the north-east, central Scotland, south Wales and Cumberland. In 1934, they were declared **Special Areas** and money was provided to help their revival and attract new industries. These policies did little to improve the

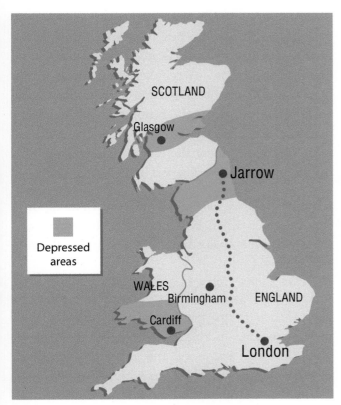

Areas affected by high unemployment in the 1930s.

increased the problems of poverty, poor housing, overcrowding and high mortality (death) rates that already plagued the town. The town had the highest unemployment and infant mortality rates in the country. Of the 8,000 skilled workers in the town, only 100 had jobs.

> **Jarrow: A Few Facts**
> - Infant mortality rate: 104 (national average: 58).
> - TB mortality per million deaths: 1,273 (national average: 702).

The local **MP**, **Ellen Wilkinson**, wrote about conditions in the town at the time:

There was no work. No one had a job except a few railwaymen, officials, the workers in the co-operative stores, and a few workmen who went out of the town … the plain fact [is] that if people have to live and bear and bring up their children in bad houses on too little food, their resistance to disease is lowered and they die before they should.

position of these regions. Matters were not helped by the system of unemployment benefit for the long-term unemployed. This financial aid was reluctantly given, subject to a means test, and was totally inadequate. Many moved in search of work to the more prosperous south. The most devastated areas were those dependent on a single industry, such as shipbuilding in Jarrow or coalmining in Rhondda in south Wales. It was the people of Jarrow that were to bring conditions in these areas to national attention.

CONDITIONS IN JARROW

Jarrow is a small town near **Newcastle upon Tyne**. On 5 October 1936, it became a household name throughout Britain when a group of 200 men from the town set out to march the 300 miles to London. They wanted Parliament to understand that they were living in a town where there was 70 per cent unemployment and to get help to tackle poverty in the town. The marchers' main demand was for a steelworks to be built to bring back jobs to their town.

The town's main employer, Palmer's Shipyard, had closed down the previous year. The closure

Ellen Wilkinson (1891–1947) was nicknamed Red Ellen. A former Communist, she was the local Labour MP and a strong supporter of the marchers.

THE BACKGROUND TO THE MARCH

Protest marches against the poverty caused by the Great Depression began in 1932. 'Hunger marches' were organised by the **National Unemployed Workers' Movement** (NUWM). These included a march of 2,000 people in 1932, two further national marches in 1934 and 1936 and a march of 200 blind people to London in 1936.

It was in this climate that in July 1936, Jarrow Borough Council decided to present a petition to Parliament. It would be delivered by men who would march the 300 miles to London in 22 stages. They called their march a 'crusade'. The name was chosen to emphasise the seriousness of their situation and partly to distinguish their march from those of the NUWM, whose connection with the Communist Party raised the fear of revolution among many people. As a result of this connection, the Labour Party had refused to support the NUWM. On the other hand, the Jarrow crusade attracted broad political support in the town, including that of local Conservatives.

KEY QUESTION

Q

What impact did the march have?

PREPARATION FOR THE MARCH

The marchers were carefully chosen. After medical examination, 200 men were selected to march. Women were not invited. A second-hand bus was bought to carry cooking equipment, and ground sheets were provided for outside rests. An advance guard was sent out to arrange overnight stops and public meetings. Finally, a religious service was held on the eve of departure to bless the crusade.

THE MARCH

The march started on 5 October 1936. Carrying blue and white banners, the Jarrow men paraded at 8:45 a.m. each morning of their 25-day march.

The petition signed by 11,000 people from Jarrow was carried in an oak box with gold lettering. A further petition was collected en route. They marched army style – 50 minutes of marching every hour, with 10 minutes' rest. On average, the men walked between 10 and 15 miles a day. As they marched, they sang and a mouth organ band was a great success, 'keeping the men swinging along all the time', according to a report in the *Shields Gazette*.

A public meeting was held at every town along the way at which Ellen Wilkinson and the mayor of Jarrow, **J.W. Thompson**, spoke about conditions in their town.

At Leeds, the Jarrow men received a donation to pay for their return trip by train. At Barnsley, the men were able to relax in the specially heated public baths. Some of the marchers needed medical aid from time to time, which was provided by medical students from the Inter Hospital Socialist Society. One helper along the route described how he saw a marcher take the ham from inside his sandwich and place it in an envelope. When asked what he was doing he replied, 'I'm sending it home … my family haven't had meat in the house for six weeks.'

The march was widely covered in the press. On 13 October, *The Guardian* newspaper described the reception the marchers received along the route of the march:

> *Harrogate welcomed the Jarrow marches to-day as cheerfully as if they were a relief column raising a siege. The police were in attendance and there was a big banner raised saying, 'Harrogate workers welcome the Jarrow marchers'. It was*

Jarrow marchers.

the same to-day all along the road from Ripon. The villagers of Ripley and Killinghall rushed to their doors to see the marchers pass; motorists waved as they went by; one shouted, 'How are you sticking it?'

There can be no doubt that as a gesture the march is a bounding success. I fell in with it this morning on the Ripon road. The marchers have with them two doctors, a barber, a group of pressmen, a Labrador dog mascot, and for a great deal of the time so far the Mayor of Jarrow (Alderman J.W. Thompson), who keeps travelling back to Jarrow to maintain touch with his civic duties and then south again to maintain touch with the marchers.

ARRIVAL IN LONDON

The march eventually reached London on 31 October. Despite considerable public sympathy, the crusade made little real impact. On 4 November, the petition was presented to Parliament. Prime Minister Stanley Baldwin refused to see the marchers or their representatives, claiming he was too busy. Delegates from the protest, including Ellen Wilkinson and Mayor Thompson, addressed a group of MPs from all parties in the largest committee room in the House of Commons.

Raising his chain of office in front of them, Thompson said:

Its links form a cable, its badge is an anchor ... symbols in gold of the cables and anchors of the thousand ships we built at Jarrow. If you are not going to help us, then this means nothing.

EFFECTS OF THE MARCH

Despite its lack of response to the plight of Jarrow, the government's policies did improve the British economy. For example, its taxes on imports increased demand for British-made goods in Britain. In Jarrow, a ship-breaking yard and engineering works were established in 1938 and a steelworks in 1939. However, unemployment remained high until World War II, when industry prospered as a result of the country's need for weapons.

Summary: The Jarrow March

- Poverty and mass unemployment (as high as 70 per cent) were caused by the Great Depression. Tyneside, West Cumberland, Scotland and south Wales were the most affected.
- In protest, 200 men from Jarrow, near Newcastle, marched 300 miles to London.
- The march had cross-party support and the marchers carried a petition containing 11,000 names. The march was widely covered in the press.
- There was a lot of public support along the route.
- The crusade ultimately made little real impact. In London, they delivered a petition to Parliament asking for a steelworks. PM Baldwin refused to meet them.
- In areas of traditional industry, the Depression continued until the rearmament boom of WWII.

The march represented the determination of one community to deal with the social and economic problems it faced. It helped to raise awareness of the poverty that existed in the north of the country. To later historians, it came to symbolise the human consequences of mass unemployment.

KEY QUESTION

Did the Jarrow March reflect conditions in Britain in the 1930s?

WAS THE JARROW CRUSADE A REFLECTION OF CONDITIONS IN BRITAIN IN THE 1930S?

The 1930s have traditionally been portrayed as a time of grinding poverty and economic hardship, highlighted by the Jarrow Crusade and books such as George Orwell's *The Road to Wigan Pier*. While this was true for some of the country, it does not reflect the experience of all of Britain. As historian **A.P.J. Taylor** has pointed out, most of Britain was enjoying a richer life than ever before in the 1930s. There were a number of reasons for this.

- The nature of the British economy had been changing in the inter-war years. While traditional industries such as shipbuilding and coalmining were in decline, industries based on new technologies such as car manufacture and electricity were growing. The traditional industries were located mainly in the north of the country, while the new industries were to be found in the south and the Midlands.

- The traditional industries were the ones that had been hit by the economic downturn, while the number of jobs in the motor industry grew from 227,000 in 1920 to 516,000 in 1938. This was more than those employed in steelmaking and shipbuilding put together. The number of workers in electrical engineering almost doubled between the wars. There was also growth in professional and clerical employment – so-called 'white collar' jobs.

- Between 1932 and 1937, national income rose by 20 per cent, industrial production by 40 per cent and income per head of the population by 18 per cent. Average weekly earnings were twice as high in 1938 as they had been in 1913.

- In addition, there had been a significant fall in the price of goods, especially of food. Real wages rose steeply in the 1930s, meaning that workers could buy more for their wages.

- Other factors contributing to prosperity included smaller families, cheap mortgages and the wider availability of consumer goods such as motor cars, music records and radios. It was also a period in which mass culture developed, such as listening to the BBC and pop music. Large numbers of Britons could now afford new pastimes, such as going to the cinema every week or going on holiday every year.

R E V I E W Q U E S T I O N S

1 What were conditions like in the town of Jarrow in 1936?

2 Was the march a non-political event?

3 'The march was well-organised.' Do you agree? Support your answer with evidence.

4 What sort of reception did the marchers get on the route to London?

5 What impact did the Jarrow March have?

6 Why was the south of England not affected as badly by the Great Depression?

KEY QUESTION

What was life like for ordinary people during World War II?

SOCIETY IN BRITAIN DURING WORLD WAR II – 'THE HOME FRONT'

The war was to have a profound effect on the lives of ordinary people in Britain. A wartime coalition was formed involving the Conservatives, Labour and the Liberals. In May 1940, discredited by the

A car plant in the Midlands. New industries such as car manufacture grew in the 1930s.

Poster encouraging people to be careful what they talked about in case the information helped the Germans.

failure of appeasement, Neville Chamberlain resigned and was replaced by Winston Churchill. He became closely identified with the determination of the British people to defeat Nazi Germany. His speeches contained some superb morale-boosting language:

> Let us therefore brace ourselves to our duties, and so bear ourselves that, if the British Empire and its Commonwealth last for a thousand years, men will still say, 'This was their finest hour'.

The country was put on a war footing and the government directed all of its efforts to winning the war.

- By 1943, over 17 million people were directly involved in the war effort as soldiers or working in factories making weapons.
- A Home Guard was formed, made up of 250,000 men who were too old to join the regular army – the famous 'Dad's Army'.
- Newspapers were strictly censored and a **Treachery Act** was passed to deal with suspected spies. About 750 Fascists, including Mosley, were arrested. Suspect enemy aliens from Austria, Germany (many of whom were Jewish or anti-Nazi refugees) and Italy were interned or deported to British colonies.
- Propaganda was extensively used to maintain morale, especially during the difficult early years of the war. As going to the cinema was a popular pastime, films served an important propaganda purpose in maintaining support for the war (see chapter 11).

MOVING THE CHILDREN TO THE COUNTRYSIDE

When the war broke out in 1939, the government expected the German air force to bomb cities and factories, so they began a mass evacuation of children from the towns to the countryside. This had been planned before the war and was called **Operation Pied Piper**. Many of the evacuees returned home during the Phoney War, but once the Battle of Britain began, the evacuation resumed. In total, around 3 million schoolchildren, teachers, mothers of children under five and pregnant women were moved to families in the countryside, causing the population of London to fall by 25 per cent.

John Maynard Keynes (1883–1946), First Baron Keynes of Tilton, was arguably the most influential economist of the 20th century. He was also a strong critic of the Versailles settlement and helped to create the climate for appeasement.

Local officials found suitable houses for the evacuees. Once selected, a host family could not refuse, but they did receive payment for hosting the children. For many of the children, this was their first taste of living in the countryside and their experiences varied widely. Some were made part of the family, while others were neglected, poorly fed and in extreme cases beaten. The evacuation also exposed the divide between the towns and the countryside. A lot of the host families were shocked at the poor health and hygiene of the children from the cities.

FEEDING THE POPULATION

Britain relied on imports to feed its population. Because of the threat of German submarines, it was not possible to get all the food that was needed, so rationing was introduced in January 1940. This system was fair and made sure that everyone was able to receive the basic amount of food necessary to keep them fit and healthy. Every man, woman and child in the country was issued with a ration book. These contained coupons that had to be handed in to the shops every time rationed food was bought. As well as the basic ration, everyone had 16 coupons each month that they could spend on what they wished.

Bacon, butter and sugar were among the first things to be rationed. Some foods such as potatoes, fruit and fish were not rationed. Beef was rationed not by weight, but by price.

The government also encouraged people to grow their own food at home and the '**Dig for Victory**' campaign was started in October 1939. It called on people to use every spare piece of land, including their gardens, to grow vegetables.

The government conducted public information campaigns to get the country to make best use of its resources. Posters, information leaflets and slogans persuaded and reminded everyone that they had a part to play in fighting the war. '**Saucepans for Spitfires**' was one of the most famous campaigns. Aluminium pans were collected so that they could be melted down to make parts for aircraft. The government did not

need the aluminium, but it believed the appeal made people feel part of the war effort and helped to keep morale up.

PROTECTING AGAINST CIVILIAN BOMBING

As we have seen, one of the greatest fears before the war had been the effects of bombing cities. The British population had been warned in September 1939 that air attacks were likely and everyone was issued with a gas mask. Civil defence preparations had been put into action. Simple corrugated steel shelters covered over by earth were constructed in gardens throughout the country, called **Anderson shelters**. Larger community shelters built of brick and concrete were built in towns.

To make it difficult for German bombers, a blackout was strictly enforced after darkness, with all houselights either covered or put out. Car headlights had to be dimmed, which led to a large number of road accidents.

SHELTERING IN THE UNDERGROUND

During the Blitz, many Londoners decided to make use of Tube stations as air raid shelters because they felt more secure there than in other shelters. It was initially discouraged by the authorities because it was felt an important service would be disrupted. However, as the war continued, platforms filled up and eventually it became necessary to provide canteens and toilet facilities for those seeking refuge in the stations.

A crowded London Tube station during the Blitz.

Churchill visits a building damaged by German bombing.

Sheltering in a Tube station may have given a sense of security, but conditions were tough. Space was limited and there was a terrible smell caused by so many people sheltering in a confined space. Nor was the Tube always as safe. In January 1941, a bomb fell above Bank Station, killing more than one hundred people sheltering below.

Despite the popular image of Londoners going to Tube stations to escape German bombs, a survey discovered that the majority of people actually stayed at home. In 1941, **Morrison shelters** were introduced that could be used in houses. They were made of very heavy steel and could be put in the living room and used as a table. They provided sleeping space for two or three people.

KEY QUESTION

What impact did the war have on British society?

WOMEN IN WARTIME BRITAIN

As men were called up to join the armed forces, more and more women were needed to replace them in the workforce. In 1941, Britain became the first country to call up (conscript) women to take part in war work. Women had to choose whether they wanted to join the armed forces or work in vital industries. At first this only applied to single women between the ages of 18 and 26, but later women up to the age of 51 were included. Women with children under the age of 14 were allowed to decide whether to work or not.

Some of the important roles that women played in wartime society are as follows.

- **Factory workers:** Women did all kinds of work except for mining. They made up over half the workforce in the chemical and explosive industry and 1.5 million women worked in the engineering and metal industries. In total, about 7 million women were employed in the war effort.
- **The military:** By December 1939, 43,000 women had volunteered for active duty in the **Women's Auxiliary Services** of the army, navy and air force. They were not allowed to fight, but supported the efforts of the military, by activities such as identifying enemy aircraft, plotting air and shipping movements and acting as motorcycle messengers. As the war

WOMEN OF BRITAIN
COME INTO THE FACTORIES
ASK AT ANY EMPLOYMENT EXCHANGE FOR ADVICE AND FULL DETAILS

Poster promoting war work for women.

went on, women were given more dangerous work to do, such as crewing anti-aircraft guns and searchlights. Women also undertook top-secret work using radar or code-breaking enemy messages. By 1944, over 450,000 women were serving in the armed forces, compared to 4.5 million men.

- **Agriculture:** The **Women's Land Army** was set up to keep farms working and providing food. The work was often hard and physically demanding. By 1943, there were over 80,000 members and they were popularly known as Land Girls.
- **Voluntary work:** During the war, many women who were exempted from war work joined the **Women's Voluntary Service**. It soon had over 1 million members. They carried out a large number of tasks, such as providing canteens at railway stations for soldiers and escorting children being evacuated. They helped people rescue their personal belongings from bombed-out houses and ran centres for those made homeless by bombing. This was dangerous work and over 200 members were killed during the Blitz.

THE BEVERIDGE REPORT

The war revealed the great gulf in standards of wealth and health care found throughout Britain. Some measures were taken to improve this situation. Free school meals were provided and improvements were made in maternity care. For most people, these changes did not go far enough and they wanted to see greater social justice and a fairer society after the war. They had been promised this after World War I but it had not happened. They now wanted a new society that would justify the sacrifice and hard work of the war effort. They believed that the government should work to create this. In 1941, responding to these sentiments, the government commissioned a report into how Britain should be rebuilt after the war.

The resulting **Beveridge Report**, published in 1942, recommended that the government should fight the five '**Giant Evils**' of 'Want, Disease, Ignorance, Squalor and Idleness'. It called for the government to provide free health care, improved education and housing, better pensions and commit to work for full employment. It caught the popular imagination and after the war the recommendations were to lead to the greatest social change ever seen in British history – the **Welfare State**.

THE END OF THE WAR

In May 1945, the war ended and a general election was called. The wartime coalition broke up and to the great surprise of many, both domestically and internationally, Churchill was soundly defeated. The Labour Party, led by **Clement Attlee**, won the election and achieved its first overall majority in the Commons. Most historians think that Churchill lost because the British people did not believe he was fully committed to the social change proposed by the Beveridge Report. The Labour Party began to introduce the Welfare State reforms proposed by Beveridge. The most important of these reforms was the creation of the free **National Health Service** in 1948.

REVIEW QUESTIONS

1 At the start of the war, why were children evacuated from the cities to the countryside?

2 How was rationing organised during the war?

3 What were conditions like in London Tube stations during the Blitz?

4 Do you agree with the view that women played an important role in Britain during the war? Support your view with evidence.

5 During the war, why was there a desire for social change in Britain?

6 Why was the Beveridge Report so important?

7 Explain why historians think Winston Churchill was defeated in the 1945 election.

Britain 1918–45: Timeline

1918	End of World War I.
1919–20	Wave of strikes and labour unrest.
1924	Formation of the first Labour government under Ramsay MacDonald.
1926	The General Strike.
1929	Wall Street Crash and the start of the Great Depression.
1931	Formation of the national government led by Ramsay MacDonald. Britain abandons the Gold Standard.
1932	Unemployment rose to over 2.5 million.
1935	Worst of the Great Depression over, although some regions still badly affected.
1936	Jarrow March. Abdication of King Edward VIII.
1938	Munich Conference – the high point of appeasement.
1939	Britain declares war on Germany.
1940	Introduction of rationing. Children moved from the cities to the countryside. Winston Churchill became PM. Battle of Britain and the bombing of London.
1942	The Beveridge Report recommended the introduction of the Welfare State.
1945	Defeat of Germany. Labour won a landslide victory in the post-war election.

ESSAY ANALYSIS

How successfully did Britain deal with the social and economic problems of the inter-war period?

SUGGESTED APPROACH

- It is very important to address the question in your introduction to show that you are going to answer the question. Remember to bear in mind "How successfully.."
- Put in dates as they are not mentioned in the question (1919 to 1939).
- Main period of focus would be the period of the Great Depression but it is not an essay just on the case study, the Jarrow March.
- The case study should be used as an illustration of the social and economic problems Britain faced at the time.
- The conclusion is very important to show that you have answered the question.

Main Points

1. What were economic conditions like in the aftermath of WWI?
2. What caused the General strike of 1926 and how did the government defeat the strike?
3. What was the impact of the Great Depression on Britain?
4. What policies did the National Government introduce to tackle the Great Depression?
5. What was the importance of the Jarrow march to London in October 1936?
6. Was the march an accurate reflection of conditions throughout Britain in the late 1930s?
7. Conclusion – How successful?

Documents A and B:

A. This is an extract from a *Guardian* newspaper article about the Jarrow March, dated 13 October 1936.

This is not a hunger march but a protest march. The unanimity of the protest that Jarrow is making to the rest of the country is indicated in the fact that the political parties represented on the Jarrow Town Council have agreed to bury the political hatchet to the extent of holding no elections this November. There is no political aspect to this march. It is simply the town of Jarrow saying 'Send us work'. In the ranks of the marchers are Labour men, Liberals, Tories and one or two Communists, but you cannot tell who's who. It has the Church's blessing; in fact, it took the blessing of the Bishop of Ripon (Dr. Lunt) and a subscription of £5 from him when it set out to-day. It also had the blessing of the Bishop of Jarrow (Dr. Gordon). With the marchers goes, prominently carried, the Jarrow petition for work, a huge book with about 12,000 signatures, which Miss Ellen Wilkinson, M.P. for Jarrow, is to present at the bar of the House of Commons on November 4.

Source: http://century.guardian.co.uk.

B. This is an edited extract from the records of a cabinet meeting about the Jarrow March and other unemployment protests in October 1936.

The Cabinet had before them a Memorandum [report] by the Home Secretary calling attention to the arrangements made ... for contingents of unemployed persons to march on London, the marchers being due to arrive on the 8th November. Two other demonstration marches had been organised, both of which were timed to reach London on the 31st October, one consisting of 200 unemployed men from Jarrow, and the other comprising about 250 blind persons, accompanied by some 50 attendants. The existing law contained no provisions by which orderly bands of demonstrators could be prevented from marching to London or elsewhere. The only course open, therefore, was to take every precaution to minimise the risk of disorder on the routes of the contingents and in London. The Home Secretary thought that the best method of informing the public on the present occasion, in order to discourage them from furnishing [giving] assistance to the marchers would be to arrange for selected journalists to be interviewed and given material for exposing the origin, motive and uselessness of the hunger march.

Source: Cabinet Conclusion 14 October 1936. March of the Unemployed on London CAB 23/85 C 57 (36) 3, British National Archives.

Comprehension

(a) From document A, what evidence is there to show that the march had widespread support in the town of Jarrow?

(b) According to document A, what was 'prominently carried'?

(c) From document B, what groups of marchers were due to arrive in London?

(d) According to document B, how did the government hope to discourage public support for the marches?

Comparison

(a) How do the documents differ in their interpretations of the marches?

(b) Which of the two sources do you think is more accurate? Explain your answer with reference to both sources.

Criticism

(a) Comment on the strengths and weaknesses of document A as a source for historians.

(b) How useful are the records of government cabinet meetings for historians?

Contextualisation

(a) Why was the Jarrow March an important event in Britain in the 1930s? (Ordinary Level, 1 A4 page)

(b) What were the causes and consequences of the Jarrow March in October 1936? (Higher Level, 1.5 A4 pages)

END OF CHAPTER QUESTIONS

1 Write a paragraph on **TWO** of the following topics. (Ordinary Level)
 ○ The general strike of 1926.
 ○ Economic and social problems in Britain in the 1930s.
 ○ Winston Churchill.
 ○ Life in Britain in World War II.

2 This topic is popular on the Leaving Certificate. Here are a number of essays that have been asked at both Ordinary and Higher level.

Ordinary Level

(a) What were the economic and social conditions in Britain that led to the Jarrow March in October 1936?

(b) How successful was Winston Churchill as a wartime leader between 1940 and 1945?

Higher Level

(c) How did the Jarrow March (October 1936) draw attention to the social and economic problems in Great Britain at that time?

(d) How successfully did Britain deal with the social and economic problems of the inter-war period?
 See analysis page 103.

(e) Which had the greater social and economic problems during the inter-war years, Britain or Germany? Argue your case, referring to both countries.

(f) What were the causes and consequences of the Jarrow March in October 1936?

(g) What was the impact of World War II on the 'home front' in Great Britain, 1939–45?

3 Was the Jarrow March an accurate reflection of conditions throughout the United Kingdom in the 1930s? Argue your case with evidence.

What do you need to know in this chapter?

Elements	Key Concepts
The Third Republic, 1920–40	Collaboration
The Vichy State	Resistance
Collaboration/resistance	

Here is an explanation of some of the terms you will meet in this chapter.

Third Republic: A period of French history from 1870 until 1940. It was the third republic established in French history – the first was from 1792 until 1804 and the second was from 1848 until 1852.

Vichy France: The government of France from 1940 until 1944, led by Marshal Petain.

Bloc National: Right-wing government that lasted from 1919 until 1924.

Cartel des Gauches: Alliance of left-wing parties that held office from 1924 to 1926 and 1932 to 1934.

Radicals: A French political group with strong support among the middle classes. It was sympathetic to reform and opposed to the power of the Catholic Church.

Anti-clericalism: Opposition to the influence of the Catholic Church, especially in education.

Devaluation: Reduction in the value of a currency, which means imports are more expensive but exports are cheaper.

In this chapter, we will examine the later years of the Third Republic and the government established after the defeat of France in 1940 – Vichy France.

INTRODUCTION

There were great divisions in French society on what the best form of government for the country was, stretching back to the French Revolution of 1789.

The Third Republic was established in 1870. Throughout its existence, it was characterised by weak coalition governments and frequent changes of prime minister. Between 1919 and 1940, there were over 30 separate cabinets or ministries formed.

The major factor causing this political instability was the large number of political parties in the Chamber of Deputies (or parliament). No one party ever got enough support in an election to govern alone, which meant that there were always coalition governments. Generally, the government was formed from right-wing or left-wing parties, although the liberal Radicals usually had a role, often providing the prime minister.

Some governments collapsed after a few days, others after two or three months; only two prime ministers served more than two years. Even though there were many governments, a small group of politicians dominated the political life of the inter-war period. It was also quite common for politicians to switch parties. For example, **Pierre Laval** started as a Socialist, later became a conservative politician and ended his career in front of a firing squad for collaborating with Nazi Germany.

DIVISION IN FRENCH SOCIETY

Despite this great political instability, the majority of French people believed that a republic was the best system of government for France and identified with the ideals of liberty, equality and fraternity from the French Revolution. On the other hand, a sizeable group in society favoured a monarchy or a strong powerful government led by a figure like Napoleon. They felt the republic was too politically unstable, run by corrupt politicians and hostile to traditional French value. Opponents of the republic were prominent in the army and in the wealthier groups in society. Some were anti-Semitic and strongly opposed to what they saw as the undue influence of Jews in French society. In the 1920s and 1930s, many who held this view were attracted to Fascism.

Another group that disliked the republic were Catholics. Most Republicans saw the Church as monarchist and opposed to progress. At the turn of the 20th century, Catholics had strongly objected to the severe anti-clerical measures introduced, especially in the area of education. There were also class divisions between the working class and the middle class and between the city and the countryside. France was a very unequal society, with the wealth of the country concentrated in the hands of a small percentage of the population. As a result, the late 19th and early 20th centuries had seen the growth of a powerful Socialist movement.

Main political groups in the Third Republic
● Leagues (Fascists)
● Monarchists
● Conservatives
● Radicals
● Socialists
● Communists

This text box shows the main political groups in France. Throughout the inter-war period, the country was governed by unstable coalitions. As it was in the centre politically, Radical politicians were involved in nearly every government.

KEY QUESTION

How did successive French governments tackle the political and economic problems facing France in the 1920s?

THE IMPACT OF WORLD WAR I

When World War I broke out, the different political groups put aside their differences to defeat the Germans. Called **L'Union Sacrée** (the Sacred Union), it resulted in political and social co-operation in pursuit of victory. For example, the trade unions agreed to preserve industrial peace. Guided by Prime Minister **Georges Clemenceau**, France won the war. However, once the war ended, the traditional divisions in French society re-emerged.

France had suffered terribly as a result of the war. Large areas of the north of the country were destroyed by four years of fighting and the scorched earth policy of the retreating Germans. Nearly 17 per cent of France's soldiers had been killed and hundreds of thousands left maimed. The **Russian Revolution** resulted in French investors losing vast sums of money and presented another problem – the threat of Communist revolution.

Despite these problems, the government hoped that the peace negotiations would remove Germany as a future threat and that reparations would pay for the damage to northern France. The resulting peace treaty negotiated by Clemenceau was harsh on the Germans. Germany was weakened but still potentially powerful. Many argued that the treaty had failed to ensure French security. The leading French general **Marshal Foch** was strongly critical, remarking, 'This is not peace, but an armistice for 20 years.'

VICTORY FOR THE RIGHT

The election of November 1919 saw a victory for an alliance of right-wing parties. Called **the Bloc National** (National Bloc), it played on patriotism and fears of Communism to win a large majority. It attracted the support of Catholics, as it promised to end the divisions between Church and state. It was also helped by a bitter split in the Socialist movement over its attitude to events in Russia. In December 1920, the party congress saw the majority of delegates support the formation of the Communist Party. This move was opposed by moderates, led by **Leon Blum**. The split weakened the Socialist movement, and in resulting elections in the 1920s, the Socialists won about 20 per cent of the votes and the Communists about 10 per cent.

Alexandre Millerand became prime minister and was later succeeded by the wartime president **Raymond Poincaré** in 1922. Poincaré was worried about France's security and was

French troops in the Ruhr. The occupation caused great resentment in Germany.

determined to enforce the peace treaty. The French also needed the reparations provided by Germany to help it out of a financial crisis caused by a shortfall in government revenue. When Germany stopped paying reparations, France invaded the German industrial heartland of the Ruhr in January 1923. The move was criticised by Britain and proved to be an embarrassing failure. This hard-line foreign policy also lost public support.

Other measures increased the government's unpopularity.

- For example, it tried to prevent civil servants from having the right to strike and attempted to extend the Church's influence in education – a move that drew strong opposition from the left.
- After the failure of the occupation of the Ruhr, Poincaré tried to raise taxes by 20 per cent, but this was rejected by the Senate. A financial crisis resulted that saw rising inflation and a fall in the value of the franc, which contributed to the Bloc National's defeat in the elections of May 1924.

Leon Blum (1872–1950) was a moderate Socialist leader and the first Jewish prime minister of France.

THE CARTEL DES GAUCHES (THE COALITION OF THE LEFT)

Before the election, the Radicals and the Socialists formed an electoral pact called the **Cartel des Gauches**. The coalition won and the new government was led by the radical politician **Édouard Herriot**. Although they supported Herriot, the Socialists stayed out of the government for fear of losing supporters to the Communists.

The new government tried to introduce anti-clerical measures into **Alsace** aimed at removing the Catholic Church from education. Popular opposition in the former German province forced the government to drop the measures.

In relations with Germany, the government pursued a more moderate course under foreign minister **Aristide Briand**, who held office from 1925 to 1932. His policy led to a period of Franco-German co-operation, the high point of which was the **Locarno Pact** (1925), which saw Germany recognise their western frontier with France as final.

There were major divisions between the Radicals and the Socialists about economic policy, especially over the role of the government in the economy. Thus, the government could not agree on what measures to take to deal with the financial crisis and the severe inflation the country faced.

Between 1922 and 1926, prices had doubled and the franc had plunged in value. In 1924, it cost 76 francs to buy £1; by 1926, this had risen to 243 francs. The government failed to tackle the problems and it was replaced by a right-wing government led by **Raymond Poincaré**. The new coalition government had the support of big business, which had little confidence in the Cartel. A series of measures including tax and interest rate increases restored financial stability. The value of the franc was fixed at one-fifth of its 1914 value, which helped exports.

THE FRENCH ECONOMY IN THE 1920s

Despite the financial problems facing governments in the 1920s, the French economy performed well. Wages for workers rose and unemployment was low. There was a massive wave of immigration from North Africa, Spain, Poland and Italy – in total, an estimated 3 million people came to France. Tourism became an important industry, with Paris becoming the centre of fashion and the arts and a refuge for writers and artists from around the world. The north of France quickly recovered from the devastation of World War I, while the return of Alsace gave France an important source of iron ore. The industrial growth relied heavily on exporting goods to other countries. Chemical and engineering factories prospered and the French car industry expanded

Aristide Briand (1862–1939) was a Nobel Peace Prize winner. Between 1906 and 1932, he was prime minister 11 times and foreign minister 17 times.

Raymond Poincare (1860–1934) was a conservative politician who was prime minister five times and president for seven years.

rapidly. Companies such as **Renault**, **Citroën** and **Peugeot** produced over 200,000 cars a year. **Andre Citroën** copied the mass production techniques used in the United States. For a time, France was the European leader in both the luxury and affordable car market.

KEY QUESTION

Why did serious political divisions develop in France in the 1930s?

THE GREAT DEPRESSION

In 1929, when Poincaré was forced to resign due to ill health, France had recovered its pre-war stability, prosperity and self-confidence. For a time, it even seemed to be unaffected by the Great Depression that began in 1929 in the US. Yet this was an illusion. By 1931, France was suffering the effects of the Great Depression and the impact was severe. To make matters worse, France was feeling the impact just as other European countries were showing signs of recovery. Two factors contributed to the economic problems faced by France.

- Overseas trade fell, which led to a balance of payments crisis – France was spending more on imported goods than it was receiving for the goods it sold abroad.
- A decline in industrial and agricultural production led to falling share prices.

THE LEFT RETURN TO POWER

Unemployment was rising quickly and in the 1932 election, the right-wing parties lost control of the Chamber to the Radicals and Socialists. A second Cartel des Gauches, led by Édouard Herriot, was formed with Socialist support, but as before, the party did not join the government. During the next two years, there were six left-wing governments, reflecting the political instability of the Third Republic. They failed to tackle France's economic problems and were subject to criticism from a rising force in French politics – the extreme right wing.

THE LEAGUES

In the 1920s, influenced by Mussolini's Italy, a number of right-wing movements called Leagues had developed. The Depression saw the Leagues grow in popularity. The most important were:

- **Action Française**, which had been founded before World War I.
- **Jennesses Patriotes**, set up in 1924.
- **Solidarité Française**, which was founded by the well-known businessman François Coty in 1933.
- **Croix-de-Feu** was the most important. It was an organisation for decorated World War I veterans.

Some Leagues were openly Fascist, while others were more traditional in arguing for a return of the monarchy. They were all strongly anti-Communist. They were also opposed to the parliamentary governments of the Third Republic, which they saw as corrupt and unable to tackle France's problems. They were hostile to immigrants and many of their members were anti-Semitic. In 1934, the Leagues were boosted by the most celebrated scandal of the inter-war period – the Stavisky Affair.

THE STAVISKY AFFAIR, 1934

The affair had all the elements that excited the right in France – a financial scandal, a Jewish villain and the strong suspicion of a political cover-up by corrupt politicians. The scandal came to light in December 1933, when a 200 million franc loan scheme collapsed. The fraud was organised by the professional swindler **Alexandre Stavisky**. When Stavisky was found dead in January 1934, police officials said that he had committed suicide. The French right believed that Stavisky had been killed to prevent the revelation of a scandal that would have involved his friends in high places, including ministers and members of the parliament. Government attempts to hush up the affair convinced the supporters of the Leagues that the Third Republic was corrupt. This seemed to be confirmed when it emerged that Stavisky had been saved from facing trial nine times since 1927 by political interference. Prime Minister **Camille Chautemps** was forced to resign when it came to

light that his brother-in-law had delayed Stavisky's trial.

The Leagues organised popular protests against what they alleged was Republican corruption. The leader of Action Française called the government 'a gang of robbers and assassins'. Their anger intensified when the right-wing head of the Paris police was dismissed. Their protests culminated in the riot of 6 February 1934 in which 15 people were killed by the police and over a thousand injured on the Place de la Concorde outside the Chamber of Deputies. The left believed that the riots were a Fascist attempt to overthrow the republic, but this is unlikely, as the riots were very disorganised. A government of national union was formed under former president **Gaston Doumergue**. This restored confidence and ended the threat to the republic. He was replaced by **Pierre Laval** in 1935, whose economic measures to tackle the Depression proved unpopular.

THE POPULAR FRONT

The immediate effect of the Stavisky Affair was an alliance of the forces on the left that became known as the Popular Front. Both Socialists and Communists realised how dangerous their feud was, given recent events and the rise of Hitler in Germany. This alliance reflected a wider movement in Europe at the time. Alarmed at the growth of Fascism, Stalin instructed Communist parties to form alliances with democratic parties to oppose it.

In 1935, the Socialists and Communists were joined by the Radicals and the three parties staged a mass demonstration in Paris on **Bastille Day, 14 July**. They also agreed on a vague programme to contest the 1936 election and the Popular Front won an overwhelming majority.

For the first time, the Socialists became the largest party, but the greatest proportional gain went to the Communists, who jumped from 10 to 72 seats. Leon Blum formed a government made up of Socialists and Radicals with the support of the Communists, but not their participation. It seemed as if a new era of social reform and economic recovery might be beginning. Throughout France, workers engaged in sit-ins and strikes. The government persuaded employers to agree to concessions such as higher wages, which ended the industrial unrest. A wave of reform measures followed, including a 40-hour week, holidays with pay, nationalisation of the arms industry and a programme of public works.

OPPOSITION TO THE POPULAR FRONT

However, the government faced many difficulties that reflected the deep political divisions in France. Upon assuming power, it faced a dilemma over what action to take over the Spanish Civil War, where a Popular Front government similar to its own was faced with a military revolt led by General Franco. In the end, responding to pressure from both the Radicals and the British, Blum agreed to a policy of non-intervention.

Blum's government had to deal with serious opposition from the right, to whom any Communist role in government was completely unacceptable. The prospect of France being ruled by a Jewish prime minister was greeted with outrage by the Leagues – the slogan 'Better Hitler than Blum' became common. Many saw the government as a Jewish or Communist plot to control France. Some extremists turned to terrorism. There was also considerable violence between right- and left-wing mobs. Blum banned the Leagues, including the Croix-de-Feu, and in response the right-wing **Parti Social Français** was formed. It soon had a membership of over 600,000 and enjoyed considerable electoral success.

Business leaders were also deeply suspicious of the government and opposed to Blum's reforms. Soon, many were investing their money abroad rather than in France. As we read earlier in the chapter, many in the Radical Party had a different economic outlook to the Socialists. While they shared the general desire for reform, they opposed many of the specific polices, as they worried about how they would be financed. This opposition saw many of Blum's reforms blocked in parliament, particularly by the upper house – **the Senate**.

Rising inflation was made worse by growing unemployment. Inflation saw prices rise 17 per cent between May and December, wiping out the benefits of the recent pay rise that workers had received. Blum was forced to halt his reform programme. He was now subject to attack from both the right and the left, and in May 1937 he resigned as prime minister. There followed a period of instability until the Popular Front government finally collapsed in April 1938.

THE GOVERNMENT OF NATIONAL DEFENCE

Faced with the rising threat from Germany, **Édouard Daladier** was chosen to lead a Government of National Defence. He was seen as a strong figure who would stand up to Hitler. His term of just under two years was very long by the standards of the Third Republic! While most of his efforts were concentrated on the worsening international situation, his government enjoyed some economic success and his policies helped to restore business confidence in the government.

THE ROAD TO WAR

France was worried by the threat posed by Germany and in 1931 started to build a series of formidable fortifications along its border with Germany that became known as the **Maginot Line**. Given that the League of Nations was completely ineffective, France had to rely on British support in the face of Germany's aggressive foreign policy under Hitler. France was forced to follow Britain's lead, as France believed they were too weak to act on their own.

Therefore, when Hitler occupied the Rhineland in 1936, France did nothing, as Britain would not support any military measures. Daladier was under no illusions about the threat Hitler posed and in a meeting with Chamberlain in 1938 he said Hitler's aim was 'a domination of the Continent in comparison with which the ambitions of Napoleon were feeble'.

Nonetheless, he did not want another war, nor did the overwhelming majority of French people. He agreed with Chamberlain's policy of appeasement and reluctantly signed the Munich Agreement that handed over the Sudetenland to Germany. This was a betrayal of France's ally, Czechoslovakia. France was forced to take action when Hitler occupied the rest of Czechoslovakia in March 1939. Along with Britain, she promised to go to Poland's aid in the event of a German invasion.

R E V I E W   Q U E S T I O N S

1 Outline some of the divisions in French society during the Third Republic.

2 Why did the French occupy the Ruhr? Was the occupation successful?

3 Why did the Socialist Party split in 1920?

4 Explain why the Cartel des Gauches became unpopular.

5 How did the French economy perform in the 1920s?

6 How was France affected by the Great Depression?

7 Outline the significance of the Stavisky Affair.

8 What problems did the Popular Government face?

9 How successful was Daladier in solving France's domestic problems?

10 Outline how France responded to German actions in the late 1930s.

K E Y   Q U E S T I O N

What was the impact of World War II on France?

THE OUTBREAK OF WORLD WAR II

On 3 September 1939, when Germany invaded Poland, France declared war. It was hoped that the Germans would suffer massive casualties in failed assaults against the Maginot Line. In reality, no aid was sent to the Poles and the war in the West was marked by inactivity. There was outrage when Russia attacked Finland in November 1939 and the outcry after the Finnish defeat the following March forced Daladier's resignation. He was replaced by **Paul Reynaud**.

FRANCE DEFEATED

In May 1940, the Germans attacked Belgium, Holland and France. In a brilliantly executed operation, they bypassed the Maginot Line and broke through the French defences at Sedan. **General Gamelin** was replaced as French commander by **General Weygand**, while the aged but respected World War I hero **General Pétain (1856–1951)** was made vice-premier. These changes made little difference, as German tanks were rapidly advancing across open countryside. The French military leadership had no response and were soon overwhelmed by events. In five weeks, the Germans took over 1.8 million prisoners. Roads were blocked with millions of refugees fleeing the Germans, which added to the chaos. The government abandoned Paris, which was captured by the Germans on 14 June 1940. Matters were made worse when the Italians entered the war on the side of the Germans.

Badly divided on the best course of action to take, the government moved to Bordeaux. The demand for an armistice increased and Reynard resigned. He was replaced by Pétain, who called for an honourable peace. A junior minister in the government, **General De Gaulle**, fled to England, where he called for resistance to continue. In England, he set up the Free French government-in-exile, but his appeal fell on deaf ears.

On 22 June, in the same railway carriage that Germany had surrendered in 1918, the armistice with Germany was concluded. As a result, France was to be divided into two zones (see the map on page 114):

- The German zone was the north of the country and included the Channel and Atlantic coasts. It contained most of the industry and good agricultural land.
- The French controlled the south of the country.
- The provinces of Alsace and Lorraine were annexed (made part of Germany).

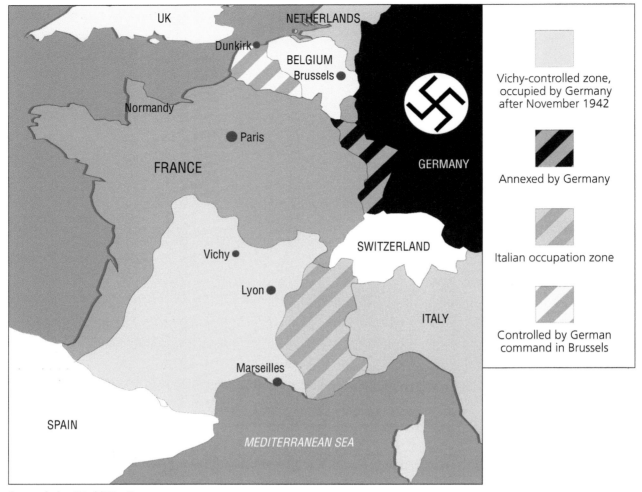

France during World War II.

The French also agreed to pay the costs of the occupying army and French POWs were to remain in German captivity until the war was over, effectively as hostages. At the time, everyone expected that this was a temporary agreement and that the war would end soon. It was believed that a German victory was inevitable.

WHY FRANCE WAS DEFEATED

Historians have put forward a number of reasons to explain the speed of the French defeat.

- The German military strategy of sending its tanks through the Ardennes caught the French by surprise and was a major factor in their defeat. The Germans also gained control of the air.
- The French tactics were poor. They had not learned the lessons of modern warfare, especially from the German success in Poland. For example, their tanks were better than German ones, but were divided out among the infantry, while the Germans formed their tanks into Panzer armies.
- Senior generals disagreed on tactics and most were incompetent. Some were more worried about a Communist revolution at home than the prospects of German occupation.

Hitler meets Pétain at Montoire in October 1940.

- Morale or the willingness to fight was poor, even though the French were defending their country. Pre-war divisions played a part as well as the false sense of security created by the Maginot Line. This unwillingness to fight resulted in the Germans capturing large numbers of French soldiers who chose to surrender rather than resist the invader.

THE VICHY GOVERNMENT

The French government now in control of the unoccupied zone chose the health resort of Vichy as its capital, hence the name **Vichy France**. It was believed that the war would soon end and the government would return to Paris, but this did not happen. Pétain assumed the title **Chief of the French State** and drew up a new constitution for France. He was the hero of the defence of Verdun in 1916 and had been widely admired for his humane treatment of the mutinies in the French army in 1917. At first he was a popular figure and the cult of the Marshal was encouraged through propaganda. Many felt he had saved France from revolution and social chaos after its defeat at the hands of the Germans.

Using the phrase the **National Revolution**, the new government hoped to see the creation of a new and better society. The new state would be based on the principles of work, the family and the homeland, replacing the liberty, equality and fraternity of the French Revolution.

- Trade unions were banned and a corporate state similar to Mussolini's Italy was introduced. It was hoped that this would represent the interests of workers and employers and replace class divisions.
- There was increased influence for the Catholic Church, with divorce being made more difficult, although attempts to restore religious control of education failed.
- Jews and Communists were removed from the civil service, resulting in 35,000 dismissals.

In 1940, the Vichy government enjoyed widespread popular approval as the successor to the discredited Third Republic. Apart from French Fascists, its main support was among big business, landowners and Catholics. The main factor that united these groups was their opposition to Communism. An **Anti-Bolshevik League** of over 12,000 men was sent to fight against the Soviets. Later in the war, thousands of Frenchmen volunteered for service in the **Charlemagne Division** of the Waffen SS.

COLLABORATION

One of the most influential political figures of the Vichy period was the foreign minister Pierre Laval. Before the war, he had served as prime minister four times. With German support, he became the dominant figure in Vichy, although major decisions still required Pétain's support.

For both Pétain and Laval, co-operation or collaboration with Germany was the means by which France might secure a better place in Europe once peace had been established. Pétain and Laval hoped that collaboration would also lead to more immediate improvements:

- The return of 1.6 million prisoners of war.
- A decrease in the war costs France had to pay.
- Assurances that Vichy's independence would be respected. It was hoped that the government would get more influence in the occupied zone as well.

They were in a very weak position and the Germans were slow to respond to Laval's insistence on the need to show the French people that collaboration brought benefits.

Most ordinary people accepted that France had been defeated and sought to make the best of things. They had to adapt to the realities of German rule and go about their daily lives, and for most this involved some form of contact with either the Germans or the Vichy government. Collaboration was a fact of life. Some took collaboration a step further and denounced political opponents to the German or Vichy authorities.

THE ATTITUDE OF THE GERMANS

Hitler was happy to see French collaboration, as it both kept France out of the war and meant that few troops were needed to control the country. Most Nazi leaders, such as Herman Göring, saw France purely in terms of its potential as a supplier of labour, raw materials and manufactured goods. They felt France should pay the price for its defeat and bear the cost of the military occupation. Many Nazis wanted revenge for the harsh peace settlement France had helped impose on Germany after World War I. This led to considerable tensions between the Vichy government and the Germans. For example, the German reannexation of Alsace and Lorraine to the Reich and the subsequent expulsion of 200,000 people soured relations between both countries.

ECONOMIC CONDITIONS IN FRANCE

Vichy faced severe economic difficulties, mainly caused by its defeat in the war and German occupation costs. The cost of occupation was about 400 million francs a day, while the division of France left 60 per cent of its agricultural land and 65 per cent of its industry under German control.

A bad harvest during the winter of 1940–41 left the country on the verge of starvation. This forced the government to introduce emergency measures such as rationing and strict control of wages and prices. By 1943, the official ration was 1,200 calories a day – well below the 1,700 considered necessary for good health. The Nazi exploitation of France became worse and occupation costs rose to 500 million francs a day. Forced labour service in Germany was introduced. This unpopular measure saw hundreds of thousands of workers sent to work in German factories. By the autumn of 1943, over 650,000 French people were working in Germany. Laval managed to secure the release of French prisoners of war in exchange for an increase in the supply of French labour to Germany. Within France, millions more worked for the occupier.

In November 1942, Allied troops landed in the French colonies of **Algeria** and **Morocco**, which surrendered after some initial resistance. In response, the Germans sent in troops to occupy Vichy France, codenamed **Operation Anton**. By this stage, the Vichy regime had become discredited in the eyes of most French people, as collaboration had failed to achieve any major benefits for France. In the words of the historian Alfred Cobban, they viewed the Vichy government as 'little more than an agency for the Nazi exploitation of France'.

THE PERSECUTION OF FRENCH JEWS

One of the darkest chapters in the history of Vichy France was its collaboration in Nazi anti-Semitic policies. In 1940, there were about 350,000 Jews in France, mostly in Paris. Over half were foreign born, including many German Jewish refugees from Nazism. After the German defeat, over 150,000 crossed into Vichy-controlled territory. The Vichy regime shared the traditional anti-Semitism of the French right, which tended to be based more on the idea that the Jews were not truly French than the racist theories of the Nazis. In October 1940, the government passed the **Statute of the Jews**, which barred Jews from holding elective office, working in the civil service, teaching and journalism. Jewish property in the occupied zone was seized with the help of Vichy officials.

Deportations began in the summer of 1942. French police rounded up Jews, mainly those without French citizenship, in both the occupied and unoccupied zones. They were sent to the **Drancy** transit camp north-east of Paris. From there, most were sent to the infamous **Auschwitz** camp. The last deportation was in August 1944. In all, 77,000 Jews were murdered by the Nazis, the vast majority of whom were foreign born.

Surprisingly, more than three-quarters of the Jews managed to survive. There were a number of reasons for this.

- Thousands of Jews fled to the south-east corner of France, occupied by the Italians in 1942. The Italian authorities refused to hand over Jews to

General de Gaulle enters Paris in August 1944.

the Germans. Later, when the Germans occupied the Italian zone in September 1943, most managed to hide or escape to Switzerland.

- Many received assistance from non-Jewish French families.
- While many Vichy officials collaborated closely with the Germans, there were honourable exceptions. Laval made an effort to protect Jews who were French citizens. In 1942, the Catholic **Archbishop of Toulouse** protested strongly at the treatment of the Jews.

THE RESISTANCE

The German invasion of Russia changed the political situation in Vichy and led to the development of the Resistance movement. Pétain described the Nazis as the defenders of civilisation against Communism, but for the first time, many in France, including supporters of the regime, began to doubt the certainty of German victory.

Prior to the invasion, any resistance that had existed had operated on a very limited scale. Now the movement was joined by a committed and

organised group: the **Communist Party**. During the alliance between Stalin and Hitler, the party had urged collaboration with the occupying troops. Now that position changed dramatically. The Communist Party possessed a widespread underground organisation (it had been banned by the government in 1939), ideal for organising resistance to German occupation.

Helped by the British and the Free French, the Resistance's main functions included gathering intelligence; establishing escape routes for political refugees, allied servicemen and Jews; sabotage; and assassination of both collaborators and Germans. Its activities were extremely dangerous and capture meant torture and death. Attacks led to reprisals, with the Germans taking hostages and shooting them in batches of 50. In 1943, after its first major success – the capture of **Corsica** – the Resistance was nicknamed **the Maquis**. Its membership grew quickly as it became clear that the Germans were losing the war. In 1944, there were about 150,000 members. The Vichy government felt it was important that it helped the Germans in defeating the Resistance and maintaining order. Its police, supported by a volunteer force called the **Milice**, helped in the fight against the Resistance.

THE ROLE OF DE GAULLE

As we read earlier in the chapter, General de Gaulle had left France just before its surrender and set up the **Free French**. He refused to recognise the Vichy government and worked hard to get Allied recognition for his government-in-exile. His relations with both the British and Americans were difficult to say the least, but his position was strengthened when more and more of the French Empire was liberated. These areas fell under the control of the Free French. In 1943, the various resistance movements in France united and looked to the Free French for support.

In November 1943, de Gaulle became head of the **French Committee for National Liberation**, which was committed to the destruction of Vichy France and the restoration of the republic. It soon had an army of 500,000 men based in North Africa and equipped by the Allies. As Cobban wrote, 'His name became identified with the idea of French national independence for millions who knew no more than his name.' The Americans remained doubtful of de Gaulle's authority over the Resistance and he was not informed of the D-Day landing until the eve of the invasion.

THE END OF VICHY FRANCE

The end of the regime came with the Allied landings at Normandy in June 1944. There was a widespread uprising by the Resistance to coincide with the invasion. It is estimated that over 100,000 fighters were involved in attacks on German forces. Their destruction of railways and bridges seriously hampered the German response to the Allied landings.

The Allies broke out from Normandy in August and a revolt began in Paris on 18 August. On 25 August, the Free French Second Armoured Division captured the city and de Gaulle entered the city in triumph. A provisional government was formed with de Gaulle at its head. It contained all of the major anti-Vichy forces, including the Communist Party. It had grown greatly in popularity on account of its prominent role in the Resistance. By the end of September, the Germans had been driven from nearly all of France. The role of the Free French forces in liberating Paris and large areas of France did much to restore national self-confidence after the dark days of 1940.

The Vichy government fled to Germany while the Resistance took revenge on suspected collaborators, especially members of the **Milice**, with at least 10,000 people shot without trial. Women who had German boyfriends had their heads shaved and were then humiliated by being paraded through the streets. The new French government soon restored order and the summary executions were halted. When the war was over, the main figures in the Vichy regime were tried. After a very unfair trial, Laval was shot. Due to his advanced age, Pétain was spared execution and was imprisoned on an island off the coast of France, where he died at the age of 95 in 1951.

REVIEW QUESTIONS

1 Outline the main events that led to the French defeat in World War II.

2 What were the terms of the German armistice?

3 Give three reasons historians have put forward to explain France's defeat.

4 What changes did the new government hope to bring to France?

5 Who supported the Vichy regime?

6 What did the Vichy leadership hope to gain by collaborating with the Germans?

7 What measures did the Germans take to exploit France?

8 Outline the treatment of Jews in wartime France.

9 What impact did the invasion of the USSR have on Vichy France?

10 What were the main activities of the Resistance?

11 Account for the collapse of the Vichy regime.

France 1919–45: Timeline

1919	Signing of the Treaty of Versailles with Germany.
	Right-wing Bloc National won the general election.
1920	Formation of the French Communist Party.
1923	French forces occupied the Ruhr.
1924	Election saw victory for the left-wing Cartel des Gauches.
1925	Locarno Treaties signed with Germany.
1931	Effects of the Great Depression hit France.
1934	Stavisky Affair led to serious rioting and a lack of confidence in the Third Republic.
1936	German troops reoccupied the Rhineland.
	Popular Front of Radicals, Socialists and Communists won the election, with Leon Blum as prime minister.
1938	Government of National Defence formed, led by Édouard Daladier.
1939	After the invasion of Poland, France declared war on Germany.
1940	Germany defeated France.
	End of the Third Republic. Vichy France was set up under the leadership of Marshal Pétain.
	General de Gaulle set up the Free French government-in-exile.
1942	Pierre Laval became prime minister of Vichy France.
	German troops occupied Vichy France.
1944	Allied troops landed at Normandy.
	Paris was liberated in August. End of Vichy France.

END OF CHAPTER QUESTIONS

Source Question

1 Read this extract from an article from the Communist Party newspaper, *L'Humanité*, on 4 May 1936 about the Popular Front victory.

> *We don't want to hide our great joy. The Popular Front has clearly won, and in its general victory the Communist Party registers its part of success. The Fascists and their allies, who claimed to be the only ones to speak in the name of France, have been chased out by the people. The workers will read with satisfaction the long list of the bitter enemies of the Popular Front who were chased from parliament yesterday.*
>
> *And now, after their defeat, the adversaries of the Popular Front will not fail to take up their insults and usual actions against the majority freely elected by the nation. They will repeat that it's the Revolution, that it's the end of the country and that tomorrow there will be disorder and chaos.*
>
> *Thus will be foiled all the hopes of the enemies of the people and the Fascists, so violently struck by yesterday's vote. These men declared before yesterday's vote ... that they would use force if the Popular Front won. It's up to all the parties of the Popular Front to more solidly preserve their unity, which assured the defeat of their bitter enemies.*

Source: www.marxists.org.

(a) Give two pieces of evidence from the article to show that the paper was a strong supporter of the Popular Front.

(b) What does it believe the attitude of the 'adversaries of the Popular Front' will be?

(c) What advice does the paper give to the parties of the Popular Front?

(d) What evidence is there from the article to show that there were great divisions in French society in the 1930s?

(e) Who became the prime minister of the Popular Front government?

2 Write a paragraph on **TWO** of the following topics (Ordinary Level):
- The impact of World War I on France.
- The Stavisky Affair.
- The Vichy state in France, 1940–44.

3 Write an essay on **ONE** of the following.

Ordinary Level
- What were the main political developments during the inter-war years, 1920–39?
- Why was France defeated in 1940?

Higher Level
- What was the impact of World War II on the civilian population of France? (Leaving Certificate question)
- What problems did the Third Republic encounter between 1920 and 1940? (Leaving Certificate question) **See analysis below.**

ESSAY ANALYSIS

What problems did the Third Republic encounter between 1920 and 1940?

SUGGESTED APPROACH
- Address the question in your introduction.
- Too broad a time frame to give a comprehensive history of the period it is better to focus in on the main problems such as the divisions between left and right or the fear of German power.
- Main period for examination should be the immediate aftermath of the war up to occupation of the Ruhr in 1923 and the 1930s leading to the defeat of France in 1940.

SUGGESTED CONCLUSION
The Third Republic founded in 1870 was ended by German invasion in 1940. After World War I it faced a host of problems some of which were tackled with a degree of success. For example the 1920s were relatively prosperous with the north of the country quickly recovering from the damage caused by World War I. In 1934 the government defeated the threat from the Right during the Stavisky Affair. However it failed in its search for security and was unable to stop a resurgent Germany under Hitler. The deep divisions in French society remained. These contributed to the lack of morale displayed by the French army during the German attack that led to French defeat in 1940.

Main Points

1 Introduction: What were the problems faced by the Third Republic?

2 What political problems faced French governments in the 1920s?

3 How did French policy towards Germany change in the 1920s?

4 What was the impact of the Great Depression?

5 What impact did the Stavisky Affair have on French politics?

6 Why did the Popular Front government of Leon Blum face such strong opposition?

7 How did the Third Republic deal with the threat posed by Hitler?

8 Why was France defeated in World War II?

10 World War II, 1939–45

What do you need to know in this chapter?

Elements	Key Personalities	Key Concepts	
Wartime alliances	Adolf Hitler	Propaganda	Resistance
Anti-Semitism and the Holocaust	Joseph Stalin	*Lebensraum*	Blitzkrieg
The technology of warfare, 1920–45	Winston Churchill	The Holocaust	
	Benito Mussolini	Collaboration	

KEY QUESTION

What were the main German successes in the early years of the war?

Here is an explanation of some of the terms you will meet in this chapter.

Allied Powers: Britain, the US and the USSR and their allies.

Axis Powers: Germany, Italy and their allies.

Blitz: German bombing of British cities.

Blitzkrieg: German military tactics using surprise, heavy bombing and concentration of tanks to overwhelm enemy defences.

Collaboration: co-operation with the German authorities in occupied Europe.

Operation Barbarossa: Hitler's invasion of the USSR in 1941.

Operation Overlord: the Allied plan to invade German-occupied France.

Operation Sealion: the German plan to invade Britain in 1940.

Operation Uranus: Russian attack that trapped the German Sixth Army in Stalingrad in 1942.

The Battle of the Atlantic: struggle to keep sea lanes open in the face of German submarine (U-boat) attack.

The Final Solution: the German plan to kill the Jews of Europe.

The Holocaust: the mass murder of around 6 million Jews.

INTRODUCTION

World War II was the most catastrophic event in human history, which left over 50 million people dead. This chapter focuses on events in Europe and looks at the main phases during the war, wartime alliances and how the different weapons developed during the war. It also examines the mass murder of Europe's Jews, an event that has become known as the **Holocaust**.

THE INVASION OF POLAND

On 1 September 1939, German troops attacked Poland. The Poles were soon overwhelmed by new German **blitzkrieg** (lightning war) tactics, which involved close co-ordination between artillery, tanks, planes and soldiers. Panzer armies smashed through the Polish defences, aided by accurate bombing from Stuka dive-bombers. The Poles thought they could hold out for six months, as they assumed that the British and the French would attack Germany.

The Poles fought bravely, but their fate was sealed when, as agreed under the Nazi-Soviet Non-Aggression Pact, the Soviet army invaded Eastern Poland. By 1 October, the war was over and the country was divided between the two dictatorships.

The Germans reclaimed the land lost after World War I and began a brutal occupation in what remained of their part of Poland, known as **the General Government**. Conditions for Poles were as bad in the Russian zone that became part of the USSR.

While the war raged in Poland, there was little activity in the west. A **British Expeditionary Force** was sent to France but saw no action. The French felt secure behind the Maginot Line – a series of fortifications on the Franco-German border. They had suffered massive causalities in World War I from attacking German troops and were reluctant to go on the offensive. This lack of fighting was nicknamed 'the Phoney War' by the American press, while British newspapers called it the *Sitzkrieg* – 'the Sitting War'.

NORWAY

In April 1940, the Phoney War ended when German troops invaded Norway and Denmark. Germany wanted to protect its supplies of Swedish iron ore that were exported through the Norwegian port of Narvik. Denmark was easily captured, but the fighting in Norway was tough. British and German troops clashed here for the first time. Helped by superior air power, the Germans won, but their navy suffered heavy losses. The British prime minister, **Neville Chamberlain**, was forced to resign on 10 May 1940 and was replaced by **Winston Churchill**, a harsh critic of appeasement. Attention had now moved to Western Europe, where the anticipated German attack on France began in May.

The German invasion of France.

BLITZKRIEG UNLEASHED ON FRANCE

In planning their attack on France, the Germans knew they could not attack the formidable Maginot Line (see page 112), so they came up with a brilliant military plan: they would send forces through Belgium and Holland to make the Allies think that this was the main direction of their invasion. While the Allies sent troops to meet this German threat, the main blow would come through a hilly wooded area called the **Ardennes**. This was lightly fortified and thought to be impassable for tanks.

On 10 May 1940, German troops invaded Belgium and Holland. French and British troops marched north to meet the Germans and fell right into Hitler's trap. Coming through the Ardennes, German tanks using blitzkrieg tactics trapped the British BEF and large French forces at **Dunkirk**. The British launched a rescue operation called **Operation Dynamo**. Using all sorts of craft, including yachts, they succeeded in rescuing over 300,000 men from Dunkirk, 100,000 of whom were French.

Hitler at the Louvre in Paris in 1940.

THE FRENCH SURRENDER

German troops then moved southwards, meeting little resistance, and on 13 June captured Paris. The World War I hero **Marshal Petain** was appointed prime minster and he began negotiations with the Germans. On 22 June, France was forced to accept German terms.

- The north of France, including the Channel coast, was occupied by Germany.
- A French government led by Petain controlled the rest of the country from the town of Vichy (for more about Vichy France, see p. 115).

WHY WERE THE ALLIES DEFEATED?

The German invasion of France was a spectacular success – Hitler had achieved in six weeks what the Germans had failed to do in four years in World War I. Contrary to popular myth, the French and the British actually had more troops and tanks, while there were about the same number of planes on both sides, but German military tactics and training were superior. French morale was poor and this saw the Germans take large numbers of prisoners.

BRITAIN STANDS ALONE

Led by Churchill, the British were determined to keep fighting. Offers of peace from Hitler were rejected, as Churchill refused to allow the Germans to remain in control of the Continent. Although the situation looked bleak, he had a number of advantages when facing a possible German invasion. Most of the British army had escaped at Dunkirk and lived to fight another day and the Royal Navy had complete control of the English Channel.

THE BATTLE OF BRITAIN

Hitler now planned the invasion of Britain, codenamed **Operation Sealion**. To stage a successful invasion, the Germans needed to destroy the British air force and gain control of the air. On 13 August 1940, **Aldertag**, or Eagle Day, saw the Germans begin attacks on the Royal Air Force (RAF). Waves of Luftwaffe planes bombed airfields and radar installations throughout Britain. The Battle of Britain had begun. The British thought the German Luftwaffe was far superior to the Royal Air Force, when in fact both sides had about the same number of fighters.

The RAF was stretched to the limit as it repaired damaged airfields and tried to stop the German attacks. Pilots had little rest, as they were involved in constant dogfights against the German fighter planes that protected the bombers. The main British fighters were **Spitfires** and **Hurricanes**. The Hurricanes attacked the bombers, while the Spitfires took on the German fighters such as the **ME 109**.

Although both sides suffered heavy losses, by the middle of September, the RAF had won the Battle of Britain. The Germans now switched to the safer night-time bombing of British cities. Turning his attention to the attack on Russia, Hitler called off the invasion of Britain. There were a number of factors that contributed to the British victory.

- The Germans made the mistake of bombing London and industrial targets, which gave the RAF time to recover and reorganise.
- The use of radar allowed the British to predict the arrival of German attacks.
- The Spitfire was an excellent fighter and better than its main German opponent, the ME 109.

THE BLITZ

Heavy German bombing of industrial, naval and civilian targets continued until May 1941, nicknamed 'the Blitz' by British newspapers. Designed to weaken both civilian morale and British industrial production, it had little effect on either. London was the main target. A raid at the end of December was so devastating that it was called the Second Great Fire of London. By the end of the Blitz, only one house in 10 in central London had been left undamaged. Other cities, including Birmingham, Manchester, Liverpool, Glasgow, Coventry and Belfast, suffered as well.

The Blitz ended in May, as the Luftwaffe was needed for the invasion of Russia. In all, over 40,000 civilians were killed and over 100,000 wounded. A significant result of the Blitz was that it convinced both the British and the Americans that civilian bombing had an important role in conducting the war. The Germans were to feel the full force of this belief from 1943 onwards.

WARTIME ALLIANCES – HITLER AND MUSSOLINI

By June 1940, Mussolini believed that Germany would win the war and he declared war on France and Britain. Jealous of Hitler's success, Mussolini's main aim was to dominate the Mediterranean region. Germany and Italy were known as the **Axis powers** and their alliance lasted until 1943. Italy's value as an ally to the Germans was doubtful to say the least, as Italian military defeats required the Germans to intervene to help their ally.

- In October 1940, Mussolini invaded Greece without consulting his ally. His poorly led troops were defeated and driven back into Albania. In April 1941, German troops were sent to Greece to help, where they defeated British troops who had been sent to help the Greeks. At the same time, German troops invaded Yugoslavia after a pro-German government had been overthrown. The country was then divided between the Germans and the Italians.

- In North Africa, the Italians attacked the British colony of Egypt in September 1940. The outnumbered British, possessing better tanks, inflicted a devastating defeat and drove the Italians back into Libya. Hitler then sent one of the heroes of the French campaign, **General Rommel**, as head of the newly formed **Africa Korps** to aid the Italians.

REVIEW QUESTIONS

1 Give two reasons why the Poles were defeated by the Germans.

2 Why were events in the West called the Phoney War?

3 What was the German plan for the invasion of France?

4 What terms did the Germans impose on France?

5 What was the significance of the British evacuation of their troops at Dunkirk?

6 Explain why the British were successful in the Battle of Britain.

7 What was the Blitz?

8 'The alliance with Italy was not of great benefit for the Germans.' Do you agree? Give evidence to support your answer.

THE ATTACK ON THE USSR – OPERATION BARBAROSSA

After his failure to capture Britain, Hitler turned his attention to the USSR. He saw the Nazi-Soviet Non-Aggression Pact as a temporary measure (as did Stalin!). He dreamed of an empire in the East populated by German settlers. He had not lost his hatred of Communism and felt the time was right for the destruction of the Soviet Union.

When the USSR attacked Finland in the winter of 1939, the Red Army had performed poorly, convincing Hitler and most of his generals that an invasion would be successful. The attack, codenamed **Operation Barbarossa**, was intended for the spring of 1941 but was delayed by the German invasion of Greece and Yugoslavia. As Niall Ferguson puts it, the 'bloodiest divorce in history' began on 22 June 1941. Over 3 million soldiers supported by 3,500 tanks and 2,500 planes unleashed blitzkrieg warfare on the Soviets. Although warned by numerous sources, Stalin refused to believe that the Germans would invade and the Russians were caught by surprise (see p. 28).

GERMAN SUCCESS AND SOVIET COUNTERATTACK

The invading army was divided into three army groups – **North**, **Centre** and **South** – and the Germans enjoyed spectacular successes along a 930-mile-long front. By the end of September, Minsk, Kiev and Smolensk had been captured, Leningrad was under siege and over 3 million Russian prisoners had been taken. However, the Germans found that things were not going all their own way.

- Although poorly led, the ordinary Russian soldier was a brave and determined opponent.
- Crucially, the weather changed and heavy rain made movement very difficult on Russia's poor roads. This delayed the German advance on Moscow, allowing the Russians to move fresh troops from the east.
- This was followed by very cold weather, as temperatures dropped to –40°C. Expecting a quick victory, the German army was not prepared for the cold.

By December, German troops had reached the outskirts of Moscow when they were driven back by a Soviet counterattack. Hitler refused to agree to a general retreat and his troops were ordered to dig in, which probably saved the German army from a greater defeat. By this time, Germany was facing the combined might of the US, Britain and the USSR.

KEY QUESTION

Why was the wartime alliance of the Allies important to the defeat of the Germans?

THE GRAND ALLIANCE

Crucial to the defeat of the Germans was the alliance that was formed between the British Empire, the United States and the USSR. The alliance was not without tensions, but all three were committed to the destruction of Nazi Germany. Their combined resources in terms of men and equipment were far greater than Germany and its allies. As the war progressed, these resources were employed more and more efficiently to defeat the Germans.

THE US AND BRITAIN

Although the US was neutral until December 1941, US **President Franklin Roosevelt** was sympathetic to the British cause but had to proceed cautiously, as a large section of the US public wanted the US to stay out of the war. Nonetheless, he helped the British with economic aid in return for British bases in Newfoundland and the Caribbean. This was called **Lend-Lease**.

The Japanese attack on the **Pearl Harbor** naval base in December 1941 ended US neutrality and the US now turned its vast industrial might towards the cause of the Allies, concentrating most of its resources on the defeat of Germany. Military co-operation between Britain and the US became very close. They shared technical and intelligence information and pooled both industrial and shipping resources. In January 1943, meeting at **Casablanca** in Morocco, both allies announced that they would only accept the 'unconditional surrender' of the Axis powers.

Both Roosevelt and Churchill enjoyed good working and personal relationships, although both pursued their own interests and there were disagreements. For example, they had different strategic objectives – the Americans believed that an invasion of France was the most important objective, while the British argued that the Mediterranean was the most important theatre of the war. Despite differences, the alliance between both countries held up well.

THE SOVIET UNION AND THE ALLIES

The relationship between the USSR and the two Western allies was not so smooth. Prior to the war, there had been a history of deep suspicion between Stalin and the US and the UK. Once Germany invaded the USSR, the British offered their support. Although he was bitterly anti-Communist, Churchill was delighted to have another ally in the fight against Hitler. The pre-war tension remained and Churchill and Stalin were never close.

Relations between Roosevelt and Stalin were better. Roosevelt saw Stalin as a practical man and both he and Stalin developed a good understanding. The US sent vast amounts of supplies to the USSR, including planes, fuel, trucks, tanks, radios and field telephones. Stalin, or **Uncle Joe**, as he was nicknamed, became a popular figure in both the US and the UK. True to his nature, Stalin distrusted the Western powers.

- He felt they were quite happy to see the Soviets bear the brunt of the fighting. He pressed for a second front to take the pressure off the Red Army.
- The Soviets shared little technical or intelligence information with the Western Allies, while a lot of sensitive information was sent to the USSR.

In November 1943, the Big Three met together for the first time at **Teheran**, the capital of Iran. They committed themselves jointly to the destruction of Nazi Germany and Stalin got the promise that the Allies would invade France and open a second front.

In 1942, the Germans suffered two crucial defeats that saw the tide of the war turn towards the Allies. These were at **Stalingrad** in Russia and **El Alamein** in Egypt.

STALINGRAD: THE TURNING POINT OF THE WAR

In the summer of 1942, the Germans resumed their offensive with the aim of capturing the oilfields in the south of the USSR. Short of oil, their capture would greatly aid the German war effort. The key town in this region was **Stalingrad**. Hitler was determined to capture the city that bore the name of his enemy, while Stalin ordered that the city be defended at all costs.

The Sixth Army, led by **General Paulus**, attacked the city. Every street and building was fought over. The Germans called it the **Rattenkrieg** – the War of Rats. Meanwhile, the Russians were preparing a trap. They committed just enough men to stop the Germans from capturing the city while the Soviet commander **General Zhukov** secretly prepared a massive counterattack. On 19 November, he

Russian troops fighting in the city of Stalingrad. The German soldier learned to respect the bravery and determination of the ordinary Russian soldier.

launched **Operation Uranus** and surrounded the Sixth Army in Stalingrad.

The Germans decided to supply the troops from the air, but this failed. Hitler refused to allow the Germans in Stalingrad to break out and escape Russian encirclement. Conditions worsened for the troops as the temperature dropped to −30°C. Food and supplies were in short supply and the German defenders started to starve to death. Seeing no hope, Paulus surrendered in February 1943. This was the decisive turning point of the war and a massive propaganda boost for the Russians. The Germans had lost an army of 300,000 men and the myth of German invincibility had been shattered. Crucially, the oilfields were now out of German reach.

EL ALAMEIN

The war also turned in favour of the Allies in North Africa. In 1942, Rommel had advanced and captured the town of **Tobruk**. His troops reached El Alamein in Egypt, where his progress was halted. The British 8th Army under **General Bernard Montgomery** patiently prepared a counterattack. He built up a two-to-one advantage in both tanks and men. He also had new American Sherman tanks, which were better than German tanks. In October 1942, he attacked and after two weeks of fierce fighting, Rommel was defeated. At the same time, American and British troops landed in **Algeria** and **Morocco**, forcing the Germans to retreat to **Tunisia**.

THE ALLIES ADVANCE

Throughout 1943, the Allies established their superiority in terms of men and equipment over the Axis powers and inflicted a number of devastating defeats on the Germans. As one British general put it, 'The Allies had begun to stop losing the war and were working towards winning it.'

- The **Battle of the Atlantic** was won by the Allies. The Germans had hoped to stop supplies reaching Britain by using U-boats to sink Allied ships. Losses of merchant ships to U-boats increased steadily through the spring of 1943, but by May 1943 the tide of the battle turned decisively in favour of the Allies. More U-boats were now being sunk than merchant vessels, forcing the Germans to call off their campaign.
- In North Africa, German and Italian troops were forced to surrender in Tunisia in May. Over 275,000 prisoners were taken and the Germans called this defeat 'Tunisgrad'. The following July, joint British and American forces captured **Sicily** and in September landed on the Italian mainland. Churchill had long argued for an invasion of Italy – the soft underbelly of the Axis, as he called it. Mussolini was removed from power and Italy surrendered (see p. 45).
- However, any thoughts of a quick Allied victory in Italy were ended by fierce German resistance. Fighting was very difficult and the Germans fought a brilliant defensive campaign, especially at **Monte Casino**. Allied troops did not take Rome until June 1944.
- In July, forewarned by Allied intelligence, the Russians defeated a German offensive at **Kursk**. The battle was fought over an area the size of Wales and included the biggest tank battle in the war. From then on, the Russians began to advance as their superiority in tanks, planes and men began to show. They had learned from their earlier mistakes and improved their military tactics. Kiev was retaken and the siege of Leningrad ended in February 1944. German resistance was fierce, with both sides committing terrible atrocities.

THE WAR IN THE AIR

In 1942, the British and the Americans began bombing German cities and factories in a move designed to weaken German morale. Using heavy

Tanks destroyed at Kursk.

bombers, they inflicted much damage and killed hundreds of thousands of German civilians. One raid on Hamburg in July 1943 saw the creation of a firestorm that led to the deaths of at least 45,000 civilians, with a further 1 million left homeless.

The Allies did not have it all their own way and the Luftwaffe shot down many bombers. The Allies then decided to target the Luftwaffe, with spectacular success. Factories involved in aircraft production and plants producing aviation fuel were bombed. Long-range fighters took on German fighters, attacking the Allied bombers. More and more fighters were moved from the Eastern Front to protect German cities and as a result, by April 1944, 500 German fighters faced 13,000 Soviet aircraft. By the spring of 1944, the Luftwaffe had been defeated and the Allies had complete control of the air. This control would be necessary for the next Allied action: the invasion of France.

OPERATION OVERLORD

The codename for the long-awaited invasion of France was **Operation Overlord**. The Allies decided to land at Normandy. Although further from Britain, it was less heavily defended than the more obvious target of **Calais**. The invasion force, commanded by the Supreme Allied Commander, **General Dwight Eisenhower**, consisted of American, British and Canadian troops. The five beaches targeted were given the codenames **Utah**, **Omaha**, **Juno**, **Gold** and **Sword**. The Allies knew that an assault against the heavily fortified German defences, known as the **Atlantic Wall**, would be difficult and were taking no chances. The Allies kept their intentions well hidden. The German commander, General Rommel, complained, 'I know nothing for certain about the enemy.'

REVIEW QUESTIONS

1 Give two reasons why the Germans invaded the USSR in 1941.
2 Why did the Germans find the fighting in Russia very difficult?
3 Why were the Germans defeated at Stalingrad?
4 How did the war turn in favour of the Allies in North Africa?
5 While they were neutral, how did the US help the British?
6 'Relations between the USSR and the Western Allies were marked by tensions.' Do you agree? Support your answer with evidence.
7 Explain why the Allies won the Battle of the Atlantic.
8 Why was the Battle of Kursk so important?
9 How did the war in the air over Germany turn in favour of the Allies?

From left to right: General Montgomery (UK) (1887–1976); Marshall Zhukov (USSR) (1896–1974); and General Eisenhower (US) (1890–1969).

Field Marshal Erwin Rommel (Germany) (1891–1944), one of the best generals of the war.

Russian troops advance in Poland.

- A successful deception operation was carried out to fool the Germans. A phantom army, with blow-up tanks, under the command of **General Patton** was created to give the impression that the attack was going to be at Calais. For days after the invasion, Hitler believed that Calais was the real target. He refused to move forces that could have defeated the Allied invasion.
- Northern France was heavily bombed, with railways, bridges and tunnels being particular targets. This made it difficult for the Germans to move reinforcements to fight the invasions.
- The armada of over 7,000 ships and landing craft assembled for the invasion was the largest in history. The invasion was supported by 12,000 planes, giving the Allies control of the air.

The invasion, or D-Day, began on 6 June 1944, when 156,000 soldiers landed along 30 miles of Normandy coast. Despite enjoying overwhelming air superiority, the Allies found fighting in Normandy very tough. The countryside, known as the *bocage*, gave the German defenders a natural advantage. There was a stalemate for two months, but in August the Allies trapped the main German army at **Falaise** and the battle was over. **General de Gaulle** led his Free French troops into Paris and the city was liberated. German troops were then driven from France.

THE DESTRUCTION OF ARMY GROUP CENTRE

Hitler's mistake of fighting a two-front war was clearly shown a few weeks after the D-Day landings, when the Soviets launched a massive offensive, **Operation Bagration**. This was directed at Army Group Centre and was a resounding success. German troops were driven from the USSR and Soviet troops entered Eastern Europe and forced Germany's allies, such as Romania, to surrender. Some Russian troops reached East Prussia. Although neglected by Western historians, the battle is seen by their German and Soviet counterparts as Hitler's greatest defeat.

> **Why the Allies Won the War**
> - The alliance of Britain, US and the USSR had vast superiority in men and equipment.
> - The industrial resources of the United States.
> - Germany was fighting a two-front war with weak allies.
> - The Allies established complete control of the air.
> - The Red Army became a powerful fighting force.

THE BATTLE OF THE BULGE

The Allies advanced on a wide front through France and into Belgium, but in September they suffered a major defeat in **Operation Market Garden** – an ambitious plan to capture the bridges over the Rhine in Holland. At **Arnhem**, British paratroopers expecting light resistance found themselves facing battle-hardened Waffen SS troops. After a fierce struggle, they were defeated and the plan was abandoned.

Despite this setback, many believed that the war would be over by Christmas. Hitler had other ideas. He decided to launch a surprise offensive in December in the Ardennes, where he had achieved such success in 1940. Known as the **Battle of the Bulge**, the German attack was launched in bad weather and caught the Allies off guard. At first they were successful, but short of fuel and ammunition, the Germans were stopped and forced to retreat. This proved to be the last major German offensive in the West.

THE DEFEAT OF NAZI GERMANY

After the Battle of the Bulge, the Allies advanced to the **Rhine**. In the east, the Soviets resumed their offensive. Advancing on all fronts, they reached and crossed the **Oder River**, the last major natural barrier before Berlin. Millions fled before the advancing Red Army, who took a terrible revenge on German civilians.

Allied bombers inflicted massive destruction on German cities. In February, the historic city of **Dresden** was targeted by waves of Allied bombers. A firestorm destroyed the centre of the city. The death toll is uncertain, but at least 35,000 people died.

Hitler called on his soldiers to fight to the last bullet and he often refused to allow trapped German armies to escape, thereby depriving the Germans of critically needed manpower. Any soldiers suspected of desertion were executed by the SS. German propaganda talked of wonder weapons such as jets and rockets that would defeat the Allies. The V2 rockets were one of these weapons, but they made little impact on the outcome of the war.

THE YALTA CONFERENCE

A few days before the bombing of Dresden, Churchill, Roosevelt and Stalin met at Yalta in the Crimea to decide what would happen after the defeat of Germany. The following were the main agreements reached.

- Germany was to be divided into four zones and occupied by the Allies.
- Stalin was allowed to keep the Polish land he had seized in 1939. The Poles were to be compensated with German land.
- Stalin promised to enter the war against Japan after the end of the war in Europe.

On the surface, the Allies were as united as ever, but there were tensions, especially over Poland, which was now under Soviet control. Free and fair elections were promised by the Soviets, but they had no intention of holding them, causing the Americans to become increasingly disillusioned with Stalin. The seeds of the Cold War were sown during the Yalta Conference.

The Big Three at Yalta (from left to right: Churchill, Roosevelt and Stalin). By the time of the conference, Roosevelt was very ill. He died two months later, in April. With the defeat of Germany, inevitable divisions began to emerge among the Allies.

THE END OF THE WAR IN EUROPE

In March 1945, the Allies crossed the Rhine and captured the main German industrial area, **the Ruhr**. German forces started to surrender in large numbers, although resistance could be fanatical at times. In April, the Russians launched a massive offensive on the **Oder River** and advanced on Berlin. By the end of the month, Russian troops were fighting deep in the city and the situation was hopeless. On 30 April, Hitler and his mistress, **Eva Braun**, committed suicide. **Admiral Donitz** was named as his successor and he quickly surrendered. The 8th of May was V-E Day, or Victory in Europe Day.

The defeated Germany was divided into four zones and occupied by the victorious Allies. In November 1945, 21 leading Nazis were put on trial in Nuremberg and 12 were sentenced to death, including Herman Göring (who managed to commit suicide) and Joachim Ribbentrop. During the trial, former foreign minister, Ribbentrop, wrote a short memoir. In it, he attributed

Soviet flag being placed on top of the Reichstag.

Germany's defeat to three factors:
1. The resistance of the Red Army.
2. The industrial might of the US.
3. Allied air power.

As we have seen, he was not far off the mark. A further factor was the wartime alliance of Britain, the US and the UK. As historian Richard Overy wrote, 'The defeat of Germany was their priority.' They were able to dedicate vast resources in terms of men and equipment to achieving this aim.

REVIEW QUESTIONS

1. What precautions did the Allies take to make sure that the Normandy landings were successful?

2. Why was Operation Bagration so significant?

3. Briefly describe what happened during the Battle of the Bulge.

4. Describe conditions for German civilians caught in the advance of the Red Army.

5. How did Hitler try to stop the defeat of the German army?

6. What major decisions were reached at Yalta?

7. Outline the main events in the last few weeks of the war.

8. In your opinion, why did the Allies win the war? Write a 400-word essay supporting your views.

1939	Germany invaded Poland using blitzkrieg tactics. Britain and France declared war.
1940	Germany conquered Denmark, Norway, Holland, Belgium and France. Churchill became British prime minister. British troops evacuated at Dunkirk. Italy joined the war on the side of Germany – formation of the Axis powers. Vichy French government formed. The Battle of Britain. German bombing of London and other British cities, known as the Blitz.
1941	German troops sent to North Africa. Germany invaded Greece and Yugoslavia. Germany attacked the USSR, called Operation Barbarossa. Japanese attacked Pearl Harbor. US entered the war, led by President Roosevelt. German advance halted at Moscow.
1942	Battle of Stalingrad. Germans defeated at Battle of El Alamein.
1943	German forces surrendered at Stalingrad. Italians and Germans surrendered in North Africa. Battle of Kursk. Allies won the Battle of the Atlantic. Mussolini removed from power. Italy declared war on Germany. Teheran Conference.
1944	D-Day landings at Normandy. Paris liberated and France freed from German control. German forces driven from the USSR. Unsuccessful attempt to kill Hitler. German counterattack defeated in the Ardennes. Heavy Allied bombing of Germany.
1945	Yalta Conference. Western Allies crossed the Rhine and Soviets attacked Berlin. Hitler commited suicide and the Germans surrendered. Atomic bombs dropped on Hiroshima and Nagasaki.

THE WAR IN THE PACIFIC

To find out about the war in the East, log on to
www.edco.ie/LCHistory

COLLABORATION AND RESISTANCE

WESTERN EUROPE

During the war, the harshness of Nazi occupation varied. In Western Europe, they saw the Danes, the Dutch and the Norwegians as being of the same racial group as the Germans. The Danish were allowed to retain their parliament and king. Anti-Communist propaganda appealed to many in these countries and a number joined the Waffen SS to fight against the USSR. The Belgian Fascist leader **Léon Degrelle** served on the Eastern Front from 1941 until the end of the war. Foreign volunteers who fought for the Germans were usually recruited into the SS and not the regular army, or Wehrmacht.

Parties that sympathised with the Nazis called for close collaboration with the German occupiers. However, there was little popular support for active Nazi sympathisers such as **Vidkun Quisling** in Norway or **Anton Mussert** in Holland, both of whom were executed after the war. In Chapter 9, we looked at the situation in France.

Most people did not like the German occupation but just wanted to get on with life. As the war progressed, resistance movements grew in these countries, although they were relatively weak and they operated in very harsh conditions. After Hitler attacked the USSR, Communist movements became active in resistance groups. Most of their activities involved spying, passing intelligence to the Allies and sabotage. The brutal response of the Germans, who shot hostages after a successful resistance attack, made resistance activities more difficult. In 1943, the Danish resistance saved the country's small Jewish community from perishing in the Holocaust. In France, the resistance, or the **Maquis**, played an important role in the D-Day landings.

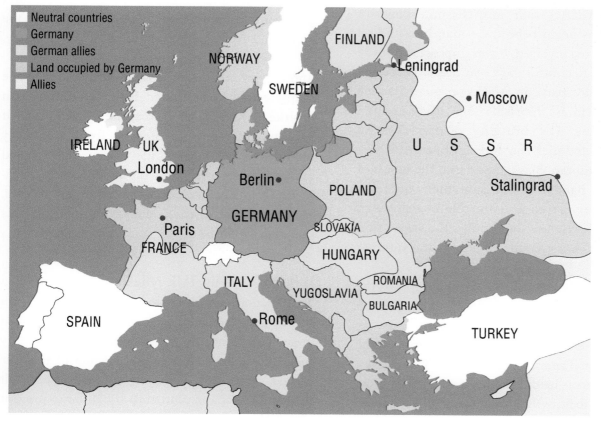

Nazi-occupied Europe in 1942.

- Neutral countries
- Germany
- German allies
- Land occupied by Germany
- Allies

FINLAND
NORWAY
Leningrad
SWEDEN
Moscow
IRELAND UK
U S S R
London
Berlin
POLAND
Stalingrad
GERMANY
Paris
SLOVAKIA
FRANCE
HUNGARY
ITALY
ROMANIA
YUGOSLAVIA
BULGARIA
SPAIN
Rome
TURKEY

EASTERN EUROPE

The situation in Eastern Europe was complex and as a general rule Nazi occupation was far more brutal than in the west.

- There were some countries that were German allies, such as Bulgaria, Hungary, Romania and Slovakia. They participated in the German invasion of Russia.

- A particularly brutal pro-German Croat Fascist regime was established in Yugoslavia, led by **Ante Pavelič**. Its violence against Serbs shocked even the Germans. There were two main resistance groups to German role: the anti-Communist **Chetniks** and the Communist-controlled **Partisans**, led by **Marshal Tito**. Supported by the British, Tito's forces grew to over 800,000 men. By late 1944, the Partisans were on the offensive and they liberated their own country from German control.

- In the USSR, German troops were greeted as liberators in the Baltic Republics and the Ukraine from what was seen as a far worse Soviet oppression. Latvians and Estonians joined the Waffen SS and others were later conscripted. Some peoples, such as the Don Cossacks and Chechens, collaborated with the Germans.

- Stalin ordered that anti-German partisan operations begin behind German lines. Given the vast area involved, it was impossible for the Germans to control their rear areas. This cruel struggle saw partisan attacks on enemy targets and German reprisals on the civilian population. The brutality of the German response and their harsh policy of control over the '**subhuman**' Slavs played into the hands of partisan bands, which saw their numbers grow. They played a major role in many Red Army offensives, including the one that destroyed Army Group Centre in the summer of 1944.

- In Poland, the largest resistance group was the **Home Guard** that was loyal to the Polish government-in-exile in London. In 1944, as Russian troops neared Warsaw, the Poles in the city revolted against German rule. This did not suit Stalin, as he did not want anti-Communist Poles to liberate their own country; he wanted a pro-Russian Communist government to run the country. Soviet troops halted on the outskirts of the city and did not help the Poles and the Soviets refused to allow US or British planes to use Soviet airbases to supply the Poles. Without Soviet help, the Poles were defeated and Warsaw was destroyed by the Germans.

As we shall see later in the chapter, for one group – the Jews – Nazi occupation was to lead to mass murder on a nearly unimaginable scale.

GERMAN OPPOSITION TO HITLER

There was little opposition to Hitler in the early years of the war, as German armies went from one victory to another. Germans also knew that the penalty for open opposition was death. A few brave men and women acted against the regime and today they are heroes in Germany.

One example of opposition was the group of students at Munich University that formed an organisation called **The White Rose**. Prominent in the group were brother and sister **Hans** and **Sophie Scholl**. They spread anti-war leaflets that called for passive resistance to the Nazis. Sophie and Hans were caught and in February 1943 were found guilty of treason along with other members of the group and executed the same day.

Another prominent opposition group met at the family estate of its leader, **Helmuth James von Moltke**, at Kriesau. Known as the Kriesau circle, it was mainly made up of men from a wealthy background who hated the Nazis. They passed information to the Allies on conditions in Nazi-controlled areas, including the treatment of Jews. Molkte was arrested in January 1944 and was executed a year later.

OPPOSITION IN THE MILITARY

There had always been some resistance to Hitler in the armed forces, though most officers placed great importance on the personal oath of loyalty they had taken to Hitler. As the tide of the war turned, opposition increased as some officers felt they had to act and plotted to kill Hitler to prevent

Hitler shows Mussolini the damage to his headquarters after the bomb on 20 July 1944.

headquarters in East Prussia and on 20 July he planted a bomb in the Führer's headquarters. It exploded but only slightly injured Hitler. Hitler's survival led to the collapse of the plot and Stauffenberg was shot, along with three other plotters. Their actions were deeply unpopular among ordinary German soldiers, who saw the event as an act of treason. The Nazis unleashed a terrible vengeance in which hundreds were executed. Hitler was shocked to find out that Rommel was involved in the plot and he was forced to commit suicide.

the complete destruction of Germany. One of the most prominent was **Colonel Claus Graf Schenk von Stauffenberg**. From a wealthy Catholic background, he was a brave soldier who had lost an eye and a hand fighting in North Africa. After he recovered, he was appointed chief of staff to the Reserve Army, a force stationed in Germany to crush any revolt. Stauffenberg and the plotters hoped to use this army to seize power. Crucially, his appointment gave him access to Hitler's

KEY QUESTION

What happened during the Holocaust?

As a result of German military successes, there were large Jewish populations in the conquered territories, especially in Poland and the USSR. The **Decree of Identification** forced every Jew to wear a yellow Star of David.

Colonel Claus Graf Schenk von Stauffenberg (1907–44), the man who almost killed Hitler. His last words were, 'Long live our sacred Germany.' Today he is a hero in Germany.

A Jewish family wearing the Star of David.

During the advance into the USSR, special SS detachments called **Einsatzgruppen** shot hundreds of thousands of Jews. Over 33,000 men, women and children were killed at **Babi Yar**, near Kiev, in August 1941.

THE FINAL SOLUTION

The Nazis were unsure what to do with the large Jewish population in the areas they conquered. Hitler came to realise that emigration was not feasible, so instead it was decided to kill the Jewish population of Europe. This was known as 'the final solution of the Jewish question' (*Die Endlosung der Judenfrage*).

In January 1942, at the Wannsee Conference near Berlin, Nazi officials led by Himmler's deputy, **Reinhard Heydrich**, planned the details of the **Final Solution**. Heydrich indicated that approximately 11 million Jews were eventually to be subjected to the Final Solution. The Nuremberg Laws served as a basis for determining who was a Jew. Other 'racial inferiors', such as Roma gypsies, Poles and Soviet prisoners of war, were also to be killed.

Jews were confined to easily controlled ghettos, the most famous of which was in Warsaw. They would then be moved to extermination camps in the east, such as **Auschwitz**, **Chelmno**, **Belzec**, **Treblinka** and **Majdanek**. Murder began in earnest in 1942.

The whole process was conducted with industrial efficiency.

- On arrival at the camps, the old and the young were mainly killed in gas chambers using **Zyklon B** or **carbon monoxide**. The gas chambers were disguised as fake shower units so as not to cause mass panic.
- The bodies were then burned in crematoria (ovens).
- The able-bodied were worked until they were murdered or died of disease. Some prisoners were also subjected to medical experiments.

It is estimated that up to 6 million Jews perished during what became known as the **Holocaust**, including 90 per cent of Poland's Jewish population of 3 million. In all, about 60 per cent of the pre-war Jewish population of Europe was killed. The programme was carried out in great secrecy and was not brought to light until the Russians began to capture the camps in early 1945.

AUSCHWITZ

Near Krakow in Poland, the Nazis established their largest and most infamous extermination camp at Auschwitz. Originally a concentration camp for Polish political prisoners, Auschwitz was greatly expanded in 1941 with the addition of a much larger camp at nearby **Birkenau**. Between 1940 and 1945, more than 1 million people were killed there. The vast majority of the victims were Jews, but Poles, Roma (Gypsies) and Russian prisoners of war were also killed. More people died in Auschwitz than the combined British and American military losses during World War II.

Guards inspected new arrivals at the camp to determine whether or not they were fit for forced labour. Most were not, and were sent directly to the gas chambers, where Zyklon B was used to kill the prisoners. In the spring of 1943, four purpose-built gas chamber and crematorium complexes were constructed and included electric lifts to carry bodies up to the crematoria. Each crematorium could handle 2,000 victims daily. In a nearby group of barracks, nicknamed 'Canada' by

Prisoners at Auschwitz.

The main camps in Nazi-occupied Europe.

the prisoners, victims' belongings were sorted for transportation to the Reich. The victims' hair was used to stuff mattresses, while gold fillings in teeth and rings were melted down and the gold deposited to an SS account.

Those who survived the initial selection were put to work in arms factories, coal mines, farms and chemicals plants as slave labour. Doctors under the infamous **Josef Mengele** conducted cruel medical experiments, especially on twins. When the Soviet army reached Auschwitz in January 1945, it found only 7,000 inmates. The TV producer and historian Lawrence Rees has written that Auschwitz 'is the site of the single largest mass murder in the history of humanity'.

REVIEW QUESTIONS

1 What was the attitude of Western Europeans to the German occupation?

2 Why was the Nazi occupation of Eastern Europe far harsher than in Western Europe?

3 Describe the activities of partisans in Russia and Yugoslavia.

4 How did the Russians respond to the rising in Warsaw against German rule?

5 What was The White Rose?

6 Write an account on the plot to kill Hitler on 20 July 1944.

7 Explain the significance of the Wannsee Conference.

8 What happened to Jews when they arrived in extermination camps?

9 Explain why Auschwitz was such an infamous place.

SUMMARY

The war led to the deaths of over 50 million people and terrible suffering inflicted on civilians on both sides. It saw the defeat of an evil and murderous ideology, Nazism, and had a number of long-term consequences.

- Germany was divided into two countries – democratic West Germany and the Communist East Germany. The country was not united again until 1990.
- The Soviet Union set up corrupt and cruel Communist regimes in Eastern Europe and the peoples of these countries were not to experience democracy until 1989.
- The spread of Communism and the rivalry between the USSR and the US led to the Cold War between both countries. Although they never went to war, it was a period of poor relations and tensions that lasted until 1989.
- In Western Europe, especially in France and Germany, there was a strong desire to promote greater European co-operation in order to prevent war in the future. This led to the formation of the European Economic Community in 1957. Today, France and Germany are no longer enemies, but close allies.
- The main colonial powers, Britain and France, were weakened by the war. Over the next 20 years they were to face independence movements in Asia and Africa and lose most of their possessions.

KEY QUESTION

How did the technology of warfare change during World War II?

DEVELOPMENTS BEFORE WORLD WAR II

Warfare and weapons change greatly during wars. World War I had seen the birth of modern 20th-century warfare. For example, by the end of the war:

- Planes were used as both bombers and fighters.
- Tanks had become common on the battlefield.
- Artillery was far more accurate.

In the 1920s and 1930s, there was a lot of research and development of new weapons. The best gun of World War II, the German 88 anti-aircraft gun, was developed secretly in the 1920s. Single-wing fighters and bombers that were made famous during World War II were built, e.g. the Spitfire in Britain and the ME 109 in Germany. Tanks were greatly improved upon from World War I. New theories on warfare were drawn up, including the **blitzkrieg** tactics employed so effectively by the Germans in World War II. The Spanish Civil War had given a taste of what a modern war might involve. The Germans used planes such as the Stuka dive-bomber. German bombing of towns such as at **Guernica** created great fear in many countries of widespread destruction in a future world war.

THE IMPACT OF WORLD WAR II

The technology of warfare was to develop greatly during World War II, since most of the industrial and scientific resources of the countries involved were devoted to the development and production of weapons. Lessons were learned from the battlefield that were then applied and improvements made. At first, Germany had the edge in military technology, but this changed as the Allies devoted their resources to developing weapons to win the war. Let's look more closely at the main changes introduced on land, in the air and at sea.

ON LAND

Tanks, or armoured fighting vehicles, to give them their correct names (called *Panzerkampfwagens* in German, hence the name Panzers), are possibly the weapon most associated with World War II. Their main use on the battlefield was to smash through enemy defences.

There are three major factors that affect how good a tank was in battle: speed, armour and firepower.

Other important factors include reliability and how far they can travel on a full fuel tank. During the war, developments were made in all of these areas, but usually some compromises had to be made between armour, speed and firepower. The best tank of the early stages of the war was French, not German – the **Char B1**. During the invasion of Russia, the Germans got a nasty shock when they encountered one of the best tanks of the war, the **T34**. Fast, and with sloping armour for greater protection and with a good gun, they were more than a match for the best German tank at the time, the Panzer **Mark IV**.

In 1942 and 1943, three tanks were introduced that played important roles in the fighting. They were the **Sherman** (Allies) and the Panzers **Mark V** (the Panther) and **Mark VI** (the Tiger). Later in the war, tanks got even bigger.

- The **Tiger II** (the King Tiger) was superior to any Allied tank.
- The Russian **Josef Stalin II** had the biggest gun of any tank used during the war.

As a general rule, German tanks were better in terms of armour and firepower, but they were slow, complicated machines that took a long time to build and repair. Both US and Russian tanks were simpler to manufacture and easier to maintain. A crucial advantage the Allies had was that their tank production dwarfed that of Germany. This meant that although the Germans would destroy more Allied tanks, the Allies could make good their losses. In Normandy, German tank crews joked that one Tiger was a match for 10 Shermans, but unfortunately there were always 11.

The Allies used trucks to move men and supplies far more than their German counterparts. For example, the US sent the Soviets over 300,000 trucks. For all its image of a highly mechanised and modern army, the Germans still relied on horses for most of their transport.

ARTILLERY

Artillery played an important role during the war in shelling enemy defences before an attack or in an anti-tank role. As already mentioned, the German 88 was the best gun of the war. During the war, **self-propelled guns** were developed. They were artillery pieces that moved around the battlefield, giving infantry mobile artillery support. Later developments saw the introduction of **tank destroyers**. Similar to tanks, they were a good defensive weapon, but the gun could only fire one way. The German **Jadpanther** was considered the best tank destroyer of the war, but only just over 400 were built.

INFANTRY WEAPONS

The main weapon used by a soldier was the rifle. The models used by both the British (**Lee Enfield**) and the Germans (**Mauser Karabiner 98k**) were similar to the ones used in World War I. Both were very accurate up to half a kilometre. The Americans used the M1 carbine and **M1 Garand** rifles.

Two of the best tanks of the war.

The T34 tank.

The Panther (Mark V) tank.

Hand-held submachine guns were ideal for close-quarter fighting, as they fired more bullets, but they had a shorter range and were quite inaccurate. The most famous British model was the **Sten gun**, while US troops liked to use the **Thompson gun**. German soldiers used the **MP 40**, while the Russian **PPSH 41** was a simple design that was popular with Red Army soldiers. In 1944, the Germans introduced the **Sturmgewehr 44** that combined the rate of fire of a machine gun with the greater accuracy and range of a rifle. Called an assault rifle, it became the model for infantry rifles after World War II and the Soviets copied it to develop the AK-47.

To counter the threat of tanks to infantry, Allied soldiers were given hand-held anti-tank weapons called **bazookas**. The German version was superior, but heavy for soldiers to carry. Later in the war, German soldiers were equipped with light and effective single-shot **Panzerfausts**.

MACHINE GUNS

As in World War I, machine guns were widely used, especially to give advancing infantry support or for defence.

- Light machine guns could be fired either in a fixed position or while the soldier was moving. The British **Bren Gun** was a fine example.
- Heavy machine guns could only be fired from a fixed position, needing two men to operate them. The US **Browning** heavy machine gun was famous for its powerful bullet that could pierce tank armour. The German **MG 42** (introduced in 1942) was the best heavy machine gun of the war. Nicknamed the Spandau, it was feared by Allied soldiers because of its rapid rate of fire. It had a range of up to one kilometre and a modified version is still in use today.

IN THE AIR

During the war, planes improved in areas such as speed, armament, ceiling (maximum height at which they can fly) and manoeuvrability. The greatest innovations were the developments of heavy bombers and jets. As with tanks and other equipment, Allied aircraft production was far greater than Germany, giving them complete control of the skies by 1944.

There were two main categories of planes used during the war: fighters and bombers.

Fighters

Fighters were usually flown by a single pilot and were designed to protect or attack bombers or to control the skies over the battlefield. Sometimes they could be fitted with bombs for close support for infantry.

- The Luftwaffe had some fine fighters, most notably the **ME 109** and the superb **Focke-Wulf 190**. The Germans were ahead in jet design and the **ME 262** was the first jet to see combat in 1944. Although superior to Allied fighters, there were not enough of them to make an impact.
- On the Allied side, the **Supermarine Spitfire** was an excellent plane that was further developed during the war. Possibly the most significant development of the war in the air was the long-range fighter, the **P51 Mustang**. Fitted with extra fuel tanks on the wing, it could accompany British and American bombers over Germany and is considered by many historians to be the best fighter of the war. The **Hawker Typhoon**, armed with bombs and rockets, provided devastating firepower to support Allied armies over the battlefield. German troops in Normandy had to move tanks at night to avoid Typhoons. Near the end of the war, the **Gloster Meteor** was the only Allied jet that saw service.
- After suffering heavy losses to the Luftwaffe in the early years of the war, the Soviets developed the **Lavochkin La 7** and **Yak 9** fighters that proved to be a match for their German opponents. The **Il-2 Shturmovik** performed the same role as the Hawker Typhoon on the Eastern Front. Flying as low as 6 metres to attack tanks, it was feared by German troops, who nicknamed it 'Black Death'.

Bombers

The Germans saw the Luftwaffe as an arm of the army and designed many of their bombers for close infantry support.

- The **Junkers 87**, or Stuka, was an accurate dive-bomber fitted with a siren and possessing unusual wings. It has forever become associated with blitzkrieg warfare. However, it was slow and suffered massive losses in the Battle of Britain. It was later fitted with cannons under each wing and employed as a tank killer on the Eastern Front.
- Medium bombers were developed, such as the **Heinkel He III** and the excellent **Junkers Ju 88**. Both could carry up to 4,000 pounds of bombs. However, the Germans did not develop a heavy bomber and therefore could not target Russian factories located east of the Ural Mountains.

The Western Allies developed a number of heavy bombers that could carry a large payload of bombs. The most important of these were:
- Four-engine British **Lancasters** that normally carried 14,000 pounds of bombs and had a range of over 2,000 miles.
- The American **B-17 Flying Fortress**, with a crew of 10, was heavily armed with machine guns and could drop over 17,000 pounds of bombs on German targets.
- Near the end of the war, the US introduced the **B-29 Superfortress**, which was used to drop the atomic bomb on Japan.

Radar played a major role in the Battle of Britain. It also led to the development of night fighters that were fitted with radar so they could detect and attack enemy bombers.

ROCKET TECHNOLOGY

The Germans developed a number of rockets called **Vergeltungswaffe**, or revenge weapons.
- The **V1** flying bomb, or doodlebug, carried an 850-kg warhead and was launched from catapult ramps or from aircraft. It was first used in June 1944 and in total over 10,000 were fired. It was not a very successful weapon, as most failed to reach their targets.
- The **V2** rocket was a major technological advance and posed a more formidable threat than the V1. It consisted of a one-ton warhead carried on a 14-metre-long rocket. It travelled at

A V2 rocket.

a speed of over 2,000 mph and dropped to earth from a height of 60,000 or 70,000 feet. Over 1,000 were fired at London alone. However, the weapon was ultimately ineffective and expensive and it diverted much-needed resources from fighter and submarine production. After the war, the German scientists who developed the rocket worked for the US military and on the space programme. The head of the programme, **Werner von Braun**, designed the Saturn 5 rocket used on the *Apollo 11* mission that travelled to the moon in 1969.

AT SEA

The Germans used submarines or U-boats to sink merchant ships bringing supplies to Britain. They operated in **wolf packs** and attacked convoys of merchant ships. U-boats were effectively surface boats that spent some time below water. They needed to stay on the surface to recharge their batteries. U-boats were slow under water and were vulnerable to attack from planes once discovered above or below the surface.

In response to the U-boat threat, the Allies used a combination of new technological developments.
- **Hedgehog mortars** fired 24 bombs at a time, and unlike depth charges did not explode unless they hit something.
- **Radar** was placed on planes that were also armed with depth charges.
- **Leigh lights** were searchlights operated by radar and gave the U-boats little warning of a plane attacking and increased their vulnerability at night.

The **Atlantic gap**, where Allied convoys had no air cover and were likely to be attacked by U-boats, was closed. This happened due to the introduction of long-range B-24 bombers and the use of **escort carriers** that accompanied convoys, providing air cover. Crucially, they also relied on decoded German messages to defeat the U-boat threat. The British built the first prototype computer to break the German **Enigma** code.

By the summer of 1943, the Allies had largely defeated the U-boat threat. Near the end of the war, in response to the Allied air threat, the Germans introduced the Type XXI model that could stay submerged while at sea. This submarine was the model for many post-war craft. During the war, well over half of the 1,100 U-boats built by the Germans were sunk in Allied attacks.

Liberty ships were cargo ships built in the US to replace those sunk by the Germans. They were cheap and quick to build, and came to symbolise the vast scale of US wartime industrial output. Another major development saw the demise of the battleship and the importance of the aircraft carrier for control of the sea. Their widespread use was seen in the war in the Pacific.

THE ATOMIC BOMB

During the war, both sides were working on using the power of the atom to make a bomb far more powerful than had ever been developed previously. The Germans did not get off the drawing board. However, the US was more successful. Fearful that the Germans might develop a bomb first, they set up **Operation Manhattan**, one of the costliest scientific projects in history. The greatest technological achievement of the war came in July 1945 with the detonation of the first atomic bomb. Atomic bombs were then used on Hiroshima and Nagasaki in August 1945 to force the Japanese to surrender. This weapon changed the face of warfare forever and created the possibility of the destruction of the world in a future war.

Devastation after the attack on Hiroshima.

REVIEW QUESTIONS

1 Identify the major technological developments in weapons in the 1920s and 1930s.

2 What were the main tanks that were developed during World War II?

3 Why were submachine guns more commonly used during the war? What was the significance of the Sturmgewehr?

4 Outline the main fighters used during the war. Which are regarded as the best?

5 What were the main bombers used by the Allies?

6 Why was the V2 rocket a significant development?

7 What technological developments helped the Allies to defeat the threat of U-boats?

8 Briefly outline how the atomic bomb was developed.

1 Source Question

Read the following account from SS officer Kurt Gerstein, describing what happened to a trainload of Jews that arrived at Belzec extermination camp.

Instructions come from a large loudspeaker: Undress completely, including artificial limbs, spectacles etc. Then the women and girls go to the hairdressers who with two or three snips of the scissors cut off their hair and put it into potato sacks. 'That is for some special purpose to do with U Boats, for insulation or something like that,' the SS officer on duty told me.

*Then the procession starts to move. They all go along with a very pretty girl in front, all naked men, women, and cripples without their artificial limbs …
And so they climb the little staircase …
mothers with their children at their breasts, little naked children, adults, men, women all naked. They hesitate but they enter the death chambers, driven on by the others behind them or by the leather whips of the SS, the majority without saying a word. After half an hour, all were dead from inhaling diesel fumes. Two dozen dentists open the mouths with hooks and look for gold.*

Source: Niall Ferguson: *The War of the World: History's Age of Hatred*, Allen Lane, 2006, pp. 507–508.

(a) According to the account, what instructions came from a loudspeaker?
(b) For what purpose was the women's hair cut and collected in sacks?
(c) How were the Jews forced to enter the death chambers and how were they killed?
(d) What do you think the author's attitude is to the scene he is describing? Support your answer with evidence from the account.
(e) What was the Final Solution adopted by the Nazi regime in 1942?

2 Write a paragraph on **TWO** of the following (Ordinary Level).
- German successes during the war.
- The main alliances in World War II.
- The battle of Stalingrad.
- Why Germany was defeated.

3 Write an essay on **ONE** of the following.
Ordinary Level
(a) What were the main advances in military technology during World War II?
(b) What role did Adolf Hitler play in World War II?
(c) What actions did the Nazis take against the Jews of Europe?

Higher Level
(d) What role did the wartime alliance of Britain, the US and the USSR play in the defeat of Hitler?
(e) What were conditions like in Nazi-occupied Europe?
(f) What developments took place in the technology of warfare during the period 1920–45?
(Leaving Certificate question)

4 Find out more about the Allied bombing of Dresden. There are a number of websites at **www.edco.ie/LCHistory** to help you. Then write a short essay (400 words) for or against the motion: 'The bombing of Dresden was a war crime by the Allies.'

(11) Anglo-American Culture, 1920–45

What do you need to know in this chapter?

Elements	Key Personalities	Key Concepts
Anglo-American culture in peace and war: radio and cinema	Charlie Chaplin Bing Crosby	Propaganda The Depression

KEY QUESTION

How did the US film industry develop in the 1920s and 1930s?

INTRODUCTION

The 1920s saw the birth of mass culture, e.g. cinema, which started to replace local cultures throughout the world. This mass culture came mainly from the US and to a lesser extent from the UK. English became the international language of entertainment. In this chapter we will look at how US film and radio came to dominate what people watched or heard throughout the World.

THE GROWTH OF HOLLYWOOD

American film production began at the turn of the 20th century in New York. Films were silent and in black and white. Just before the start of World War I a number of film makers moved to the Los Angeles suburb of Hollywood attracted by the space the area provided to shoot films. The town grew rapidly and became the centre of the US film industry. In the US the 1920s were an era of prosperity known as the "Roaring Twenties" and people had more money to spend on entertainment. The film industry grew dramatically and as early as 1920 over 90 percent of the films shown in Europe, Asia, South America and Africa were made in Hollywood.

THE BIG FIVE

Movies were big business worth over $2 billion a year. The 'Big Five' major film-making studios dominated Hollywood; Warner Brothers, Paramount Studios, RKO, Metro Goldwyn Mayer (MGM) and Fox Film Corporation. They produced more than 90 percent of the films in America and also distributed their films internationally. About 800 films were released a year in the US.

The Big Five also owned their own cinemas or **picture palaces** where they showed their films. In 1927 the largest movie palace in the world the 6000-seat Roxy Theatre, owned by the Fox Film Corporation, opened in New York City.

CATEGORIES OF FILMS

Films were organised into **genres** or categories such as historical extravaganzas or biblical epics, e.g. *The Ten Commandments* directed by Cecil B. DeMille or Westerns (cowboy) films such as *The Covered Wagon* (1923). There were also horror films, war films, romances and comedies.

THE MAIN STARS

Two of the biggest silent movie stars of the era were **Douglas Fairbanks** and **Mary Pickford**. In 1920 their marriage was a major media and cultural event. He was famous for his costumed adventure films called Swashbucklers such as *The Mark of Zorro*, *Robin Hood* and *The Iron Mask*.

The Hollywood studios could now afford to buy up the best talent from Europe including directors **Ernst Lubitsch**, **Fritz Lang** and actors **Peter Lorre** and **Greta Garbo**. The German actress **Marlene Dietrich** appeared in her first Hollywood feature film in 1930, signed by Paramount as a rival to MGM's Garbo. This exodus confirmed the lead of the US over the rival film industries in Europe.

THE IMPORTANCE OF CHARLIE CHAPLIN

During the silent era it was American comedy that reached the widest worldwide audiences. This was due mainly to the comedy genius of **Charlie Chaplin, Buster Keaton, Harold Lloyd, Stan Laurel** and **Oliver Hardy**. The popularity of Charlie Chaplin was already established through his famous tramp character. His career continued to prosper with films such as *The Kid* and *The Pilgrim*. In 1925 he made what he later thought was his best film, *The Gold Rush* a story about a lonely gold prospector in Alaska.

THE USE OF SOUND IN FILMS

By the late 1920s the studios were working on ways to use sound in films. In 1927 Warner released the first feature-length talking film (and the first musical), *The Jazz Singer*. By the early 1930s the silent movie had practically disappeared and US cinemas were wired for sound. In Great

Charlie Chaplin (1889–1977). Born in London he began to star in silent comedy films in 1914. In 1919 he set up his own studio, United Artists, with Mary Pickford among others. In 1940 he made his first talkie and most successful film *The Great Dictator*. This film was an attack on Hitler and fascism. After World War II his left-wing views were regarded with deep suspicion and he left the US in 1952, moving to Switzerland where he died in 1977.

Britain the success of talkies from the US resulted in a rush to wire cinemas as well.

Many silent actors and actresses found it hard to adjust to making films using sound. Both Fairbanks and Pickford could not make the transition and retired. Some made the change successfully including Joan Crawford and Greta Garbo. The introduction of sound encouraged new types of films such as gangster films that reflected real life events in American cities such as Chicago. Musicals also became very popular, usually successful shows from Broadway brought to the silver screen. The dancing partnership of **Fred Astaire** and **Ginger Rogers** dominated Hollywood musicals in the late 1930s.

Another technological advance was the use of colour. In 1926 the first feature-length colour picture was *The Black Pirate* starring Douglas Fairbanks. However it was not until the 1930s that colour films became commonplace. In 1927 the Academy of Motion Picture Arts and Sciences (AMPAS) was founded to recognise excellence

Top Five Films (US Box Office) – 1920 and 1930s	
1920s	**1930s**
The Big Parade (1925)	Gone with the Wind (1939)
The Four Horsemen of the Apocalypse (1921)	Snow White and the Seven Dwarfs (1937)
Ben-Hur: A Tale of the Christ (1925)	The Wizard of Oz (1939)
The Ten Commandments (1923)	Frankenstein (1931)
What Price Glory? (1926)	King Kong (1933)

within the film industry. It announced the first Academy Awards in 1929. These awards were soon nicknamed the Oscars and became a very important measure of the quality and success of a film.

CENSORSHIP

In the 1920s Hollywood films represented glamour and were seen as a challenge to the strict morality of the period. The content of some films drew strong criticism. Scandals that rocked Hollywood in the 1920s such as the trial of the popular comedian **Fatty Arbuckle** for rape and murder increased this concern. In response the industry set up the Motion Picture Producers and Distributors of America to regulate the content of films. Its first president **William Hays** wanted Hollywood to produce family orientated films so a production code called the Hays Code was drawn up in 1930. It laid down strict guidelines about the content of films. It came into operation in 1934 and required that there would be no nudity, excessive violence or criticism of ministers of religion. Activity seen as sinful such as criminality or sex outside marriage could only be portrayed if it was punished or if it ended in misery. This code remained in force until the 1960s.

THE GOLDEN AGE OF HOLLYWOOD

The 1930s has been called "The Golden Age of Hollywood". This was the decade of the colour revolution and saw the advance of the 'talkies'. In 1931 Hollywood started dubbing films in the different languages of the countries to which they were exporting their output. This was to overcome the difficulty foreign audiences had understanding films with sound. In 1932 a new three-colour camera was developed and this led to true full-colour that was known as **Technicolor**. In 1939 two of the most popular films of the decade were both produced with Technicolor: *The Wizard of Oz* and *Gone with the Wind*. However the process was expensive and most films were still made in black and white.

THE EFFECTS OF THE DEPRESSION ON THE FILM INDUSTRY

The Great Depression had a major impact on the film industry. Attendance at theatres declined and to survive, the industry cut salaries, production costs and closed a third of the nation's cinemas. To boost attendance, theatres reduced admission prices and put on two films (double bills). As a result, movie attendance was still between 60–75 million per week.

THE MAIN STARS

Clark Gable was known as the King of Hollywood and made his name in films such as *Mutiny on the Bounty* and *The Call of the Wild*. In 1939 he starred in his most successful film *Gone with the Wind* which was the top grossing film of the decade. It was the first colour film to win an Oscar for best picture and Hattie McDaniel's Best Supporting Actress Oscar win made her the first African-American Oscar winner.

The biggest star of the 1930s was **Shirley Temple**. In 1932 Fox signed her as a 4 year-old. She was a tremendous success in hits like *Bright Eyes*, *Heidi* and *The Little Princess*. Another major star was the greatest swashbuckling actor of all time **Errol Flynn** who made films such as *Captain Blood* and *The Adventures of Robin Hood*.

COMEDY IN THE 1930S

Charlie Chaplin was one of the few silent screen comedians to survive the arrival of sound by deliberately remaining silent in his two comedy films in the 1930s! He realised the words would reduce the international appeal of his brand of comedy. One of his finest films was *City Lights* released in 1931. The **Marx Brothers** dominated comedy in the 1930s, their biggest hit was the 1935 musical *A Night at the Opera*. The popular comedy pair Stan Laurel and Oliver Hardy also adapted to talkies.

FILM IN BRITAIN

In 1933 the success of Hungarian-born director **Alexander Korda's** British-made costume drama *The Private Life of Henry VIII* helped to resurrect England's film industry. Korda established London Films which had success with *The Four Feathers*, *The Thief of Bagdad* and *The Jungle Book*. Director **Alfred Hitchcock** became widely-known in both the UK and the US with the release of his thrillers such as *The 39 Steps*, and *The Lady Vanishes*. Brought to Hollywood, Hitchcock made his first US film in 1940.

THE GROWTH OF RADIO IN THE US AND UK

Guglielmo Marconi is credited with inventing the radio (wireless) in 1895. In 1920 the first commercial radio broadcast was made by the station RDKA in Pittsburgh, USA. Soon there were hundreds of American stations, but dependant on advertising revenue over half quickly went bankrupt. Despite the early chaos radio established itself as a new form of communication bringing the world to the living room with a turn of a dial. Programmes included plays, serials, music and news. Soon sporting events were broadcast live. Radio ownership grew quickly even during the Depression.

Famous radio stars included the comic **Will Rogers** and the singer **Bing Crosby** both of whom also had very successful Hollywood acting careers. Crosby had his own radio show on NBC called *Kraft Music Hall*.

Bing Crosby (1903–77). An American singer and actor, in the 1930s he became a radio star and is credited with inspiring Frank Sinatra and other later pop singers. Crosby's most famous song *"White Christmas"* was for many years the biggest-selling single of all time. He starred in his first film in 1932, his most famous being the seven 'Road To' films in which he co-starred with Bob Hope. In 1944 he won the Oscar for Best Actor for his role in the film *Going My Way*.

REVIEW QUESTIONS

1 How did Hollywood become the centre of the US film industry?
2 What different types of films were made by the Hollywood studios?
3 How did the Big Five studios control the movie industry?
4 Write a short piece on two of the main stars of the 1920s.
5 What was the impact of the introduction of sound on Hollywood actors?
6 Why was censorship introduced in Hollywood and how did it make the pictures different to those of today?
7 Who were the main stars in the 1930s?

In Britain the government was reluctant to follow the free for all that had occurred in the US but after pressure from Marconi among others it agreed to the formation of the **British Broadcasting Company** in 1922 (later changed to British Broadcasting Corporation in 1927). It was funded by a radio licence rather than advertising. By 1926 there were two and a quarter million licences increasing to eight and a half million by 1938. In 1925 the building of a long range high-transmitter meant that it was possible for nearly all of Britain to hear the BBC.

KEY QUESTION

How did cinema and radio plays support the war effort in the US and the UK during World War II?

HOLLYWOOD AND WORLD WAR II

After war broke out in Europe in 1939 Hollywood was broadly sympathetic to the Allied cause. In 1940 *The Great Dictator* written, starring and directed by Charlie Chaplin, in his first talking role was released. It was an attack on the Third Reich featuring a dictator Adenoid Hynkel who ruled the kingdom of Tomania.

In 1941 after the attack on Pearl Harbor Hollywood became an important part of the propaganda machine to improve morale. The US government set up a propaganda agency **The Office of War Information** in 1942 coordinating its efforts closely with the film industry. In 1942 the Office also established the **Voice of America** radio station to broadcast to Japan and German-occupied Europe.

Many of the movies produced during the war emphasised patriotism, group effort, and the value of individual sacrifices for a greater cause. Many wartime films featured female characters playing a role in the war by serving as combat nurses or working in factories. The most famous of all

wartime propaganda films was *Casablanca*, released in 1942. It is about a nightclub owner, played by Humphrey Bogart, and a former lover, played by Ingrid Bergman, separated in Paris by WWII.

SUPPORTING THE WAR EFFORT

Off screen, leading actors and actresses led recruitment drives and urged people to buy bonds to raise money for the war effort. Bing Crosby, a popular figure among US troops, visited bases singing to troops and made propaganda broadcasts in German to the enemy who nicknamed him Der Bingle. After World War II he topped a poll of US soldiers as the man who did most to maintain their morale ahead of President Roosevelt and General Eisenhower. Directors like Frank Capra, John Ford, and John Huston made propaganda documentaries to explain, "why we fight". Over 25% of all film industry employees entered the armed forces, including Clark Gable and Henry Fonda. Like other wartime industries Hollywood faced many shortages and to cut costs colour was rarely used. Nevertheless, the war years proved to be profitable for the industry with movie attendance at record levels of 90 million a week.

BRITISH CINEMA AND RADIO IN WARTIME

British cinema played a major role in the war effort. Although all cinemas initially closed in 1939, they soon reopened and between 1939 and 1945 weekly attendance trebled. The most celebrated British war film was the naval adventure *In Which We Serve* released in 1942, written by the playwright and composer **Noel Coward.** In 1944 **Laurence Olivier** directed and starred in *Henry V*, dedicated to the fighting forces and the bravery of the British people in resisting the Nazis.

As in Germany, BBC radio played a propaganda role reporting on the fighting and carrying speeches from politicians such as Winston Churchill. **Vera Lynn's** programme *Sincerely Yours* won her the title of "Forces' Sweetheart". The BBC's wartime radio services spread the Allied message in Nazi-occupied countries. By the end of the war, the BBC was broadcasting in 40 languages and Josef Goebbels was said to have admitted that BBC Radio had won the "intellectual invasion" of Europe.

R E V I E W   Q U E S T I O N S

1   How did radio develop in the United States?

2   Why was the BBC so important to the development of radio in the UK?

3   In what ways did Hollywood films help to support the US war effort?

4   Would you agree that Bing Crosby was an important figure during World War II?

5   What was probably the greatest film made in the US during the War?

6   How did cinema and radio help the British war effort?

History of Cinema and Radio: Timeline

1920	First commercial radio broadcast
1922	British Broadcasting Corporation (BBC) formed
1926	Death of Rudolph Valentino
1927	Release of *The Jazz Singer* – the first film with sound
1929	First Academy Awards or Oscars as they soon become known
1931	Depression had major impact leading to a fall in profits
1934	Hays Production Code placed strict controls on the content of films
1939	A Golden year for Hollywood with films such as *The Wizard of Oz* and *Gone with the Wind*
1940	Release of Chaplin's film, *The Great Dictator*. British radio and film industry devoted to supporting the war effort. Churchill made a number of radio broadcasts designed to maintain morale.
1941	Entry of US into World War II – both radio and film played major propaganda role.
1942	Release of *Casablanca*

1 Source Question

During World War II, the Office of War Information examined the contribution that each film made to the war effort. Read this edited extract from its report about the film *Casablanca* and answer the questions that follow:

From the standpoint of the war information program, Casablanca is a very good picture...Many excellent points are scored:

(1) The film presents an excellent picture of the spirit of the underground movement. We learn that people of all nationalities meet secretly everywhere, despite the danger, planning the destruction of the oppressor. Their courage, determination and self sacrifice should make Americans proud of these underground allies.

(3) It is shown that personal desire must be subordinated to the task of defeating Fascism. The heroine and the man she loves sacrifice their personal happiness in order that each may carry on the fight in the most effective manner.

(5) America is shown as the haven of the oppressed and homeless. Refugees want to come to the United States because here they are assured of freedom, democratic privileges and immunity from fear.

(7) The film presents a good portrayal of the typical Nazi. In the arrogant Major Strasser, with his contempt for anything not German, his disregard for human life and dignity, his determination that all peoples shall bow to the Third Reich, we get a picture of the Nazi outlook.

Source: http://www.digitalhistory.uh.edu/historyonline/ bureau_casablanca.cfm

(a) How does the film portray the underground movement opposing the Nazis?

(b) According to the extract how is the US shown?

(c) What does the Office of Information consider is "a good portrayal of the typical Nazi"?

(d) Would you agree with the view that *Casablanca* was a propaganda movie? Explain your answer.

2 Write a paragraph on **TWO** of the following:
- The growth of Hollywood in the 1920s
- The British film industry in the 1930s and 1940s
- Hollywood during World War II
- The development of radio as a popular form of entertainment

3 Write an essay on **ONE** of the following:
- How did Bing Crosby and/or Charlie Chaplin become stars of popular culture during the period 1920–45? (Ordinary Level)
- How did Anglo-American culture develop in the area of radio and cinema in the period 1920–45? (Higher Level)
- What role did radio and cinema play in supporting the war effort in the US and the UK during World War II? (Higher Level)

VLADIMIR ILYICH LENIN (1870–1924): REVOLUTIONARY AND POLITICAL LEADER

Vladimir Ilyich Ulyanov was born in **Simbrisk**, a town on the Volga River, in 1870. His father was the local school inspector and he was an excellent student who went to university. In 1887, his brother, Alexander, was executed for involvement in a plot to kill the Tsar. Lenin became a follower of Karl Marx and a revolutionary. He was later arrested and sent to Siberia. On his return, he married **Nadezhda Krupskaya** and joined the Russian **Social Democratic and Labour Party**. In 1901, he was forced to live in exile abroad and adopted the revolutionary name **Lenin**, after the River Lena in Siberia.

The Social Democratic Party split in 1903. The majority, led by Lenin (**Bolsheviks**), wanted a small party with a membership of dedicated revolutionaries. His opponents (**Mensheviks**) believed the party should be modelled on the German Socialist Party. He played little role in the 1905 revolution and spent most of the next 12 years in exile in Switzerland. When the Tsar was overthrown, he returned home to Russia in April 1917. He was opposed to any co-operation with the new **provisional government** and attacked the government for continuing the war and opposing land reform. Aided by severe economic problems and defeat on the battlefield, support for the Bolsheviks grew, especially in the cities.

Sensing his opportunity, he ordered a revolution and, aided by **Leon Trotsky**'s organisational skills, the Bolsheviks seized power in October 1917. Lenin ordered an immediate ceasefire with the Germans but was later forced to agree to the harsh **Treaty of Brest-Litovsk** in March 1918. He also started land reform. Election results proved disappointing for the Bolsheviks and he ordered the assembly closed, which marked the end of democratic government in Russia.

Lenin's government was opposed by many Russians and a civil war broke out. Lenin ordered the use of terror to defeat his enemies, which came to be known as the **Red Terror**. The **Cheka**, or secret police, was set up to deal with political opponents. Thousands were shot, including the Tsar and his family in 1918. By 1920, Lenin's supporters, the **Reds**, had defeated the **Whites** in the Civil War. Russia was renamed **the Union of Soviet Socialist Republics (USSR)**.

During the Civil War, Lenin ordered the introduction of **War Communism**, under which private enterprise was banned. Although it helped to feed the workers, it led to famine in the countryside and proved to be a disastrous failure. In 1921, the sailors at the **Kronstadt** naval base outside St Petersburg revolted. Although crushed, the revolt worried Lenin and he abandoned War Communism and introduced the **New Economic Policy**. This allowed for a return to limited private business activity and proved successful.

Lenin's health was always poor and in 1922 he suffered two strokes that left him paralysed. He could do little to stop the growing power struggle in the party between Stalin and Trotsky to succeed him. A further stroke followed in 1923 and in January 1924 he died of a fourth stroke. His body was preserved in a mausoleum in Red Square in Moscow and St Petersburg was renamed Leningrad in his honour. In Soviet propaganda he became a God-like figure who could do no wrong.

JOSEPH STALIN (1879–1953): POLITICAL LEADER AND DICTATOR

Stalin was born to a very poor family in **Gori** in **Georgia in 1879**. His real name was **Joseph Vissarionovich Djugashvili**. His father was a cobbler and his mother was a washerwoman. In 1894, he attended a seminary at **Tiflis**, where he studied for the **Orthodox** priesthood. He became involved in Socialist activity there and was expelled in 1899. He became a professional revolutionary and was involved in bank robberies. He was sent to Siberia seven times, from where he escaped on six occasions. Stalin married his first wife, **Yekaterina Svanidze**, in 1904, but she died in 1907.

Stalin was a loyal supporter of Lenin and in 1912 he was elected to the **Central Committee** of the party. He adopted the revolutionary name **Stalin: the 'man of steel'**. After the **February Revolution in 1917**, he became editor of *Pravda*, the Communist Party newspaper. He played little part in the **October Revolution**, although his role would be greatly exaggerated after he came to power.

He was appointed **Commissar for Nationalities** in the new government. In 1919, he married his second wife, **Nadezhda Alliluyeva** (she committed suicide in 1932). During the **Civil War**, he served as a commander on a number of fronts, where he frequently came into conflict with **Trotsky**. Stalin was appointed **General Secretary of the Communist Party** in 1922. He used this position to build up his power base, appointing his supporters to posts throughout the country.

After Lenin's death in 1924, Stalin gradually outmanoeuvred his rivals in the party, especially Trotsky, who was forced into exile. By 1928, Stalin was effectively the dictator of the Soviet Union. Stalin believed that Socialism must be built in Russia first before exporting world revolution. He called his policy **Socialism in One Country**. He introduced his policies by means of three **Five-Year Plans**, which involved the introduction of heavy industry, the collectivisation of agriculture and a huge transfer of population from the countryside to the cities. These changes were supported by massive propaganda. Stalin was portrayed as the rightful heir to Lenin, a living god who could do no wrong.

Terror was used on a scale rarely witnessed in human history. The secret police, the **NKVD**, spied on the population. Giant concentration camps, called **Gulags**, were to be found throughout the country. The forced **collectivisation** of agriculture cost millions of lives, especially in the Ukraine. The policy of **industrialisation** made his country militarily strong and helped it defeat Nazi Germany, but provided little material benefit for its citizens. Many of the great industrial projects were built using slave labour.

The assassination of **Sergei Kirov** led to the worst period of political violence, called the **Great Terror**, or the Purges. Stalin acted against any real or imagined threats to his control of the Communist Party and Soviet society. Many prominent figures in the party were tried in a series of **show trials** and later shot. Thousands of army officers were also killed. These executions weakened the fighting ability of the Red Army and partly explained the massive German victories of 1941.

Deeply suspicious of the Western powers, he agreed to an alliance with Hitler in 1939 called the **Nazi-Soviet Non-Aggression Pact**. He was caught by surprise when the Germans attacked in June 1941. However, he recovered and provided decisive, if cruel, leadership during the war. Soviet industry was dedicated totally and successfully to the war effort – production of tanks and planes was far greater than that of Nazi Germany.

After World War II, Stalin extended Soviet control over Eastern Europe and helped to start the Cold War with the US. In 1949, the USSR gained superpower status when it tested their first atomic bomb. Increasingly distrustful of everyone, Stalin started a new round of purges. In March 1953, he died after a brain haemorrhage and was buried next to Lenin.

BENITO MUSSOLINI (1883–1945):
FOUNDER OF FASCISM AND DICTATOR OF ITALY

Benito Mussolini was born in **Predappio** in central Italy in 1883. His father was a blacksmith and his mother was a schoolmistress. He was a difficult pupil and was expelled on one occasion from his school. Influenced by his father, he became involved in Socialist politics. In 1912 he became editor of the Socialist Party newspaper, *Avanti* (Forward). When World War I broke out he supported Italy's entry into the war. He broke with the Socialist Party and set up his own newspaper, *IL Popolo d'Italia* (The Italian People), which was secretly funded by the Allies. When Italy entered the war in 1915, he joined the army. In 1917, he was wounded and returned to editing his paper. In the same year he married Rachele Guidi and they had five children. Mussolini was not faithful to his wife and had a string of mistresses, including the love of his life, **Clara Petacci**.

Conditions in Italy after the war were poor, with waves of strikes and political demonstrations. Hoping to take advantage of the political situation, Mussolini formed the Fascist Party (**Fascio di Combattimento**) in March 1919. Opposed to Communism, he promised to bring order to Italy. He was also strongly against the terms of the peace settlement after World War I and pledged to make Italy a great power. He received the support of many unemployed war veterans. He organised them into armed squads known as **Blackshirts**, who terrorised their political opponents. He received a lot of support from wealthy businessmen who were worried by the possibility of a Communist revolution.

His party went from strength to strength as the weak coalition governments seemed to be doing little to solve Italy's political and economic conditions. In October 1922, the Blackshirts marched on Rome and Mussolini demanded to be appointed prime minister. Refusing to use troops, **King Victor Emmanuel III** invited Mussolini to form a government.

Mussolini then gradually dismantled the institutions of democratic government. He received the power to issue decrees and an electoral law was passed that gave two-thirds of the seats in parliament to the party that won the most votes. The Fascists duly won the 1924 election. In 1925 he made himself dictator, taking the title **Il Duce**. He introduced a new form of government called the **corporate state**, which Mussolini claimed was an alternative to capitalism and Communism. Mussolini used propaganda to promote a **cult of personality**. However, his rule was nowhere near as brutal as Hitler's or Stalin's. In fact, he became a respected international statesman who spoke French, English and German.

He set about attempting to re-establish Italy as a great European power. In 1935, Mussolini invaded **Abyssinia (now Ethiopia)** and incorporated it into his new Italian empire. He provided military support to **General Franco** in the Spanish Civil War. Increasing co-operation with Nazi Germany led to the 1936 **Rome-Berlin Axis** and the 1939 **Pact of Steel**. Influenced by Hitler, Mussolini introduced anti-Jewish legislation in Italy, but it was only enforced half-heartedly.

His declaration of war on Britain and France in June 1940 exposed Italian military weakness. Jealous of Hitler's successes, he launched his own military adventures. However, Italy's forces suffered a series of defeats in **North Africa** and **Greece**. In July 1943, Allied troops landed in **Sicily**. Mussolini was overthrown by the king and imprisoned. Italy then signed an armistice with the Allies and changed sides. Rescued by German commandos, he was installed as the leader of a new government called the **Salo Republic** but had little power. As the Allies advanced northwards through Italy, Mussolini was captured trying to escape to Switzerland. He was shot along with his mistress, Clara Petacci, on 28 April 1945.

ADOLF HITLER (1889–1945): DICTATOR AND WAR LEADER

Adolf Hitler was born in **Braunau am Inn** in Austria in 1889. His father was a customs official. In 1907, he went to **Vienna** to study at the Viennese Academy of Fine Arts but was refused entry. Vienna was home to a large Jewish and Slavic population and Hitler came into contact with racist and anti-Semitic ideas. In 1913, he moved to **Munich**. He welcomed the outbreak of World War I and joined the German army and was awarded the Iron Cross First Class. Hitler was shocked by the German surrender in 1918. After the war, he remained in the army and was ordered to spy on the small **German Workers' Party**. He joined the party and rapidly became the party's leader and star speaker. In 1920, the party was renamed the **National Socialist German Workers' Party (NSDAP)**. The uniformed **Sturmabteilung**, or **SA (Brownshirts)**, was set up under the command of **Ernst Röhm**, with the **Schutzstaffel (SS)** acting as Hitler's personal bodyguard.

He was strongly opposed to the Treaty of Versailles, Communism and the influence of Jews in German life. In 1923, he tried to stage a rebellion, or putsch. This failed and he was sentenced to five years in jail, of which he served only nine months. While in prison he wrote *Mein Kampf*, where he set out his political views. The years between 1924 and 1929 were tough for Hitler and the Nazi Party, as they had little popular support. This was to change with the onset of the **Great Depression**. As economic conditions worsened, more and more Germans supported Hitler. In July 1932, his party became the largest in Germany. In January 1933, he was appointed chancellor, or prime minister, by **President Hindenburg**.

He quickly established complete control over Germany. Taking advantage of a mysterious fire in the Reichstag, he banned the Communists. The **Enabling Act** was passed, which gave Hitler the power to pass laws without getting the approval of parliament. Hitler was now the **Führer**, or dictator, of Germany. The following year he ordered the execution of the leadership of the **Brownshirts** in an event that became known as the **Night of the Long Knives**. The death of President Hindenburg in August 1934 allowed Hitler to merge the offices of chancellor and president.

Aided by a well-oiled propaganda machine directed by **Dr Josef Goebbels**, Hitler was a popular figure with most Germans. The German economy recovered dramatically from the Great Depression. His policies of dismantling the **Treaty of Versailles** and uniting German speakers in one country, e.g. the takeover of Austria, were welcomed by most Germans. On the other hand, political enemies were arrested and placed in newly established **concentration camps**. The secret police, the **Gestapo**, kept a close eye on the population. Jewish people suffered from severe discrimination, which caused many of them to emigrate.

Hitler's aim of building a German empire in Eastern Europe led him to attack **Poland** in 1939, which started World War II. He took command of the army, which at first enjoyed spectacular successes, including the conquest of France in 1940. The following year, he launched the invasion of Russia and after the Japanese bombing of Pearl Harbor, he declared war on the United States. The war then started to go badly for the Germans. Hitler made matters worse by interfering in military decisions and refusing permission for troops to retreat. At **Stalingrad**, his refusal to allow the German forces to break out contributed to the destruction of the Sixth Army.

During the war, he ordered the destruction of the Jewish people of Europe. Called the **Final Solution**, this policy of mass extermination in camps such as **Auschwitz** resulted in the deaths of 6 million people. The Nazis also proved to be brutal occupiers of conquered countries, such as Poland and Yugoslavia. As the war went from bad to worse, Hitler ordered his troops to fight to the last man. His health deteriorated and he was probably suffering from Parkinson's disease and heart problems. On 29 April 1945, with Russian troops only a few hundred metres away from his headquarters, he married his mistress and the following day both committed suicide. The movement that he had created died with him.

DOCTOR JOSEPH GOEBBELS (1897–1945): NAZI POLITICIAN AND PROPAGANDA CHIEF

Joseph Goebbels was born in Rheydt in the Rhineland in 1897. Goebbels was less than five feet tall with a bad limp caused by a childhood operation. A very good student, he achieved a PhD (hence the title 'Doctor') in philosophy from Heidelberg University.

Goebbels joined the Nazi Party in 1924. Hitler admired Goebbels's abilities as a writer and speaker and they shared an interest in propaganda. He was made **Gauleiter**, or party leader, of Berlin in 1926. This was a difficult job, as Berlin was a stronghold of left-wing parties opposed to the Nazis. A talented journalist, he became editor of the newspaper *Der Angriff* (The Attack). In 1928, he was elected to the Reichstag and became the party's propaganda chief. His skill as an organiser and propagandist contributed to Hitler's rise to power. He also helped to develop the cult of personality around Hitler – **the Führer Myth**.

When Hitler became chancellor in January 1933, he appointed Goebbels as **Minister for Public Enlightenment and Propaganda**. This position gave him complete control over the radio, press, cinema and theatre, although he interfered little in cinema, art or music. However, as a former journalist, he was very interested in the press. Most newspapers, especially Jewish-owned ones, were taken over by the Nazi publishing company, **Eher Verlag**. He also promoted the distribution of inexpensive radio receivers (the **Volkasempfänger**), which ensured that millions of people heard the output of the Reich's propaganda ministry.

He was an excellent orator, seen as second only to Hitler in the party, and in the staging of mass meetings and parades he had no equal. He largely succeeded in presenting a favourable image of the Nazi regime to the German people. Although married, he had an affair with a Czech actress that reduced his influence with Hitler in the late 1930s. Strongly anti-Semitic, he used his position to attack Jews and their role in German society. In 1938, he played a central role in the attack on Jews in Germany that became known as *Kristallnacht*.

As the tide turned in World War II, Goebbels returned to prominence, playing an important role in maintaining morale in the face of Allied successes. He waged a constant propaganda campaign, arguing for **total war**. He talked about miracle weapons that would win the war. When the Russians advanced into Germany, he moved into the bunker in Berlin. He was the only one of the main Nazi leaders to remain in the bunker. On 1 May 1945, after poisoning their six children, Goebbels and his wife committed suicide.

LENI RIEFENSTAHL (1902–2003): ACTRESS AND DIRECTOR

The famous filmmaker was born in Berlin, where she studied painting and ballet. A talented dancer and actress, she set up her own production company and began directing her own films. This was a brave move, as film directing was dominated by men. In 1932, she wrote, directed, produced and starred in *The Blue Light*. Hitler was impressed by her work.

After 1933, with the support of the Nazi Party, she directed a film about the 1933 Nazi Party rally at Nuremberg called *Triumph of Faith* (1933). Her most famous film, *The Triumph of the Will* (1935), documented the 1934 party rally at Nuremberg. It used advanced techniques, such as moving cameras, that produced wide panoramas and striking close-ups. The film emphasised the unity of the party and introduced the German people to many of the party leaders.

Ever since, a debate has raged as to whether the film is a documentary or a piece of propaganda. The film did bring her widespread attention and international praise. She was commissioned to film the 1936 Berlin Olympics (*Olympia*, 1938). This film was also hailed for its technique and won international awards.

The two films are landmark documentaries, and Riefenstahl is considered to be one of the great innovators in moving pictures. Although she never joined the party, Riefenstahl's connections with the Nazis led to her imprisonment for four years after 1945. Because of her association with Hitler, she was unable to direct films and turned to photography instead.

For over half a century, she tried to shrug off her reputation as Hitler's favourite film-maker and the Third Reich's most gifted and glamorous female propagandist. 'I had no political reasons for making these films,' she said in 2002. 'There was one Hitler and one government. Everyone shouted: "Heil Hitler." It was normal at that time. You have to put yourself in the past to look at it from the right perspective.'

SIR WINSTON CHURCHILL (1874–1965): POLITICIAN AND WAR LEADER

Winston Churchill was the son of the prominent Conservative politician Lord Randolph Churchill. He was born into the English aristocracy and attended Harrow and Sandhurst before joining the army. During the Boer War, he was captured while reporting for a London paper, *The Morning Post*. He escaped from captivity and his exploits brought him widespread attention in Britain.

His political career began in 1900 when he became Conservative MP for Oldham. He changed his views and joined the Liberals in 1906. In 1911, he was appointed as the **First Lord of the Admiralty** in charge of the navy. During World War I he was forced to resign this position after the disastrous **Gallipoli campaign.** In 1917, he was appointed Lloyd George's **Minister of Munitions**. He was a strong opponent of the Bolshevik Revolution in Russia, which he argued should be 'strangled at birth'.

Rejoining the Conservative Party in 1924, he was made **Chancellor of the Exchequer** (Minister of Finance) by Prime Minister **Stanley Baldwin**. As chancellor, he presided over the return to the **Gold Standard**. This decision helped to plunge the British economy into deep recession and led directly to the general strike of 1926. A determined opponent of Socialism, he was instrumental in helping to break the strike.

The fall of the Conservative government in 1929 saw his political fortunes decline and it was believed that his career was over. Sitting on the backbenches, he was strongly critical of Neville Chamberlain's appeasement policy and called for rearmament. When war broke out, he was reappointed to his old post in the Admiralty. In May 1940, Neville Chamberlain resigned and Churchill was appointed prime minister with the support of the Labour Party. Even though he promised nothing more than 'blood, toil, tears and sweat', he mobilised and inspired courage in an entire nation.

Throughout the war, he worked tirelessly to defeat the Germans. He built good relations with US **President Roosevelt** and developed an alliance with the Soviet Union. His belief in air power and bringing the war to Germany through bombing helped to bring about eventual victory. However, his tendency to interfere in military matters brought him into conflicts with some of his generals, including the chief of staff, **Sir Alan Brooke**. He dismissed generals and admirals he did not like and frequently showed poor military judgement, especially over his belief that the Mediterranean theatre was the key to victory. By 1943, his influence on military decisions was reduced by the emergence of popular generals such as **Bernard Montgomery**.

Even though he had led Britain to victory, the British people did not believe he would establish a better society in the country and he lost power in the 1945 post-war election. However, he remained a powerful international voice. He popularised the use of the term 'the Iron Curtain' and encouraged the European and Atlantic unity that led to NATO.

In 1951, he returned as prime minister at the age of 77. He was forced to resign due to ill health in 1955 but continued as a backbencher until 1964. He died after a series of strokes in 1965 and was given a state funeral. As well as his many political achievements, he was a very talented writer whose works include a six-volume, 5,000-page history of World War II. He won the Nobel Prize for Literature in 1953. In a poll conducted by the BBC in 2002, he was voted the greatest Briton of all time.

JOHN MAYNARD KEYNES, FIRST BARON KEYNES OF TILTON (1883–1946): CIVIL SERVANT AND ECONOMIST

Keynes was arguably the most influential economist of the 20th century, with a school of economic thought named after him – **Keynesian economics**. He was also a financier, patron of the arts and a prominent civil servant.

Keynes was born in Cambridge into a wealthy academic family. His father was an economist, while his mother became the town's first female mayor. He excelled academically at Eton as well as King's College, Cambridge, where he studied mathematics, history and philosophy.

After graduating, Keynes entered the civil service. Following the outbreak of World War I, he joined the Treasury. He attended the Paris Peace Conference, where he was opposed to the Treaty of Versailles. He resigned his position and wrote *The Economic Consequences of Peace*, which criticised the demands for war reparations from Germany. He prophetically predicted a German desire for revenge. The book became a best-seller and had a major influence in developing the view in Britain that Germany had been treated unfairly at the peace conference and contributed to the policy of appeasement in the 1930s.

During the inter-war years, Keynes became a wealthy man by investing in stocks and shares. He also taught at Cambridge and married the Russian ballerina **Lydia Lopokova**. At the same time, he developed the economic theories that were to establish him as the foremost thinker on the subject. He defended the policies being introduced in both the US and the UK to deal with the Great Depression.

His best-known work, *The General Theory of Employment, Interest and Money*, was published in 1936. He believed that in a time of economic depression (falling investment, declining production and rising unemployment), the government must play a major role in helping economic recovery. He argued it should boost demand for goods and services by increased spending funded through borrowing. The money should then be paid back when the economy recovered.

When World War II broke out, he was reappointed to the Treasury. In 1944, he played an important role at the **Bretton Woods Conference**, which saw the creation of the **World Bank** and **International Monetary Fund (IMF)**. However, the excessive workload had taken its toll on his weak health and in 1946 he died of a heart attack. His economic policies were to play a major role in the 1950s and 1960s.

CHARLIE CHAPLIN (1889–1977): COMEDY ACTOR AND DIRECTOR

Charles Spencer Chaplin was born in London in 1889. Both of his parents were entertainers in music halls. He first appeared on stage at the age of eight, and by the age of 17 he started a career as a comedian with the **Fred Karno Repertoire Company** and travelled with the company to the US in 1910. He was very popular with American audiences and was offered a motion picture contract with **Keystone Pictures**. He made silent comedies with a number of film companies between 1914 and 1917.

His '**Little Tramp**' character and distinctive moustache were a big hit with audiences. He played the role in over 70 films during his career and became a wealthy man, paid the astronomical sum of $1,000,000 for eight pictures by **First National** in 1917. His most famous films from this period include *One A.M., The Pawnshop, Easy Street* and *The Adventurer*. His success was based on the **star system** – films were sold to audiences based on the featured performer rather than the plot or the title.

In a desire for more freedom, he had his own studios built in Hollywood and now directed his own films. In 1918, he made a national tour on behalf of the US war effort. In 1919, Chaplin joined with **Mary Pickford** and **Douglas Fairbanks** to found the **United Artists Corporation** to control the distribution of films. In 1921, he made one of his classic films, *The Kid.*

In 1923, Chaplin changed direction with the romantic comedy *A Woman of Paris*. Unlike all his other films, he only made a brief appearance. This film was followed by the classic comedies *The Gold Rush* and *The Circus*, two of Chaplin's most commercially successful films. The latter film won Chaplin his first Oscar. During the filming of *The Gold Rush*, he had an affair with and later married 16-year-old actress **Lita Grey**. This was his second marriage to a child actress and like his first to Mildred Harris in 1918, it soon ended in divorce. His divorce from Lita proved to be one of the most sensational of 1920s Hollywood.

He made two films in the 1930s – *City Lights* and *Modern Times*. *City Lights* was a critical success. In 1940, Chaplin released his first 'talkie', *The Great Dictator*. This famous film was an attack both on the Nazis and anti-Semitism. He played two roles in the film – a Jewish barber who has lost his memory and Adenoid Hynkel, the dictator of Tomania.

He played little active role in supporting the US war effort, although his two sons fought in the army. His reputation was damaged by a paternity dispute and a series of court battles with the actress **Joan Barry**. In 1943, he wed his fourth wife, 18-year-old **Oona O'Neill**. His fourth marriage was successful. Eight children were born and it lasted until his death in 1977.

After the war, his left-wing views were a source of deep suspicion in the era of **McCarthyism** and it was suspected that he might be a Communist sympathiser. In 1952, on a brief trip to Britain to promote his new autobiographical film *Limelight*, Chaplin found that his US re-entry permit had been cancelled. He decided to settle with his family in Switzerland. In 1966, he produced his last and only colour film, *A Countess from Hong Kong*.

Chaplin was also an author and a talented musician and composed the background music for his films. He was knighted in 1975 and died on Christmas Day, 1977.

BING CROSBY (1903–77): ACTOR AND POPULAR SINGER

The most successful recording artist ever was born **Harry Lillis Crosby** in Tacoma, Washington in 1903. He received the nickname 'Bing' after his favourite character in a cartoon series. His family moved to Spokane (Washington) and he studied law at Gonzaga University, though he left before graduating to pursue his first love, music.

His singing talents were soon recognised and his big break came when he was asked to join the Paul Whiteman Jazz Orchestra. Crosby was part of a three-man vocal group called the **Rhythm Boys**. It soon became clear that he was the star attraction. In 1931, he made his first solo debut on radio and by 1936 he was a major radio star and had his own radio show. During the dark days of the Depression, he was a trusted voice of optimism. He is credited as being the inspiration to most of the male singers of the era that followed him, such as **Frank Sinatra**, **Dean Martin** and **Perry Como**. In 1942, he recorded his most successful single, '**White Christmas**'.

Hollywood also recognised his talents and in 1932 he starred in his first film, *The Big Broadcast*. In all, he starred in 55 feature films between 1932 and 1971. In 1940, the first of the Road movies, *Road to Singapore*, was released. These films saw the creation of one of the most successful comedy partnerships in film history between Bing Crosby and Bob Hope. In 1944, Bing won an Academy Award for his performance in *Going My Way*.

During World War II, he played an important role in the war effort. His radio show regularly attracted an unprecedented audience of 50 million listeners. Crosby placed great importance on making personal appearances to American troops fighting in Europe. At the end of the war, an army poll declared him the individual who had done the most to boost wartime morale.

The post-war years represented the peak of Crosby's success. He married his first wife, **Dixie Lee**, in 1930. They had four children, but she died in 1952. In 1957, he married actress **Kathryn Grant**. They had two sons and a daughter. Bing continued his radio shows and making hit records and movies into the 1960s. Always interested in sport, he starting spending more time on the golf course and the racing track. He died on a golf course in Madrid in 1977.

Bing played an important role in the development of three industries that didn't even exist when he was born: recordings, motion pictures and broadcasting. He helped to transform and define the cultural life not only of the United States, but the world. He made more studio recordings than any other singer in history. During his career, spanning from 1927 until 1962, he had a total of 383 top 30 hits, compared to 85 for Elvis and 69 for the Beatles. He is also ranked as the third most popular film actor in history, behind Clark Gable and John Wayne.

INDEX

A

Abdication crisis, 94
Abyssinia, 45
Acerbo Law, 40
Albania, 45-46, 124
America, 10, 30, 54, 88, 94, 125, 138-39, 144
America, WWI, 1
Anschluss, 3, 75, 83
Anti-communist, 110
Anti-Semetism, 71, 81, 93, 107, 110, 116
Appeasement, 75, 94, 99
April Theses, 8
Arnhem, 130
Aryan Race, 70, 72, 79
Auschwitz, 116, 136-37
Austria, 45, 73, 74, 99
Austrian Empire, 1, 2, 7, 36
Aventine Secession, 40
Axis powers, 124, 127

B

Babi Yar, 136
Baldwin, Stanley, 90-91, 94, 97
Balilla, 42
Battle of Britain, 28, 99, 123, 141
Battle of Stalingrad, 29
Battle of the Atlantic, 127
Battle of the Bulge, 129, 130
Beer Hall Putsch, 55
Belgium, 3, 113, 122, 129
Belzec, 136
Beria, Lavrentiy, 22
Berlin , 69
Berlin Olympics, 64
Beveridge Report, 102
Blackshirts, 38
Blitz, 100, 102, 124
Blitzkrieg, 121, 122
Bloc National, 108
Blum, Leon, 108, 111-12
Bolsheviks, 6, 8, 10, 11, 37
Bonhoeffer, Dietrich, 67-68
Brest-Litovsk, Treaty of, 10
Briand, Aristide, 109
Britain, 10, 27-28, 41, 45, 72-73, 74, 76, 88, 125, 138, 144
British Broadcasting Corporation (BBC), 79, 98, 148
Brownshirt, 63
Bruning, Heinrich, 56
Buchenwald, 62
Bukharin, Nicholas, 26, 27

C

Cartel des Gauches, 109-10
Casablanca, 38, 43, 67-68, 107-9, 115, 148
Central Powers, 1
Centre Party, 51, 62, 67
Chamberlain, Neville, 75, 94, 99, 112, 122
Chaplin, Charles, 145, 147-48, 159
Cheka, 11-12
Chelmno, 136
Chelyabinsk, 29
Churchill, Winston, Sir, 90, 99, 102, 122-23, 125-27, 130, 157
Civil war, 10, 12
Clemenceau, Georges, 2, 107-8
Collaboration, 116
Collectivism, 18, 20
Comintern, 11
Command Economy, 18
Communism, 5, 12, 37-39, 49, 50, 70, 58, 61, 93, 107, 111, 112
Communist, 56, 62, 80, 91
Communist Party (KPD), 51, 96
Conciliation, the, 44
Confessing Church, 67
Conscription, 3
Corporate State, 41, 46, 115
Crosby, Bing, 147-48, 160
Cult of personality, 19, 41, 78, 83
Czechoslovakia, 3-4, 75, 112

D

Dachau, 61-62
Daladier, Edouard, 112
D'Annunzio, Gabriele, 37
Danzig, 3, 75-76
Dawes Plan, 53
D-Day, 129
De Gaulle, General, 113, 117-18, 129
Demilitarised zone, 3
Denmark, 3, 122
Depression, 93
Dietrich, Marlene, 53, 145
Drancy, 116
Dresden, 130
Duma, 6
Dunkirk, 122-23

E

East Prussia, 3, 75, 129, 135
Ebert, Frederick, 50
Egypt, 45, 124
Einsatzgruppen, 30, 136
Einstein, Albert, 70
Eisenhower, Dwight, General, 128

Munich Agreement, 45, 112
Munich Conference, 28, 75-76
Mussolini, Benito, 37-46, 55, 73, 75, 110, 115, 124, 127, 153

N
Nagasaki, 142
National Socialist German Workers Party (NSDAP), 51, 55
Nazi, 56-58, 62, 65, 71, 78, 83, 126, 133
Nazi Party, 49
Nazi regime, 60, 99
Nazi-Soviet Non-Aggression Pact, 28, 76, 122
Neuilly, Treaty of, 3
New Economic Policy (NEP), 12, 18
Niemoller, Martin, 67
Night of the long knives, 62
NKVD, 21-22, 24-25, 27, 29
Non-Aggression Pact, 124
Norway, 122, 133
November Criminals, 50
Nuremberg Laws, 70-71, 84, 136
Nuremberg Rallies, 83

O
Old Bolsheviks, 22
Olympics, 1936, 71, 73, 81
Operation Bagration, 129
Operation Barbarossa, 28, 30, 125
Operation Manhattan, 142
Operation Market Garden, 129
Operation Overload, 128
Operation Sealion, 123
Orlando, Vittorio, 2
Owens, Jesse, 82

P
P51 Mustang, 140
Pacific, The, 142
Pact of Steel, 45, 74
Panzer, 121, 138
Papen, Franz von, 56-57, 61
Partisans, 46, 134,
Partisan units, 29
Paulus, General, 126
Pearl Harbor, 125
People's community, 83
Permanent Revolution, 17
Petain, General, 113, 115, 118, 123
Petrograd, 7, 8, 10
Petrograd Soviet, 8
Phoney war, 99, 122
Piccole Italiane, 42
Pickford, Mary, 145
Picture palaces, 144
Poincare, Raymond, 108-10
Poland, 3, 10, 28, 75-76, 83, 121, 134-36
Polish Corridor, 3, 75
Pope Pius XI, 43-44, 67-68

Pope Pius XII, 44
Popular Front, 111
Pravda, 8, 16
Propoganda, 41
Protective Custody, 62
Provisional government, 8
Purges, 22

R
Radek, Karl, 26
Radical Party, 112
Radicals, 107, 109 111
Rasputin, 7
Red army, 12, 29, 124
Red Guards, 9
Red Terror, 11
Reds, 10
Reichskirche, 66
Reichstag, 50, 57, 61-62
Reparations, 3, 4, 107-8
Resistance, 117
Rhineland, 73, 83, 112
Riefenstahl, Leni, 81, 85, 156
Rohm, Ernst, 55, 63,
Roma, 136
Roman Question, 44
Rome-Berlin Axis, 45, 74
Rommel, General, 124, 127-9, 135,
Roosevelt, Franklin, President, 125, 126, 130
Royal Air Force (RAF), 123
Ruhr, 52-54, 109, 131
Russia, 5, 113, 139

S
SA, 67, 71, 83-85, 61-62
Saar, 3
Saarland, 73
Salo Republic, 46
Schutzstaffel, 55
Scorched earth policy, 29
Self-determination, 2, 4
Sevres, Treaty of, 3
Slovakia, 134
Social Democrats (SPD), 51, 61
Social Revolutionaries, 7
Socialism in One Country, 17
Solovetsk, 23
Somme, 1
Soviet Union, 138
Spartacus League, 50
SPD, 62, 80
Speer, Albert, 84-85
Spitfires, 123, 138
SS, 62-63, 71, 83-85, 137
St Germain, Treaty of, 3
St. Petersburg, 6
Stakhanite movement, 20
Stalin, Joseph, 9, 13, 16, 21-31, 41, 73, 76, 111, 117, 125-26, 130, 152
Stalingrad, 30-31, 126-27